# explore & discover

A PHOTO-LOCATION AND
VISITOR GUIDEBOOK

# THE INNER HEBRIDES

## VISIT THE MOST BEAUTIFUL PLACES, TAKE THE BEST PHOTOS

### CHRISTOPHER SWAN

**explore ⊗ discover**

# THE INNER HEBRIDES
## CHRISTOPHER SWAN

Publisher: Mick Ryan – *fotoVUE Ltd*.
fotoVUE Scotland Series Editor: Dougie Cunningham.
Additional research: Mick Ryan and Martyna Krol.
℗ Design and layout by Ryder Design – *www.ryderdesign.studio*

All maps within this publication were produced by Don Williams of Bute Cartographics.
Map location overlay and graphics by Mick Ryan. Maps contain Ordnance Survey data
© Crown copyright and database right 2016.

A CIP catalogue record for this book is available from the British Library.

ISBN 978-1-7395083-1-9
10 9 8 7 6 5 4 3 2 1

**Front cover**:       Kilmory Bay on Rum at dawn, with the Cuillin of Skye across the water. Fujifilm X–T2, 10–24mm f/4, ISO 200, 1/170s at f/8. Aug.
**Rear cover left**:   The Needle at The Quiraing. Fujifilm X–T2, 10–24mm f/4, ISO 200, 1/75s at f/8. Aug.
**Rear cover right**: Puffin on Staffa. Fujifilm X–T1, 55–200mm f/3.5–f/4.8, ISO 200, 1/4000s at f/4.8. Jul.
**Opposite**:          A glimpse into Camasunary Bay from Elgol. Fujifilm X–T2, 55–200mm f/3.5–f/4.8, ISO 200, 1/320s at f/11. Sep.

Printed and bound in China by Latitude Press Ltd.

*From the lone shieling of the misty island*
*Mountains divide us, and the waste of seas-*
*Yet still the blood is strong, the heart is Highland,*
*And we in dreams behold the Hebrides.*

**The Canadian Boat Song,**
**Anonymous**

# CONTENTS

*Fishing boat in the reeds at Gallanach on Muck. Fujifilm X–T2, 10–24mm f/4, ISO 200, 1/600s at f/8. Jul.*

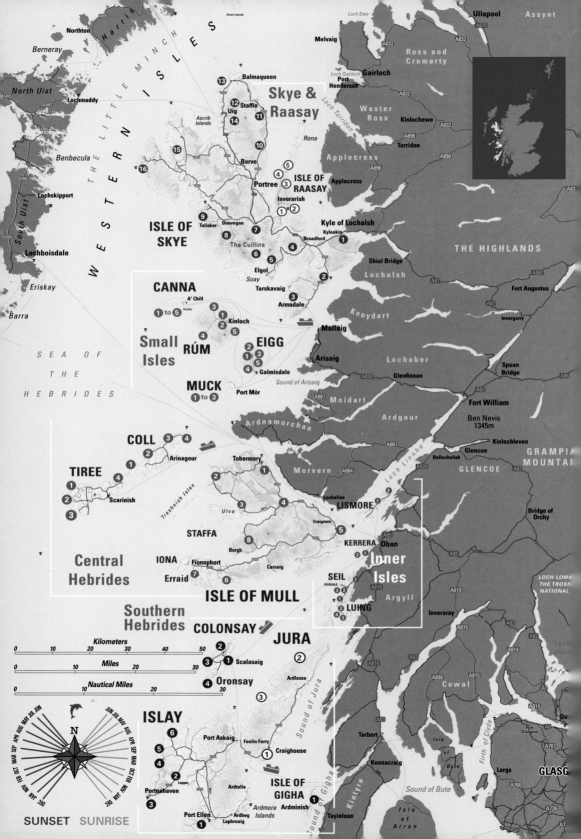

# ACKNOWLEDGEMENTS

Firstly, I'd like to thank Mick and Dougie at fotoVue for giving me the opportunity to visit, explore and photograph so many incredible Hebridean Islands. From the moment we discussed the project over a curry in Glasgow I have been so excited about it and it has been a huge part of my life for the past 5 years. There have been many challenges over the course of it: undertaking all the trips, the unpredictability of the weather, a pandemic and subsequent lockdowns, making the images and writing the book itself, but it really has been a dream commission. Thanks to Don for the brilliant maps and Nathan for both the excellent layout and putting up with my constant image changes.

To Joanne, my partner, thank you for being there with me on so many of these trips. For your love and encouragement, for always believing in me. Thank you for the endurance you've shown in waiting *"just another 10…20…30 minutes for the light"* as the rain beats down, and for spending all your holidays in the Hebrides with me.

To Mum, Dad, Stewart and Jenna, thank you for all your love and support. It has been amazing to spend time with you in many of these places. Thanks to Dad who not only taught me the basics of how to use a camera, but how to see and compose an image; without you this book wouldn't have happened. Thank you to Andy Hall for the inspiration and encouragement over the years.

To my best friend Nick. Sorry for chucking your anchor off the boat when it wasn't tied on. It's somewhere off the coast of Jura if anyone finds it.

To everyone who has shown an interest in the project, who has either commented on social media or asked about my trips, thank you, it has meant so much to me. Writing this book has been a long process and the encouragement from friends and family has been so important to me, particularly during lockdown when I could no longer visit the islands and these wonderful places seemed so far away.

Lastly, I'd like to thank the islands, which mean so much to me. There is a beautiful word in the Gaelic language which is *'cianalas'*. It doesn't directly translate into English but roughly equates to 'a homesickness or a longing for a place' and is what a Gael feels when they are far from home. These islands aren't my home (yet), but I do feel a yearning for them when I'm not there and after your visit, I'm sure you will too.

**Christopher Swan**
September 2023

*Looking across to Rum from Laig Bay on Eigg.*
*Fujifilm X–T2, 14mm f/2.8, ISO 200,*
*120s at f/8. Apr.*

**All art is about storytelling.**

At its root art can be seen as a form of escapism, transporting someone from their normal day to day life and taking them to another world. Whilst creating something of value an artist's aim will be to tell a story – to either give a sense of something that she has experienced herself or to create something from his imagination.

As a musician who is deeply affected and inspired by the landscape around me in the Highlands it is wonderful to become connected with a visual artist who shares my passion for our homeland, embodying within their work a real spirit of the outdoors.

Christopher Swan's beautiful book *'Explore & Discover The Inner Hebrides'* demonstrates a deep understanding as well as an artistic and creative interpretation of the world around him. Within the pages of this book there is the realisation that the land makes us what we are, we are part of it, just as it is part of us. There is a perceptible connection between man and land which resonates outwards from every page.

The realities of nature and land provide experiences that people everywhere share and understand similarly. Whether you know the Inner Hebrides intimately or not, these wonderful images will play with both your emotions and your intellect and bring you closer to this incredible land we call home.

**Duncan Chisholm**
September 2023

BLACK CUILLIN
duncan chisholm

SANDWOOD
duncan chisholm

**Duncan Chisholm** is one of Scotland's most recognised and accomplished fiddle players and composers. His art is deeply rooted in the landscape which provides much inspiration clearly heard in the compositions of his two latest albums, the evocative Black Cuillin and Sandwood, the latter winning 2018 Scots Trad Music Awards 'Album of the Year'. Born and brought up near Inverness in the Highlands of Scotland, Duncan travels extensively performing throughout the UK, Europe and the USA and often tours with multi-instrumentalist Hamish Napier and the Scottish Gaelic singer Julie Fowlis' band. He is also a founder member of the folk rock group Wolfstone. He played fiddle for Runrig.

Find out more about Duncan including forthcoming performances at: *www.duncanchisholm.com*

*Sgùrr nan Gillean from Sligachan. Fujifilm X–T1, 18–55mm f/2.8–f/4, ISO 200, 2s at f/11. Dec.*

# INTRODUCTION

**The Inner Hebrides, *Na h-Eileanan a-staigh*, are some of the most incredible and beloved island landscapes in the world. This diverse archipelago situated off the ragged western seaboard of Scotland, and southeast of the Outer Hebrides (Western Isles), *Na h-Eileanan Siar*, stretches for 150 miles from Islay in the south to Skye in the north. The archipelago is composed of almost 100 islands, with 35 of them inhabited. Skye, Mull, and Islay are the largest, and have the highest populations.**

Islay in the south is a place of pilgrimage for devotees of heavily peated malt whisky with a plethora of distilleries to sample across the island. To Islay's east is tiny Gigha with its crystal blue waters and palm-tree fringed beaches. Across the Sound of Islay is the rugged and wild Jura; formerly home to George Orwell and now to thousands of deer who roam freely across the uninhabited interior. Just to the north is Colonsay, with a glorious arc of golden sands lining Kiloran Bay or the ancient priory on Oronsay which can only be reached at low tide.

A stone-skim from the Argyll coast are the Slate Isles: Easdale, Luing and Seil, where you can see abandoned slate mines, the flooded quarries of the islands that roofed the world. Sheltering the harbour of Oban is Kerrera with its fascinating ruined castle at its southern tip. Then there is Lismore at the mouth of Loch Linnhe, the great garden, a geological outlier of limestone which created a lush and green island of meadows and fertile farmland.

In the centre of this archipelago is Mull, a haven for wildlife, home to sea eagles and otters, and the multicoloured harbour town of Tobermory, delighting adults and children alike. Off the coast of Mull are yet more beguiling islands; the sacred Isle of Iona, where Christian missionaries arrived from Ireland, before travelling throughout Scotland, replacing pagan rituals with Christian sermons, and its neighbour Erraid, immortalised as the island which trapped David Balfour in Robert Louis Stevensons 'Kidnapped'. To the west is Staffa with its basalt columns, a geological moment frozen in time above a boiling sea. Further west are the low-lying isles of Coll and Tiree with their sun-kissed beaches.

North of the Ardnamurchan peninsula are the Small Isles, four islands which all have their individual and distinct qualities. Wild and mountainous Rum is perfect for those who want to get off the beaten track. Tranquil Canna with its honesty shop, excellent restaurant and sandy beaches. Eigg is community owned and powered by renewable energy, a model of sustainability. Eigg also has one of the finest beaches in the Hebrides at Laig Bay which is a seascape photographers' dream for its fascinating geological features and the iconic view across to Rum. Then there is Muck, small and perfectly formed, a peaceful farming island with glorious views in all directions.

Skye, the largest of the islands, is undoubtedly the most well-known and popular of all the Inner Hebridean islands and it is easy to see why. From the jagged Cuillin hills to the wild pinnacles of the Storr and the crazy land-slip geology of the Quiraing, Skye has an upland landscape which is unrivalled in the British Isles. There are waterfalls, beaches, castles and villages to explore, fantastic restaurants serving local produce and seafood straight off the boat. There is enough variety on Skye to last a lifetime. Across the water is Raasay, which not only is a delightful island in itself, but its distinctive hill of Dun Caan grants one of the finest panoramic views in Scotland.

The Inner Hebrides are more than just islands; they are a world of their own, where you can immerse yourself in nature, culture and history. They are islands where you can reconnect with yourself and connect with others. They are islands where you can find adventure or peace, excitement or serenity, challenge or comfort. They are islands which are simply unforgettable.

**Christopher Swan**
September 2023

*Golden hour on Traigh Bousd. Fujifilm X–T2, 18–55mm f/2.8–f/4, ISO 200, 1/13s at f/11. Oct.*

# USING THIS GUIDEBOOK TO GET THE BEST IMAGES

**fotoVUE Explore & Discover photo-location and visitor guidebooks give you the information and inspiration to get to beautiful locations and take the best photographs.**

## In the right place

Each location chapter has a grey box titled 'How to get here' where there are written directions to the location along with four co-ordinates to the nearest car park or lay-by, including a scannable location QR-code. On the maps are location and sometimes viewpoint pins, and parking symbols.

**Viewpoints 1–3**
**🅿 Lat/Long**:   55.627610, -6.2209583
**🅿 what3words**: ///bronzes.misted.screaming
**🅿 Grid Ref**:   NR344452
**🅿 Postcode**:   PA42 7AZ

## The QR-code

Using your smart phone camera point the lens at the QR-code and your camera will scan the code that contains the parking location information as a lat-long co-ordinate. On some older phone operating systems you may have to have a QR-code reader app. Once read, your browser will open in Google maps and you can get directions from where you are to the parking spot of your chosen location.

## ///What3Words

### Download the free app at *what3words.com*

Postcodes are great if you are going to a specific building but not ideal for getting to the middle-of-nowhere. Latitude/longitude is precise but it is a hassle to type 16-digits into a navigation app or sat-nav. Better is *what3words*, which assigns each 3m square in the world a unique three-word address that will never change. Download the free *what3words* app then either say, type or scan in the *what3words* of a location, click on navigate, open a map app and you will get directions to the location. You can save locations on your phone, which is useful if you plan on visiting several locations in a day or are on a trip; you can save them all before you set off. The *what3words* app can also take photographs and stamp the *what3words* location on your image as a useful reference source for where your images were taken. In the UK most emergency services use *what3words* so if you get into trouble whilst exploring in a remote location, use the app to help 999 know exactly where to find you.

## Ordnance Survey maps

The relevant OS Explorer map (1:25 000) for each location is given at the beginning of each location section next to the introduction. There are several apps that allow you to download the relevant OS maps in return for a subscription. However, it is not recommended to rely solely on a mobile phone or tablet for navigation as batteries can run out and wireless connections can be lost.

Before you set off, study a map so that you know where you are going and give yourself plenty of time to get to your destination. Also, read the accessibility notes to check the distances and terrain to a location's viewpoints.

## The fotoVUE maps

Our maps are created by the talented Don Williams of Bute Cartography, then an overlay is added with location and viewpoint pins along with points of interest and services.

## Our map symbols

Our maps are detailed but with few symbols. The symbols that are important are:

### A location chapter

A location chapter is marked by a numbered circle or pin and its name.

### A location viewpoint

A viewpoint is marked by a small circle sometimes with the name of the viewpoint by it, or a reference to a viewpoint in the text such as VP1, VP2, V3 etc.

### Footpaths   --------------

Not all footpaths are marked on our maps, only footpaths that are useful to get to a location and its viewpoints.

### Walking man symbol

Paths with a walking man represent longer walks of a few miles, often involving steep uphill walking. These may require navigation and use of map and compass. Sometimes we use them to clarify a right of way.

## TRAVEL: ROADS

A846 Main A road
B8017 B road
Drivable track or minor road
Fuel/EV charging
Parking
Ferry
Harbour or Port
Airport

## FACILITIES

Restuarant
Cafe
Bar/pub
Whisky Distillerly
Other Distillerly
Grocery shopping/supermarket
Souvenir shopping
Vibrant nightlife
Church
Visitor centre/information
Botanical gardens
Museum
Bus terminus
Public toilets/restroom
Hospital/medical centre
Swimming pool
Golf Course

## TRAVEL: OFF ROAD

Footpath/trail with hiker
River crossing on foot
National Trail
Long bike packing routes

## PROTECTED AREA

National Park or Nature Reserve
NATIONAL TRUST for SCOTLAND
UNESCO World Heritage site / area

## LOCATIONS

**6**
**The Cove** Location name, number
**VP1: Beach** & viewpoints
**VP2: Rocks**

## NATURAL & CULTURAL FEATURES

Waterfall
Graveyard
Castle
Estate/Historic House
Point of cultural interest
Shipwreck
Lighthouse
Beinn Bheigeir △ 491m  Peak name & elevation
Wild swimming spot
Surfing spot

## ACCOMMODATION

Hotel/chalets/glamping
Hostel/highland dorm
Bothy
Campsite
Motorhome/van & camp site
Parking for campervans

## WILDLIFE

Good red deer habitat
Dolphins seen here
Seal watching spot
Whale watching spot
Coastal bird watching
Puffins common here
Inland bird watching spot
Corn crake habitat
Eagles common
Mountain hare habitat
Otters seen here
Wild goats
Highland coos

# MAP KEY

---

## At the right time

Each location in this book is accompanied by detailed notes on the optimum time of year and day to visit a location to get the best photographic results. Good light can occur at any time, however. Often the best time to visit a location is when conditions are rapidly changing, such as after a storm.

## Weather

Check the weather forecast a few days before and the day before a planned outing. Recommended apps are *metoffice.gov.uk* and *yr.no*

## Sun

Topography, sun position and weather determine how light falls on the land. Use the sun position compass on the front flap of this guidebook for sunrise and sunset times, to find out where the sun rises and sets on the compass (there is a big difference between summer and winter) and sun elevation (how high the sun rises in the sky).

Useful websites and apps include **The Photographer's Ephemeris** (*photoephemeris.com*), **photopills** (*photopills.com*) and *suncalc.org*

## Exploration

This guidebook will help get you to some of the best photographic locations and viewpoints in the Hebrides. It is by no means exhaustive; use it as a springboard to discover your own viewpoints. Study a map to look for locations or just follow your instinct to discover your own.

# CAMERA, LENSES AND CAPTIONS

Aesthetically, my approach to photography is always to strive for strong, graphic compositions with a desire to simplify the scene into its base elements. I grew up using film and like to get it right in-camera, minimising the amount of time I spend processing images. I do enjoy using long exposures, mainly to simplify water and skies, and create an ethereal atmosphere but aside from long exposures my images are intended to convey a realistic but artistic impression of the landscape.

## Equipment list

### Camera bodies
- Fujifilm X-E3
- Fujifilm X-T1
- Fujifilm X-T2
- Fujifilm X-100S

### Lenses
- Fujinon XF 10–24mm f/4
- Fujinon XF 18–55mm f/2.8-f/4
- Fujinon XF 55–200
- Fujinon XF 35mm f/1.4
- Fujinon XF14mm f/2.8

### Filters
- Lee Seven 5 Filter System

### Tripods
- Gitzo Mountaineer Tripod
- Manfrotto Magnesium Head

*Waiting for the light on Dun Caan, Raasay.*
*Fujifilm X–T2, 55–200mm f/3.5–f/4.8,*
*ISO 200, 1/200 at f/8. Apr.*

## Photo captions
The photo captions in fotoVUE guidebooks are in two parts:

### 1 Descriptive caption
First is a caption that describes where the photograph was taken, mentioning any references to viewpoints (e.g. VP1) in the accompanying text and any other useful information.

### 2 Photographic information
The second part of the caption lists the camera, lens, exposure, and the month the photograph was taken. This information is from the Exchangeable Image File Format (EXIF data) that is recorded on each image file when you take a photograph.

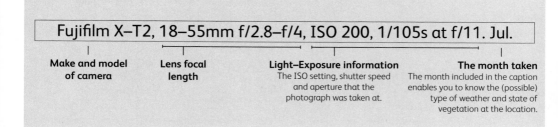

Fujifilm X–T2, 18–55mm f/2.8-f/4, ISO 200, 1/105s at f/11. Jul.

| Make and model of camera | Lens focal length | Light–Exposure information | The month taken |
|---|---|---|---|
| | | The ISO setting, shutter speed and aperture that the photograph was taken at. | The month included in the caption enables you to know the (possible) type of weather and state of vegetation at the location. |

# ACCESS AND BEHAVIOUR

Being outdoors means living life to the full and should be enjoyed by all, but we have to share it with others and stay safe. Here is some information and guidelines on accessing the outdoors and looking after yourself.

## The Scottish Outdoor Access Code

The Scottish Outdoor Access Code provides detailed guidance on the exercise of the ancient tradition of universal access to land in Scotland, which was formally codified by the Land Reform (Scotland) Act 2003. Under Scots law everyone has the right to be on most land and inland water for recreation, education and going from place to place providing they act responsibly. The basis of access rights in Scotland is one of shared responsibilities, in that those exercising such rights have to act responsibly, whilst landowners and managers have a reciprocal responsibility to respect the interests of those who exercise their rights. The code provides detailed guidance on these responsibilities. From: *www.outdooraccess-scotland.scot*

## Be a respectful photographer

The obvious is always worth stating: do not climb over walls or fences, shut all gates, don't drop litter, pick up litter others have dropped, keep dogs at home or on a lead, drive slowly in rural and urban areas, give way to cyclists, agricultural vehicles and horse riders, park considerately, don't scare livestock and keep quiet (don't play music or fly drones near others) but always say hello to fellow outdoor enthusiasts. In short, follow the **the Scottish Outdoor Access Code**.

## Respect other people

- Consider the local community and other people enjoying the outdoors
- Park carefully so access to gateways and driveways is kept clear
- Leave gates and property as you find them
- Follow paths but give way to others where it's narrow

## Enjoying Scotland's outdoors

In Scotland, you can enjoy the outdoors on most land and inland water, as long as you act responsibly and follow the Scottish Outdoor Access Code.

SCOTTISH **OUTDOOR** ACCESS CODE
outdooraccess-scotland.scot

These rights of responsible access include things like:

- walking
- cycling
- sightseeing and picnicking
- dog walking, provided your dog is under proper control
- swimming
- watching wildlife

but do not include:

- access with motor vehicles
- hunting, shooting and fishing

Responsible access can be enjoyed over most of Scotland including:

- parks
- hills and woods
- beaches and the coast
- lochs, rivers and canals

Exceptions include:

- houses and gardens
- other buildings
- school grounds
- most land where crops are growing
- places which charge for entry

## How to follow the Code

Key principles are to:

- take responsibility for your own actions
- respect the interests of others
- care for the environment

### When you're out and about

- Paths are shared with others – let people know you are coming so you do not alarm them, and slow down, stop or stand aside if needed.
- Respect the needs of other people enjoying or working in the outdoors and follow any reasonable advice from land managers.
- Don't disturb or damage wildlife or historic places.
- Park sensibly and do not create an obstruction.
- Take your rubbish home.

### Walking your dog

- Do not allow your dog to approach animals or people uninvited – where possible avoid animals.
- Always keep your dog in sight and under control – if in doubt use a lead.
- Always bag and bin dog poo, or take it home.

### On farmland

- Access rights do not usually apply to farmyards, but if a well-used path goes through a farmyard, you can follow this.
- Leave gates as you find them.
- Keep to unsown ground, field edges or paths.
- Never let your dog worry or attack farm animals. Do not take your dog into fields containing young animals or growing crops.
- Keep a safe distance from cattle. If they act aggressively, take the shortest safest route out of the field. If you have a dog, release it and let it find its own way to safety.

### Be a responsible camper

- Access rights include responsible lightweight camping in tents, in small numbers and for two or three nights in any one place. Keep well away from buildings and roads.
- Leave no trace of your campsite.
- Carry a trowel and bury your own waste and urinate well away from open water, rivers and burns.
- Use a camping stove. Never light open fires, barbeques or fire bowls in dry periods or near to forests, farmland, buildings or damage trees. Never cut down or damage trees.
- Follow all local advice at high risk times and places.

**NatureScot**
**NàdarAlba**
Scotland's Nature Agency
Buidheann Nàdair na h-Alba

SCOTTISH **OUTDOOR** ACCESS CODE
outdooraccess-scotland.scot

For more information and further guidance on different activities, visit the Scottish Outdoor Access Code website.

outdooraccess-scotland.scot

## Mobility ♿

If you can't walk far or up steep slopes, or if you use a wheelchair or have an injury and need to know whether a location is suitable for you, each location chapter has a brief Access Notes section describing the terrain and distance from the road to a viewpoint. Most locations in this guidebook are usually not far from the road and some are roadside.

If a location or viewpoint has the wheelchair symbol, part or all of it will be accessible by wheelchairs. Bear in mind that access for wheelchair users may not be exactly as described in the text, and you should use your own judgment as to how far you proceed at any given location. And don't forget, driving around the countryside will present many superb photographic opportunities; just be careful where you stop – avoid stopping in passing places for more than a quick shot and always be aware of traffic.

## Coastal locations

If you or others are in trouble call 999 and ask for the Coastguard. If you don't have a mobile phone, shout for help. Many locations in this guidebook are by the sea, on beaches and on rocky shorelines including cliff edges.

## Before you go

- Wear appropriate clothing and footwear.
- Let someone know where you are going and at what time you plan to return.
- Take a fully charged mobile phone with you.
- Check the tide timetables so that you know when high and low tides will be.

## Once outside

- Take extra care on rocky beaches that are often slippery and sharp.
- Stay away from cliff edges, especially if it's windy or if the ground is wet.
- Avoid walking below cliffs as many are unstable.
- Obey warning signs and don't climb over fences.
- If you get stuck in mud or quicksand, spread your weight, avoid moving and call for help.
- Always take a head torch with you for night photography.
- If you're taking a selfie, be safe.

## Protect the natural environment

- Leave no trace of your visit; take all your litter home
- Don't have barbecues or fires
- Keep dogs under effective control
- Bag, and bin, dog poo

## Enjoy the outdoors

- Plan ahead, check what facilities are open, be prepared
- Follow advice and local signs, and obey any social distancing measures

## Busy viewpoints

As photography becomes more popular, some accessible locations and viewpoints can become busy in times of good light. In some circumstances this can cause conflict between photographers as they look for the best spot from which to compose their shot. If you arrive at a location and someone is already set up, give them space and don't get in their way. Talking and negotiating helps; they may be OK with you setting up next to them, or with you using their spot after they have finished. There are usually alternative viewpoints, but just make sure you aren't in their line of fire. If there is a crowd at a particular spot, it's often best just to find another viewpoint.

**Getting to the Hebrides is all part of the fun. Whether you are sailing across on the ferry or flying in a small plane you will get a great perspective of the islands on your journey. There is also the potential for photography, particularly on the ferries, with both regular sightings of whales and dolphins and also the distinctive views of the islands you get from being on the water. Whilst public transport is available in the Hebrides, travelling by car is the best way to ensure you get to the right place at the right time.**

## Ferry

Apart from Skye (which is connected to the mainland by the Skye Bridge) the most likely way you will arrive on a Hebridean island is by ferry. For me the boat over is always a delight, and whether it's a stormy day, or it's clear and calm; the journey across the water is always a symbolic one. Run by Caledonian Macbrayne (Calmac), their distinctive red, black and white boats have plied the waters of the Hebrides for over a century, an essential, lifeline service for the islanders bringing the majority of their supplies over from the mainland. They are increasingly popular and in the summer months booking is essential.

The ferry timetables are often co-ordinated with other public transport services both on the mainland and on the islands and there are connections to the rail network at Oban and at Mallaig see (*www.scotrail.co.uk*). If you are visiting more than one island, then Calmac provide discounted Hopscotch tickets for a number of island groups.

Check *www.calmac.co.uk* for full timetables and each islands introduction chapter in this book.

The main ports than ferries run from are Oban, Mallaig and Ullapool with several other small ports. You can also travel between some islands by ferry.

## Air

There are number of airports in the Hebrides and with a journey time of an hour from Edinburgh or Glasgow of an hour this is an excellent way of making the most of your time. Car hire is available at the airports making a fly-drive trip a possibility but it is essential you book prior to travel. Viewing the Hebrides from the air and in particular flying to Barra, and landing on the only sand runway in the world might just be the highlight of your trip!

**Loganair** (*www.loganair.co.uk*) fly to and from Stornoway, Benbecula, Tiree and Islay.

**Hebridean Air Services** (*www.hebrideanair.co.uk*) fly from Oban to Coll, Tiree, Colonsay and Islay.

| FERRIES FROM MAINLAND TO ISLANDS | Destinations | Duration | Car Ferry | |
|---|---|---|---|---|
| **PORT** – calmac.co.uk | | | | |
| Tayinloan | Gigha | 20m | Yes | – |
| Kennacraig | Port Ellen, Islay | 2hrs, 20m | Yes | |
| | Port Askaig, Islay | 2hrs | Yes | – |
| | Scalasaig, Colonsay | 3hrs, 56m | Yes | |
| Oban | Arinagour, Coll | 3hrs, 31m | Yes | |
| | Scalasaig, Colonsay | 3hrs, 3m | Yes | |
| | Craignure, Mull | 50m | Yes | |
| | Achnacroish, Lismore | 1hrs | Yes | – |
| | Port Askaig, Islay | 3hrs, 55m | Yes | |
| | Scarinish, Tiree | 4hrs, 52m | Yes | |
| Lochaline | Fishnish, Mull | 18m | Yes | – |
| Arisaig (arisaig.co.uk) | Eigg | 1hr | No | – |
| (MV Shearwater, Arising Marine Ltd) | Muck | 2hrs | No | – |
| Mallaig | Armadale, Skye | 30m | Yes | |
| | Canna | 4hrs, 10m | Yes | – |
| | Eigg | 1hr, 20m | Yes | Vehicle permit for island required |
| | Muck | 1hr, 40m | Yes | Vehicle permit for island required |
| | Rum | 1hr, 20m | Yes | Vehicle permit for island required |
| **INTER ISLAND FERRIES** | | | | |
| Port Askaig, Islay | Feolin, Jura | 15m | Yes | |
| | Scalasaig, Colonsay | 1hr, 10m | Yes | – |
| Tobermory, Mull | Kilchoan, Ardnamurchan | 35m | Yes | – |
| Sconser, Skye | Raasay | 25m | Yes | – |
| Fionnphort, Mull | Iona | 10m | No | |
| **FLIGHTS** (Loganair – loganair.co.uk) | | | | |
| Glasgow to Islay | – | 45m | – | – |
| Edinburgh to Tiree | – | 1hr | – | – |

## DISTANCES AND DRIVING TIMES TO MAIN PORTS

| | TAYINLOAN | KENNACRAIG | OBAN | |
|---|---|---|---|---|
| **Glasgow** | 113 miles (2hrs, 58m) | 100 miles (2hrs, 42m) | 90 miles (2hrs, 30m) | |
| **Edinburgh** | 161 miles (3hrs, 45m) | 148 miles (3hrs, 30m) | 122 miles (2hrs, 59m) | |
| **Carlisle, England-Scotland Border** | 212 miles (4hrs, 4m) | 198 miles (3hrs, 47m) | 189 miles (3hrs, 38m) | |
| **London** | 516 miles (9hrs, 45m) | 503 miles (9hrs, 29m) | 494 miles (9hrs, 16m) | |

## Bus

There are regular bus connections to all the ferry terminals on the mainland at Ullapool, Mallaig, Oban and Tayinloan. Tickets can booked at (*www.citylink.co.uk*). On the islands themselves there are number of local services, which may only be once daily or even more infrequent. With enough planning it is possible to get around by bus however you will be constrained somewhat by the timetable.

## Car

Travelling by car is the easiest way to get around the Hebrides however visitors may initially be unfamiliar with single track roads with passing places. We drive on the left hand side of the road in the UK with distances on road signs measured in miles and speed limits shown as miles per hour (mph). Speed limits in built up areas are 30mph unless otherwise indicated. On dual carriageways and motorways (none of these in the Hebrides!) the speed limit is 70mph unless you are towing or driving a van when it is 60mph. Rural roads are 60mph or 50mph respectively. Drink driving laws are strict with the legal limit set at 50mg of alcohol in 100ml of blood. Essentially this can mean that a single pint of lager can put you over the limit. If you are visiting distilleries, make sure you take your tasting dram with you. Throughout the Hebrides you may come across animals in the road. Sheep and cows wander freely and should be given time to get off the road. Deer are a menace on the road at dusk and dawn and will often cross the road when you least expect. Otters, rabbits, hares and even goats are to be seen wandering the roads.

## Navigation

Phone reception can be patchy at best or at times non-existent in The Hebrides so downloading any maps you require for navigation prior to your visit is advisable. 3G and 4G signals are becoming more widespread throughout the islands but depends greatly on the network. See each islands 'fact file' in the island's introduction chapter in this book for more information.

| LOCHALINE | ARISAIG | MALLAIG | UIG, SKYE | ULLAPOOL |
|-----------|---------|---------|-----------|----------|
| 126 miles (3hs, 36m) | 138 miles (3hrs, 31m) | 145 miles (3hrs, 39m) | 225 miles (5hrs, 21m) | 223 miles (4hrs, 12m) |
| 156 miles (4hrs, 8m) | 178 miles (3hrs, 58m) | 185 miles (4hrs, 12m) | 250 miles (5hrs, 41m) | 211 miles (4hrs, 20m) |
| 223 miles (4hrs, 49m) | 235 miles (4hrs, 40m) | 243 miles (4hrs, 50m) | 322 miles (6hrs, 39m) | 307 miles (5hrs, 21m) |
| 536 miles (10hrs, 32m) | 549 miles (10hrs, 26m) | 556 miles (10hrs, 35m) | 653 miles (12hrs, 9m) | 615 miles (10hrs, 52m) |

## Single Track Roads

Once you venture off the main roads you will be travelling on what are known as single track roads. These roads are only wide enough for one vehicle at a time and have regular passing places which allow you to get passed vehicles coming in the opposite direction. Many roads are steep, windy and very narrow and for drivers who are unfamiliar with them can be a daunting experience. These roads require care, caution and concentration and will take longer to negotiate than the milage suggests.

There is an etiquette in driving single track roads which will make driving them a much more pleasant experience for you and for other road users. Passing places are marked with a diamond or circular white sign and indicate where the road widens. If the passing place is on the left hand side and a vehicle is approaching, pull into the left. If in the same circumstance, the passing place is on the right hand side, stop in the centre, allowing the approaching vehicle to pass you via the passing place. In short, stop on the left hand side. There are a few golden rules to follow:

- **Passing places are not for parking**. In popular areas, there is a problem with visitors parking in passing places. This is inconsiderate, blocks the road, annoys locals and can cause a problem for emergency services.
- **Passing places should be used to allow overtaking**. Check your mirrors often, if there is somebody behind, pull in to the next passing place and allow them to overtake.
- **Do not pull up onto the verge to allow a vehicle to pass**. This causes a lot damage to road verges and can lead to cars getting stuck. If you approach a vehicle and there are no passing places, one driver will have to reverse.
- **Take particular care** passing bikes and pedestrians on single track roads.
- Give way to vehicles coming uphill.
- If you are visiting The Hebrides in a campervan, motorhome or with a caravan it is vital that you are confident in reversing.
- Wave! Give a cheery wave if a driver has pulled in for you.

## Welcome. How are you?
## Fàilte. Dè do chor?

There is no better source of information about where to stay, eat and buy provisions in the Inner Hebrides than the individual island websites, the **Visit Scotland** website: *www.visitscotland.com/places-to-go/islands* and *www.southernhebrides.com*. Most of these sources are kept up to date and you can book accommodation direct rather than through a third party. They are also a mine of information about what to do and island culture.

*www.visitscotland.com* (VisitScotland is Scotland's national tourist board.)

| | |
|---|---|
| **Islay** | islayinfo.com |
| **Jura** | welcometojura.com • jurawhisky.com |
| **Colonsay** | visitcolonsay.co.uk • colonsay.org.uk |
| **Gigha** | visitgigha.co.uk • gigha.org.uk |
| **Mull** | isle-of-mull.net • visitmullandiona.co.uk |
| **Iona** | welcometoiona.com • visitmullandiona.co.uk |
| **Coll** | visitcoll.co.uk |
| **Tiree** | isleoftiree.com |
| **Lismore** | isleoflismore.com lismoregaelicheritagecentre.org |
| **Kerrera** | isleofkerrera.org • kerreramarina.com |
| **Seil** | seil.oban.ws • slateislands.org.uk |
| **Easdale** | easdale.org • easdaleisland.scot slateislands.org.uk |
| **Luing** | isleofluing.org |
| **Eigg** | isleofeigg.org |
| **Rum** | isleofrum.com |
| **Canna** | theisleofcanna.com |
| **Muck** | isleofmuck.com • islemuck.com |
| **Skye** | isleofskye.com • isleofskye.net |
| **Raasay** | raasay.com • raasaydistillery.com |

## Island fact files in this book

In addition, in the introduction to each island in this book is an island fact file which gives further information including whether vehicles are allowed, main towns, car and bike rental, public transport information, accommodation, festivals and events, eating out and provisions.

## Support the islands: provisions and eating out

Buy provisions locally, grab a coffee and cake, a beer or dram, buy locally-made gifts and eat out when you can, (don't miss the locally caught and smoked fish, and venison if you are an omnivore) and you will be making a positive contribution to the economies of the island communities.

## Accommodation

There is a wide range of accommodation including hotels, hostels, B&Bs and self-catering cottages on the islands. Book accommodation early as places fill up fast. As well as the websites previously mentioned, the following sites are also useful:

| | |
|---|---|
| scottishcamping.com | hostelworld.com |
| hostel-scotland.co.uk | hostellingscotland.org.uk |
| lhhscotland.com | cottages.com |
| unique-cottages.co.uk | airbnb.co.uk |

## Wild camping

Wild camping is also permitted, but anyone wild camping should always follow the guidance given in the **Scottish Outdoor Access Code**.

### The code defines wild camping as:

Lightweight, done in small numbers and only for two or three nights in any one place. You can camp in this way wherever access rights apply, but help to avoid causing problems for local people and land managers by not camping in enclosed fields of crops or farm animals and by keeping well away from buildings, roads or historic structures. Take extra care to avoid disturbing deer stalking or grouse shooting. If you wish to camp close to a house or building, seek the owner's permission.

### Leave no trace by:

- taking away all your litter
- not causing any pollution
- removing all traces of your tent pitch and of any open fire. Wherever possible, use a stove rather than light

an open fire. If you do wish to light an open fire, keep it small, under control, and supervised – fires that get out of control can cause major damage, for which you might be liable. Never light an open fire during prolonged dry periods or in areas such as forests, woods, farmland or on peaty ground or near to buildings or in cultural heritage sites where damage can be easily caused. Heed all advice at times of high risk. Remove all traces of an open fire before you leave.

# Campervan and motorhomes

Campervan and motorhomes have grown increasingly popular in recent years and are catered for very well across the islands. Please note that The Outdoor Access Code states that access rights do not apply to motor vehicles – **sleeping in a van is not wild camping**.

## Plan ahead
Check an islands website for campsites, designated parking spots and aires, the location of chemical toilet disposal points, public toilets, grocery shops & fuel stations, calor gas suppliers and laundrettes.

## Overnight stays in campervans, motorhomes and roof-top tents
Access rights do not include motor vehicles. If public or private land owners restrict or regulate parking on their land, you must comply with this.

## At all times, minimise your impact by:
Following the Highway Code and the guidance in the Scottish Outdoor Access Code, including the specific advice on car parking. Respect the interests of others, care for the environment and take responsibility for your own actions.

Planning ahead and booking into managed caravan/camp sites and other provision for campervans and motorhomes where possible.

More info about campsites and caravan parks can be found at Scottish Camping; Visit Scotland; and at VisitScotland iCentres. From: *www.outdooraccess-scotland.scot*

**The Hebrides are the stronghold of the Gàidhlig language and culture. On your visit to the islands you may notice the language spoken in shops or pubs, you will hear it sung if you listen to traditional music and you will definitely see it written on road signs. Thought to have been spoken since the 4th Century, this Celtic language was once used widely across Scotland, with many place names able to trace their etymological roots to the Gaelic language. The language declined in use throughout much of Scotland, however it always remained in the Hebrides and along the western coast of the mainland.**

Gaelic now is enjoying a resurgence. There is a Gaelic language TV station; BBC Alba. Gaelic schools are becoming more widespread throughout the country and the popularly of language-learning apps like Duolingo has brought Gaelic to a new audience, however it is in the Hebrides that you are more likely to come across it on a day to day basis. When visiting you can easily get by without knowing any Gaelic, after all, the vast majority of Gaelic speakers also speak English and the road signs are bi-lingual however learning some of the language will enrich your understanding of the landscape immeasurably and can even benefit your photography.

I believe an understanding of the landscape is fundamental to creating good landscape photography, and an excellent way to gain an understanding of the landscape is through the people who named it. No matter where you are in the world, the interaction between people and their landscape can reveal so much – I'm always amazed when studying maps at just how much of the landscape has been named, although it can be puzzling if you cannot understand the words! It is clear from reading maps today how important the landscape was to the Gaels of old, and we can definitely learn about the landscape from what features they chose to name.

Take for example the Gaelic word Dearg, meaning Red. If you see this applied to a mountain, it is a safe bet to assume that when the sun is low in the sky, the rocks will take on a bright red hue. Or the word Garbh, meaning

'rough or rugged'. This could be a particularly craggy hill with a bouldery slope which might offer some good foreground opportunities for a wider view, or its could just be a tricky walk! How about Darach or Daraich, meaning Oak? The chances are that if you encounter oakwood along the Atlantic coast you will find some interesting gnarled specimens worthy of investigation. On your journeys throughout Scotland you might encounter the place name Tarbert or Tarbet and notice that they are all positioned on a neck of land between two water bodies. This is from the Gaelic An Tairbeart, which essentially means "carry across" – it is a portage site for people to move boats from one water body to another!

The wealth of intrigue that opens up from just a basic grasp of landscape names can add so much to your enjoyment and understanding of the landscape, hopefully the list below sparks your intrigue. The following list gives a number of common Gaelic place names or landscape features which will aid your understanding of the landscape and if you would like to understand more, the book "Reading the Gaelic Landscape" by John Murray is a fantastic resource.

| | | | | |
|---|---|---|---|---|
| **Abhainn** | River | | **Eagach** | Jagged |
| **Achadh** | Field | | **Eilean** | Island |
| **Àrd or Aird** | High | | **Garbh** | Rough or Rugged |
| **Acarsaid** | Anchorage | | **Gorm** | Blue blue/grey |
| **Aiseag** | Ferry | | **Inbhir** | Mouth of watercourse |
| **Allt** | Stream | | **Iolaire** | Eagle |
| **Bàta** | Boat | | **Làirig** | Pass |
| **Bàn** | White | | **Liath** | Grey |
| **Bealach** | A mountain pass or col | | **Maol** | Bald |
| **Beag** | Small or little | | **Mhor or Mór** | Large or great. |
| **Beith** | Birch | | **Òr** | Gold |
| **Beinn** | Hill | | **Ròn** | Seal |
| **Caol** | Strait (Kyle) | | **Sneachda** | Snow |
| **Ceann** | Head (Usually anglicised to Kin – for example Kinloch Rannoch is The Head of Loch Rannoch | | **Sròn** | Nose shaped |
| | | | **Tiobar** | Well |
| | | | **Tigh** | House |
| **Cnoc** | Hillock | | **Uaine** | Green |
| **Bòidheach** | Beautiful | | **Uisge** | Water. As in Uisge beatha / Whisky (the water of life) |
| **Dearg** | Red | | | |
| **Darach** | Oak | | | |
| **Dubh** | Black | | | |
| **Eas** | Waterfall | | | |

*"If you don't like the weather, then just wait 5 minutes"*

It's a phrase which could easily have been written with the Hebrides in mind. The whims and vagaries of the weather on the islands off the west coast of Scotland are the stuff of legend and a source of constant discussion. The predominate prevailing wind in Scotland is from the west and the first land mass that wind hits is the Hebrides. It can therefore be windy and wet. That's not to say it's all cloud and rain, there are beautiful clear sunny days where the water is calm and you might brave the waters of the Atlantic for swim. But the days when the clouds scud over the land, with heavy downpours and occasional blasts of illumination? Those are the days when the Hebrides are absolutely magical. Get your jacket on, and get out there because that is when the best images are made.

### SPRING – March, April, May

Spring is a fantastic time to visit the the Hebrides. As the land wakes up from its slumber, the days begin to lengthen and the quality of the light is almost as good as winter. It is not uncommon to have a long spell of settled clear weather in spring. There may still be snow on the higher hills, particular on sheltered north faces where it delicately traces out the lines of gullies and crags. The gorse begins to bloom in May and in the sheltered woodlands and on some coastal areas bluebells flourish. The yellow flag iris also brings a bright pop of yellow to marshy areas and the machair begins to bloom at the end of spring. Puffins and corncrakes return form their winter grounds in May and common dolphins start to be seen in the Atlantic. Unfortunately the end of spring brings about the start of the dreaded midge season.

### SUMMER – June, July, August

Summer can be a frustrating time for photography in the Hebrides. Often the settled spring weather will give way to a *dreich* and damp summer with low cloud obscuring the hills. On sunny days, out of the golden hours, the light can be harsh and sometimes frustratingly hazy. On days like this, head to the beach, the sun on the turquoise sea is idyllic and once you're done with photography, make the most of the sun; it doesn't happen too often! Sitting at a latitude of 56 degrees north, the days are very long with sunrise at the summer solstice around 4:30 and sunset at 22:15. It therefore takes some dedication to make the most of the golden hour, however photographing a warm summer sunset in the Hebrides is a lovely experience. The heather comes into bloom in August and brings a beautiful

purple hue to the hills. The machair is at its best between July and August with species changing as the season progresses. The best areas of machair is in South Uist however, it can be found in many coastal locations in the Hebrides on the low-lying ground on the landward side of the dunes. It is an amazing sight, with a huge number of wild flower species creating carpet of colour buzzed by bees and insects. Of great interest to the macro photographer, studies of the machair can also be undertaken with great results on overcast days when the colours appear at their most saturated.

## AUTUMN – September, October, November

Autumn is a great season in the Hebrides. Whilst not blessed with many areas of woodland to experience the changing colours, there are some areas to photograph this stunning yearly spectacle. The hills turn russet as the bracken dies back and the marram grass on the dunes begins to yellow, looking especially good in the slanting low sun at the now lengthening golden hours at both ends of the day. The nights draw in and on clear nights the milky way makes an appearance again after the twilight of summer nights. October is the rutting season and the roaring of stags may often be heard, Rum in particular has a huge population of deer at Kilmory Bay. The midge and tick season comes to a welcome end at the end of September.

## WINTER – December, January, February

In winter the Hebrides can be a very wild place, but also incredibly photogenic. Atlantic storms lash the coast with huge waves breaking onto the shoreline making for some powerful images. Be very careful in these conditions, you will often be far from help. The hours of daylight are very short, sometimes only 7 hours long, but with the sun siting low in the sky you are blessed with a day-long Golden Hour.

Once the sun has set, the jet black skies, devoid of light pollution are perfect for astrophotography. The northern lights are often seen on clear nights in winter and it is worth subscribing to alerts from Glendale Aurora *www.glendaleskye.com/aurora-alerts-app.php* to make sure that you don't miss them. Whilst the colours are not as intense as the lights seen further north in Iceland or Canada, just seeing the lights is a magical experience. Whilst the Hebrides are at a northerly latitude, snowfall is not that common and the salt air tends to disperse it quickly from low lying areas. Skye occasionally gets a decent dump of snow and on those days the Cuillin take on an even more alpine appearance.

# THE INNER HEBRIDES CLIMATE

**Whether it is sunny, or wet and windy, the Hebrides are always dramatic. The islands take the full force of westerly Atlantic storms and the Butt of Lewis has been recorded as being the UK's windiest spot, however in summer, due to the Gulf Stream, the Hebrides' sea temperatures can be as warm as Cornwall at the south-west tip of UK; great if you like swimming. It is because of the Gulf Stream, that brings warmer waters across the Atlantic from the south-east USA, that the Hebrides have a mild climate, despite their northerly latitude. Whilst inland, when the Highlands are snow-covered, the average winter temperature in the Hebrides is 6 °C (44 °F) and snow is rare on most westerly islands. Topography and land mass however also play a part and the high peaks, especially on Skye, are regularly snow covered, with the glens often filled with cold low-lying mist and fog.**

The Outer Hebrides, generally, get slightly more sun and less rain than the Inner Hebrides, the latter getting more frosty days and snow. Average maximum temperatures are 12 °C (53 °F), average minimum is 6 °C (44 °F). May is the sunniest month, April to June the driest, December and January the wettest. Climate change and the movement of the jet stream have an influence and some years are seeing less rain and more sun, whilst it can be raining on the mainland, you won't need an umbrella in the Hebrides, some summers have seen only 10% of the average rainfall.

Weather can be localised, on one side of an island you may get rain, whilst on the other side there will be glorious sunshine.

Pack a jacket in summer, night temperatures drop quickly at sunset with the lowest temperatures just before sunrise. In high summer the days are long, and the nights short, making sunset late and sunrise very early (see the sun compass on the front flap for sunrise/sunset times and day length) and in June it never gets completely dark and in the depths of winter the sun stays low on the horizon all day in a perpetual golden hour (cloud cover dependent) for 6 or 7 hours.

*"Azure. Turquoise. Cerulean. Aquamarine. I'm struggling to find enough words to describe the different shades of blue that I encounter on my travels across the length and breadth of Lewis and Harris in the Outer Hebrides."*
Audrey Gillan

The Hebrides are renowned for their changeable weather (lots of rainbows and squalls) and celestial light, which when combined with the rich blues of the sky and the sea, make the Hebrides a visual delight at any time of year.

# Met office weather station averages

**Outer Hebrides**: Stornoway, Lewis

**Location:** 58.214, -6.325
**Altitude:** 15m above mean sea

**Inner Hebrides**: Lusa, Skye

**Location:** 57.257, -5.809
**Altitude:** 18m above mean sea level

☀ **SUN /** Average hours of sunshine per month
(1256 hours per annum)

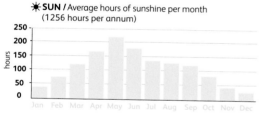

☁ **RAIN /** Average days rain/month and precipitation in mm
(1235mm/206 days per annum)

| | Jan | Feb | Mar | Apr | May | Jun | Jul | Aug | Sep | Oct | Nov | Dec |
|---|---|---|---|---|---|---|---|---|---|---|---|---|
| mm | 145 | 111 | 105 | 74 | 69 | 65 | 74 | 87 | 103 | 132 | 127 | 139 |

🌡 **TEMPERATURE /** Average min/max per month C/F
(yearly average 12°C/6°C)

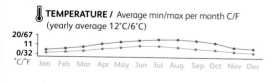

❄ **FROST /** Average days of frost per month
(22 days per annum)

| days | Jan | Feb | Mar | Apr | May | Jun | Jul | Aug | Sep | Oct | Nov | Dec |
|---|---|---|---|---|---|---|---|---|---|---|---|---|
| | 4 | 5 | 4 | 1 | 0 | 0 | 0 | 0 | 0 | 0 | 1 | 5 |

☀ **SUN /** Average hours of sunshine per month
(1200 hours per annum)

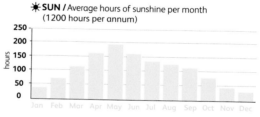

☁ **RAIN /** Average days rain/month and precipitation in mm
(2019mm/220 days per annum)

| | Jan | Feb | Mar | Apr | May | Jun | Jul | Aug | Sep | Oct | Nov | Dec |
|---|---|---|---|---|---|---|---|---|---|---|---|---|
| mm | 240 | 185 | 172 | 114 | 111 | 96 | 114 | 137 | 180 | 217 | 209 | 240 |

🌡 **TEMPERATURE /** Average min/max per month C/F
(yearly average 12°C/5°C)

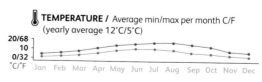

❄ **FROST /** Average days of frost per month
(35 days per annum)

| days | Jan | Feb | Mar | Apr | May | Jun | Jul | Aug | Sep | Oct | Nov | Dec |
|---|---|---|---|---|---|---|---|---|---|---|---|---|
| | 8 | 7 | 5 | 2 | 1 | 0 | 0 | 0 | 1 | 1 | 3 | 8 |

Bortle Class 1 excellent dark sky | Bortle Class 2 dark sky | Bortle Class 3 rural sky | Bortle Class 4 rural/suburban | Bortle Class 5 suburban sky | Bortle Class 5 bright suburban | Bortle Class 7 suburban/urban | Bortle Class 8 urban city sky | Bortle Class 9 inner city sky

*Graphic representation of the Bortle Scale.*

## Light Pollution

The Hebrides have excellent dark skies, generally unspoiled by light pollution unless you are near a large town. This means that not only are the Hebrides great for witnessing and photographing the Aurora Borealis but also the Milky Way, stars and planets. In the February edition of Sky and Telescope magazine an American amateur astronomer, John Bortle came up with a light pollution scale that rates the darkness of a site. Generally the Hebrides skies are very dark, from Bortle Class 1 to Bortle Class 3. In fact the island of Coll was designated a 'dark sky community' in 2013 by the International Dark Sky Association and the Isle of Gigha has created a non-profit community group, Dark Skies Gigha, which has been named as a Dark Sky Discovery Site by the UK Dark Sky Discovery Partnership.

In each islands' introduction fact file, its Bortle scale is listed.

## Aurora Borealis (Na Fir Chlis 'The Nimble Men' in Scottish Gaelic folklore)

Caused by electrons from the sun exciting atoms and molecules in the Earth's atmosphere to subsequently release photons of light, the Aurora Borealis or northern lights are a magical phenomenon and can be seen in the Hebrides and the rest of Scotland. While the aurora is active all year it requires dark skies to see clearly, making the longer nights from autumn to spring the best time to view them. The best season generally extends from late August to mid-April. Avoid light polluted areas when taking Aurora Borealis images, and look for interesting foregrounds.

We are currently in period of high solar activity when the sun has the highest number of sunspots, solar flares and coronal mass ejections (CME) and, therefore is most active. When CMEs collide with Earth's magnetosphere they can cause geomagnetic storms and aurorae. So for the next few years (2024 onwards) you stand a good chance on a clear night of witnessing them.

## KP Northern Lights forecast

**Glendale Skye** have produced an app which you can download from: *aurora-alerts.uk*

It is worth subscribing to get aurora alerts to make sure that you don't miss them.

One measurement of aurora activity is the KP index which has a range from 0–9, the higher the KP number the further south you can see the aurora and the more intense it will be. It's always worth going out for a look even if the KP index is low; also the forecast can change quickly, the KP can be high and it may not appear. However, cloud cover is your biggest enemy, clear skies are best.

**KP 1–3**: Quiet activity and feint, predominant colour is green.

**KP 4–6**: Very active, yellow, bluish, or purple tones. Possibility of ribbons, bands and pillars.

Aurora coronas are also possible.

**KP 7–9**: Strong aurora storms, very active. High chances of multiple colours including red.

A KP Index of 5 is common in the Hebrides, and some have witnessed spectacular Aurora coronas.

## Photographing the Northern Lights

### For DSLR and mirrorless cameras
• Bring a tripod and plenty of spare batteries.
• Aperture: f/1.4–f/3.5.
• Shutter Speed: Your shutter speed will be largely influenced by how fast the aurora is moving.

*The Aurora Borealis at Clachan Shannda. Fujifilm X–T2, 14mm f/2.8, ISO 1000, 30s at f/2.8. Mar.*

- 15–30 seconds for slow moving aurorae like arcs and diffuse glows.
- 5–15 seconds for bright dancing bands and pillars.
- 1–5 seconds for bright overhead coronas.
- ISO: 800–6400: use the ISO as the final control of the overall exposure.

If your image is too dark, increase the ISO (or vice versa).

- Focal Length: 14–24mm would be ideal.
- Focusing: use manual focus but don't twist your focus ring to the furthest left, or put the arrow in your viewfinder by the infinity symbol – as on most lenses this is not infinity. Better to manually focus on a bright star or planet or focus on a distant house/streetlight on the horizon. This will set your lens at infinity, some then use gaffer tape to fix it in position.

## For smartphone cameras

- Make sure your battery is fully charged.
- Turn off all apps to save power.
- Attach your phone to a phone tripod in andscape orientation.

- Set your phone camera to manual mode or use a camera app (there are specialist aurora apps available) if it doesn't have a native manual camera app.
- Use the same settings as described above for a DSLR or Mirrorless camera.
- Some phones have native Night Modes, some that take multiple images and combine them, and some of these can be used handheld without the need for a tripod.

If you want to learn more about night sky photography, fotoVUE have published the definitive bible to night sky photography, *Photographing The Night Sky* by Alyn Wallace. You can buy a copy at **fotovue.com** and get **20% off** by using the coupon code: **COLL**

Swans in flight over Oronsay with Jura in the background. Fujifilm X–E3, 55–200mm f/3.5–f/4.8, ISO 200, 1/2000 at f/8. Nov.

The varied habitats from sea and lochs to mountain top, and the influence of the Gulf Stream make the islands of the Inner Hebrides a haven for wildlife with a rich diversity of species — from sea eagles to seals the islands, and the seas around them, are packed with fascinating creatures. Some are easier to spot than others, sightings of red deer for example are commonplace but seeing, and not just hearing, a corncrake is a massive stoke of luck. In order to maximise your chances of being lucky, planning and fieldcraft are essential. For more information on learning these skills check out *Photographing Wildlife in the UK (fotoVUE)* by Andrew Marshall.

*Atlantic white sided dolphin. © Hollandvk.*

In each islands fact file there is a list of common animal species that inhabit the island. Also check each islands website. Here are some key species to look out for and where to find them. Binoculars are useful, as is a zoom lens.

### Whale, dolphin, porpoise, basking sharks

The waters around the islands of the Inner Hebrides teem with sea-life due to a combination of the Gulf Stream and its intersection with the cold waters of the Atlantic creating the ideal conditions for the growth of plankton, the microscopic organism at the base of the food chain.

*Basking shark. © Martin Prochazkacz.*

Patience, and luck is needed to spot whales, dolphin, and porpoise (collectively known as cetaceans). Twenty-three species have been recorded in Hebridean waters. There is an app and website, the **Whale Trail** – *whaletrail.org*, that will help you spot and identify these wonderful creatures. There is an interactive map that records recent sightings at the website which will help you locate cetaceans. Several species of dolphin and porpoise, including the harbour porpoise, Atlantic white-sided dolphin, bottlenose dolphin, orcas (killer whales) — present but rarely seen — and the humpback whale can be seen year-round in open and coastal waters. In summer look out for the common dolphin. Risso's dolphin have been seen feeding and breaching off the Oa cliffs on Islay. Minke whales and basking shark migrate into the Sea of the Hebrides during the summer and can be seen feeding at the surface

*Minke whale – Coll. © Katie HM.*

between June and October each year. There are several boat trip operators, based on most of the islands, specialising in dolphin, shark and whale spotting.

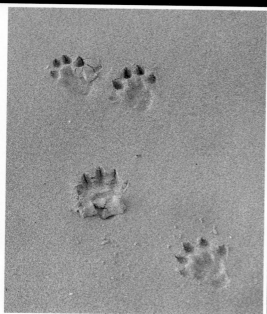

Otters. © Andrew Marshall.

Otter footprints.

Grey seal.

## Seals and otters

You stand a great chance of spotting seals and otters on the coast of the Inner Hebrides. Common and grey seals are often seen basking on the rocks and are frequently seen in and around harbours. Grey seals have their pups in October, please keep your distance. The European otter—they aren't sea otters—are common all around the coast, in saltwater lochs and inland freshwater, to spot them being stealth-like is important as otters are elusive and shy. Lookout for a bobbing head, a disappearing tail out to sea or a trail of bubbles, and if you do, be still and quiet and as always with wildlife spotting, let the subject come to you. Your best chance of seeing one is at dusk or dawn, particularly on an incoming tide when they feed. Their tracks are often seen in the sand.

Common seal.

**If you want to learn more about wildlife photography, fotoVUE have published *Photographing Wildlife in the UK* by Andrew Marshall. You can buy a copy at fotovue.com and get 20% off by using the coupon code: HEB**

*Puffins in flight.*

*Bonxie.*

## Puffins

These characterful little birds are an absolute delight and make their summer homes on a number of Hebridean islands. Completely unafraid of humans it is possible to get quite close to the birds, and photograph them in their natural habitat. Puffins arrive at the end of April and start to leave in August. Puffins can be seen on Staffa and Lunga in the Treshnish Isles west of Mull, on Canna on the Small Isles and on Skye (hard to find). From the Inner Hebrides you can also take boat trips to islands in the Outer Hebrides that are home to puffins including St Kilda (home to136,000 pairs of Atlantic puffins, about 30 percent of the UK total breeding population), the Shiants, Flannan Isles, Sula Sgier, Rona and Mingulay.

*A juvenile razorbill.*

## Great Skuas

Also known as Bonxies, these pirates of the skies are famous for dive-bombing unfortunate walkers. They can be found throughout the Hebrides in summer and are fierce scavenging birds who will often harass other smaller birds for food. If you are entering bonxie territory – beware!

## Birds – general

Three hundred and twenty seven species of birds have been recorded and more than 100 breed. Seabirds that inhabit the coastal areas of the islands include shag, northern gannets, northern fulmars, kittiwakes,

*Gannet.*

Little owl. © Andrew Marshall.

White-tailed eagle. © Andrew Marshall.

Corncrake. © Gergosz.

Greylag geese.

guillemots and multiple species of gull. Oystercatcher, ringed plover, bar-tailed godwit and dunlin are the most numerous species on the sand flats and the Atlantic beaches are particularly important to turnstones, purple sandpipers and sanderling. On the machair, oystercatcher, ringed plover, lapwing and dunlin are dominant. In the winter visit Islay's RSPB reserve at Loch Gruinart where over a thousand white-fronted geese settle each day to roost.

## Birds of prey

Birds of prey in the Inner Hebrides include the spectacular golden eagles and white-tailed eagle (aka. the sea eagle), hen harrier, merlin, short-eared owl and if you are lucky, peregrine falcons which nest on sea cliffs, Most of these species can be seen across all the islands. With a wingspan of over 2 metres, the golden eagle is a true giant of the skies. Once you have seen one, you are unlikely to get it confused with the buzzard (AKA the tourist eagle) ever again. The white-tailed eagle or sea eagle was reintroduced to the Hebrides in 1975 after being hunted to extinction in the 1920s.

## Corncrake

The corncrake is a shy and elusive bird known for its distinctive "crek crek" call. It returns to the Hebrides in April and makes its home in long grass and reeds within costal locations. Once a common bird, it is now only found in a few locations in Scotland. The RSPB reserve on Coll provide some of the best opportunities to see corncrakes and they have been spotted on Iona.

*Red deer.*

*Feral goats.*

## Red Deer and other mammals

*"Red deer are one of the symbols of Scotland, as much a visual shorthand for the Highlands and islands as the thistle."* **The Scotsman**

Red deer are found on most islands and are usually at their most active around dusk and dawn. October sees the deer coming down from the higher hills for the rut, during which the males fight for the females – the best times to witness the rut is just after sunrise. The bellowing of stags echoing around the hills is an atmospheric indicator of autumn. On Jura there are over 6,000 red deer and a similar number on Mull. On Rum there is a long standing research project investigating the behaviour and population dynamics of red deer. There are no red deer on Colonsay, Gigha, Coll or Tiree. Another large mammal to look out for are feral long- haired goats on Rum and Colonsay. On Islay and Tiree there are brown hares, and on Skye, Raasay and Mull there are mountain hares, easy to spot in winter with their white coats.

*Highland coo.*

## Highland Coo

Shaggy-haired, horned and with a lovely docile temperament, highland cows are found throughout the Hebrides and will usually stand still for long enough to take the classic postcard shot.

*Border collie.*

*Border collie.*

## Border Collie

Crazy farm dogs who will occasionally follow you along the beach or up a hill, the Border Collie is an exceptionally clever animal and a vital member of the team when it comes to rounding up the wandering sheep at shearing time. Approach with caution, they will often pester you into throwing sticks for hours.

## Resources

Island websites:
- The Sea of Hebrides (see a story map at: *www.storymaps.arcgis.com*)
- *www.whaletrail.org*
- *www.nature.scot*
- *www.rspb.org.uk*

## Nature Reserves

- Islay's RSPB reserves at the Oa and Loch Gruinart
- RSPB Oronsay
- RSPB Coll
- Rum National Nature Reserve
- Isle of Eigg Wildlife Reserve

# MACHAIR

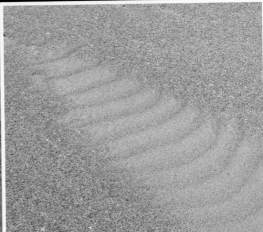

Unique to the west coast of Scotland and Ireland, Machair, a Gaelic word meaning fertile, low-lying grassy plain, is the flat or undulating carpet of wild flowers and grass found on west facing coastlines in the Hebrides. They are fascinating to visit and photograph, both the flora and birds, and are a perfect place to spot dolphins and seals. The machair was formed by calcerous shell fragments brought in by waves and then blown in by the wind, forming an alkaline soil low in nutrients, ideal for flowering plants, herbs and grasses. The machair is a semi-natural habitat, traditional Hebridean farming, tree clearance, low density grazing and the spreading of seaweed as natural fertiliser, aided its development into the beautiful and diverse carpet of plant species we see today. In the Hebrides there is a balance struck between food production and nature conservation.

Plant species include common meadow grass and red fescue, red clover, bird's-foot-trefoil, yarrow and daisies and rarer species such as lesser-butterfly orchid, Hebridean spotted orchid, marsh orchid and, on Coll and Barra, Irish lady's-tresses. You may spot iris, silverweed, ragged-Robin and poppies.

Kelp washes up on the machair, protecting it from erosion and as the kelp decays it provides food for insects which in turn are prey for wading birds and gulls. This habitat, because of its rich insect diversity, is also home to corn crake, twite, dunlin, common redshank, linnets, corn buntings and ringed plover and also several insect pollinators including several species of bumble bees.

Spring is the best time to visit for bird watching, with the machair in full bloom in June and to mid-August. The machair is under threat from rising sea levels and increasing storms which erodes it and also because of the decline of traditional farming and grazing.

## Where to find machair

### explore & discover THE OUTER HEBRIDES

### explore & discover THE INNER HEBRIDES

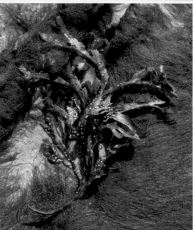

The coastline and open water of the Hebrides is rich with marine algae, the collective name for seaweed. Many types are found here including green, red and brown, with over 389 species recorded. Seaweed is used as food for both humans and livestock; as a fertiliser in the old run-rig system and for modern farming today; it was burnt to provide alkali for making soap and glass, and iodine was extracted from it. Today it makes a significant economic impact in the Hebrides. It's exported as fertiliser and dried as a nutritious snack, it's used in processed foods; as a biofuel; as a cosmetic and in skincare products. With the increase in the popularity of foraging you will often see people in the littoral zone in rocky areas as the tide goes out wearing wellingtons with scissors and a plastic bucket in hand gathering it to make into a variety of highly nutritious and tasty umami meals. Seaweed also makes beautiful macro studies.

It's quite apt that the authors of the best books about identifying, the history of, foraging for, and cooking with seaweed live in the Hebrides – both books are highly recommended.

Miek Zwamborm, who lives on Mull, is the author of *The Seaweed Collector's Handbook*, and Fiona Bird, who lives on Uist, is the author of *Seaweed in the Kitchen*.

There are so many classic locations to visit and photograph in the Inner Hebrides, it is difficult to whittle it down to a top ten. Here is a mix of my personal favourites and those that are well-known and considered classic. If your visit is short, make sure to put these on your itinerary. These are not in order of rank.

**1  CALGARY BAY**  P.136

**2  DUN CAAN**  P.436

**3  EASDALE**  P.266

**4  ELGOL**  P.356

| 5 KILORAN BAY | P.102 | 6 LAIG BAY | P.292 |

| 7 THE BAY AT THE BACK OF THE OCEAN | P.174 | 8 THE TWIN BEACHES | P.119 |

| 9 TRÀIGH CHORNAIG | P.212 | 10 WEST LOCH TARBERT | P.92 |

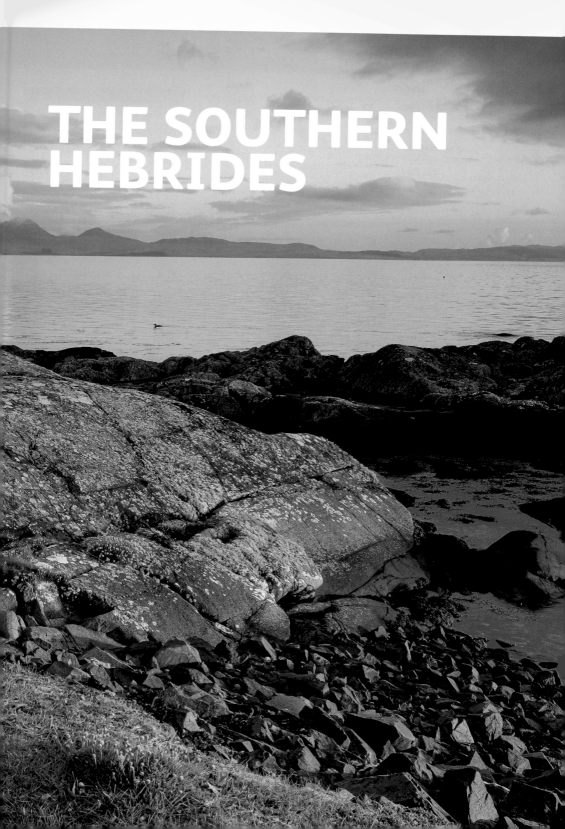

# THE SOUTHERN HEBRIDES

**The Southern Hebrides section encompasses the islands of Islay, Jura, Colonsay and Gigha. Four incredibly varied islands, each with their own distinct identity and all worth spending as much time as you can exploring.**

The largest island of the Southern Hebrides and the most famous is Islay. The spiritual home of single-malt whisky, Islay itself is more of a blend. Rugged cliffs on the Oa peninsula, wild sandy shores on the western edge, open moorland and peat bogs in the centre and picturesque villages throughout. Much like the whisky, Islay is an island to savour over time.

Jura is wild and rugged, with its quartz tipped conical hills a fixture on the Hebridean horizon. An island where deer outnumber people 35 to 1 and served by a single-track road which runs along the southern and eastern shores. Beyond the road, paths lead off into some of the most rugged and remote land in the Hebrides, there is even a whirlpool, the infamous Corryvreckan at its northern tip.

The isle of Colonsay and neighbouring Oronsay are small but perfectly formed. Kiloran Bay at the northern tip of Colonsay is one of the finest beaches in the Hebrides and on the west coast of Oronsay, the beaches have some of the whitest sand you will see, as well as a beautiful outlook to Jura.

Gigha is the smallest of the four, but is another lovely island. Located just off the Mull of Kintyre it is green and lush with a number of fantastic beaches.

*Previous spread*: looking across to Jura from the north of Gigha. Fujifilm X–T2, 18–55mm f/2.8–f/4, ISO 200, 1/9s at f/10. May.

ROSS OF MULL

SCARBA

Cruach Scarba
449m

Fladda

Dubh Artach

SUNSET  SUNRISE

0      miles      5

COLONSAY

Gulf of Corryvreckan
whirlpool

Glentrosdale Bay

Glengarrisdale Bay

Kinuachdrachd

2 Kiloran Bay
VP1-3
Uragaig
Balnahard

Barnhill
Where George Orwell
wrote 1984

Crinan

Kilchattan
B8086

1 Loch Fada
& Riasg Bhuidhe

Glengarrisdale

Glengarrisdale Bay

bothy

Raised Beaches
& Ruined Forts
VP1: Raised Beaches
VP2: Tràigh an Tobair Fhuair
& Dùn Ghallain

3

Scalasaig

Garvard

B8005

Glendebadel Bay

JURA

Corpach Bay

Beinn Bhreac
467m

Lussa
Gin

Ardlussa

Tayvallich

RSPB Oronsay

VP1
VP2

Shian Bay

Loch
Righ Mòr

Lussagiven

Oronsay 4
VP1: Crossing the Strand
VP2: The Eastern Beaches
VP3: The Priory

VP3

Ruantallain

3

bothy

Tarbert

Loch Tarbert

Taynish NNR

Loch Sween

Lagg

ISLAY

Ruvaal

Nave Island

Ardnave
Point

S
o
u
n
d

Beinn an Oir
785m

Paps of Jura

Skervuile

Sound of Jura

Argyll

6 Sanaigmore
VP1: Sanaigmore Beach
VP2: Rocks at North of Beach

Kilnave Church
& Cross

VP1  VP2

Sanaigmore

Port
Askaig

o
f

A846

Leargybreck

Ardfernal

Small Isles

RSPB Loch Gruinart

Finlaggan
Castle

Feolin Ferry

B8018

I
s
l
a
y

5 Saligo Bay

B8017

Loch Gruinart

Ballygrant

Craighouse

1 Craighouse

Kennacraig

Coul Point

Loch
Gorm

Kilchoman

Cabrach

West Loch
Tarbet

4
Machir Bay
VP1: Dunes
VP2: Shipwreck
VP3: South

THE
RHINNS

Bruichladdich

Brigend

A846

Bowmore

Lossit
Bay

Port Charlotte
Port Mòr
Centre

2 Port
Charlotte

A847

Loch Indaal

Beinn Bheigeir
491m

McArthur's
Head

Ardtalla
Beach

Gamhna
Gigha

VP3

A83

Rhinns
Point

Port Wemyss

A846

Laggan
Bay

B8016

Claggain
Bay

GIGHA
VP1: The Bays
VP2: Creag Bhàn
VP3: Twin Beaches
VP4: Port Mòr &
Palm Tree Beach

VP4

3 Portnahaven
VP1: Village
VP2: Shore
VP3: Isle Orsay & Lighthouse

Machrie Hotel
& Golf Links

Kintra
Farm

Islay
Airport

Kidalton Church
& Cross

Ardmore Point

VP2
VP1

Ardminish VP1

Achamore

RSPB The Oa

VP1
VP2
VP3

Port
Ellen

Tayinloan

American
Monument

Ardbeg

Texa

Cara

Sound of Gigha

ISLAY DISTILLERIES
1. Laphroaig
2. Lagavulin
3. Ardbeg
4. Caol Ila
5. Ardnahoe
6. Bunnahabhain
7. Bowmore
8. Bruichladdich
9. Kilchoman
10. Port Ellen

Mull of
Oa

1

OA PENINSULA

Carraig Fhada
VP1: Kilnaughton Bay
VP2: Carraig Fhada Lighthouse
VP3: The Singing Sands

KINTYRE
PENINSULA

Loch
Fyne

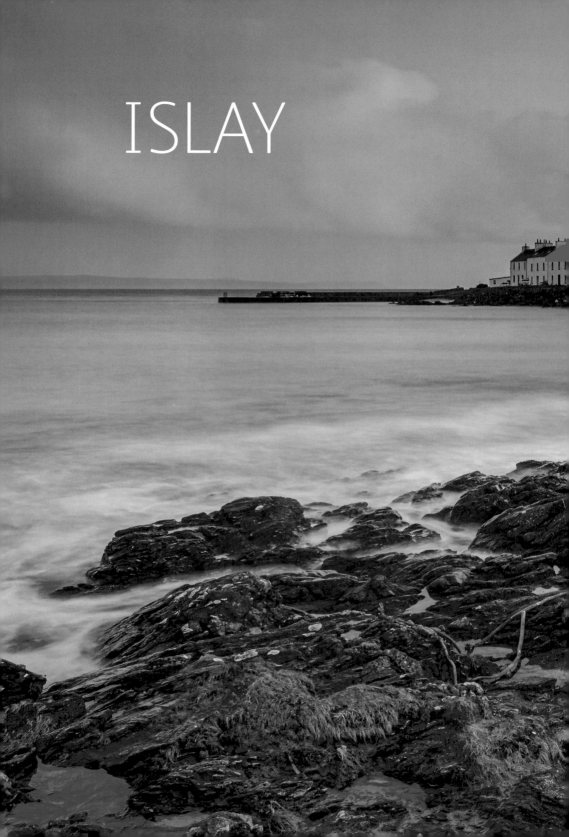

# ISLAY

**Islay is the largest and southernmost island of the Southern Hebrides and is famed for its stunning coastline, picturesque villages, and world-renowned single malt whisky. Known as the Queen of the Hebrides, Islay is a beautiful island and enjoys a fantastic situation, with far reaching views from its coastline to Ireland 30 miles away to the south, Jura to the east and Colonsay and Mull to the north.**

The island's main settlements are Bowmore (the islands largest town) and Port Ellen (the main ferry port), where you can stock up on provisions at the local shops. There are smaller local shops in Bridgend, Port Askaig, Bruichladdich, Port Charlotte and Portnahaven. Depending on which ferry you catch you will either arrive at Port Ellen or at Port Askaig on the east coast. The ferry to Jura is from Port Askaig.

Islay's whisky industry is one of the island's main attractions with nine working distilleries, each with their own heritage, style and flavour. It is famed in particular for its peaty and smoky whisky, the result of drying barley over smoking peat fires. The island's whisky is considered by many to be the finest in the world and with most distilleries offering tours and tasting it would be rude not to visit some (if not all) of them! In May *Fèis Ìle*, the Islay Festival takes place, a gathering of whisky enthusiasts from all around the globe who flock to Islay to celebrate the culture with a ten day festival of tastings, music and dances,

In addition to its whisky, Islay is also renowned for the beauty of its landscape. The island's wild western coastline is home to beautiful beaches, and the island's interior is a mix of rolling hills, peatlands and farmland. Some of the coastline is wild and rocky contrasting starkly with the bucolic pastoral farmland.

The island is home to a variety of wildlife, including seals, otters, and a wide range of bird species. The RSPB reserve at Loch Gruinart is a fantastic place to see the annual migration of Greenland geese, when thousands of barnacle and white fronted geese descend on Islay to spend the winter on the fields and estuaries. Whooper swans can also be seen at this time as they make a pitstop on their way south to Ireland, with golden and sea eagles found on the Oa peninsula. Perhaps the easiest wildlife to spot are the famous seals of Portnahaven which bask just metres offshore in the sheltered harbour.

Islay is also rich in history. It is ancient settled land, suffused in Celtic myths and legend; Kildalton Church with its beautiful 8th century carved Celtic cross, Kilnave Chapel, roofless and isolated above Loch Gruinart or Loch Finlaggan home to the island stronghold of the Lords of The Isles. All offer a spine-tingling look back into the past.

Photographically Islay offers so much, from the ferocious waves and beautiful beaches of the west coast to the distilleries and their artisan processes to the ancient ruins and Celtic history. It is an island very much like its whisky, one to savour and return to.

## How to get to Islay

The Calmac ferry to Islay leaves from Kennacraig on Kintyre, landing at Port Ellen (2 hours 20 minutes) or Port Askaig (from 1 hour 55 minutes) and they run all year-round. Vehicle reservations are recommended.

Kennacraig is 106 miles (3 hours) drive from Glasgow passing by Loch Lomond then down the Kintyre peninsula and just south of Tarbert is Kennacraig on the west coast. The Citylink bus from Glasgow to Kennacraig takes just over 3 hours.

Islay Airport operates daily flights to and from Glasgow (Loganair), with once-weekly flights to nearby Colonsay and Oban (Hebridean Air Services).

*Previous spread*: Port Charlotte in the blue hour. Fujifilm X–T2, 18–55mm f/2.8–f/4, ISO 200, 8s at f/11. Mar.

| ISLAY | |
|---|---|
| Scottish Gaelic | Ìle (Yula's isle). |
| Area | 239 sq. miles (619 sq. km). |
| Length/breadth | 25 × 15 miles. |
| Highest Elevation | Beinn Bheigeir, 491m (1,611ft). |
| Owned by | Multiple |
| Population | 3228 |
| Largest settlement(s) | Port Ellen, Bowmore. |
| Vehicles allowed | Yes |
| Car/Bike rental | Islay car hire: *islaycarhire.com*<br>Islay cycle hire: *islaycycles.co.uk • islay-bikehire.co.uk* |
| Public transport | Islay Coaches: **01496 840 273**. Links all main towns and villages.<br>There are many taxi services. |
| Day trips from mainland? | Yes, get early ferry |
| Internet/mobile phone coverage | Broadband. 3G/4G dependent on carrier. Wifi in many hotels and businesses. |
| Power | Grid, oil. |
| Island website(s) | *islayinfo.com • islay.scot • islaymuseum.org • islaynaturalhistory.org<br>southernhebrides.com • visitscotland.com • scotland.org.uk* |
| Festivals/Events | Islay Festival, *feisile.co.uk* (May/June)<br>Islay Book Festival, *islaybookfestival.co.uk* (September),<br>Beach Rugby Tournament, Port Ellen (June). |
| Accommodation | There are 12 hotels, over 30 B&Bs, over 100 self-catering properties, a youth hostel and three camping/camervan sites. Book direct at *islayinfo.com/stay* |
| Provisions/Eating Out | The island is well served by supermarkets and shops in the main towns and villages. For restaurants and bars visit: *islayinfo.com/do/where-eat* |
| Wildlife | Grey seals, dolphins, brown hares, otters, red, fallow and roe deer, over 100 species of birds, including Greenland barnacle and Greenland white-fronted geese, golden eagles, corncrakes. |
| Night Sky Bortle Scale | Class 2 away from towns/villages. |

## LOCATIONS

## Maps

• OS Landranger 60: Islay: 1:50 000

You may have noticed the unusual lighthouse at Carraig Fhada if you have arrived by ferry into Port Ellen. This squat, square lighthouse sits on a promontory to the west of Port Ellen and was commissioned in 1832 by Walter Frederick Campbell who also was responsible for the villages of Port Ellen and Port Charlotte, naming them after his wife and his mother. The square shape of the lighthouse makes it very distinctive compared to the many other lighthouses you will see around the Hebrides and it is a very recognisable Islay landmark.

## What to shoot and viewpoints

The lighthouse is the main attraction in this location, however, the beaches nearby are also very interesting and offer some excellent opportunities in their own right as well as a foreground to the lighthouse.

### Viewpoint 1 – Kilnaughton Bay
From the parking area head back down the road you have driven up from Port Ellen and turn right onto a track at the woodland. Follow this track down across the dunes to the beach. You arrive at the eastern end of the beach and this spot give a splendid view west along the beach to the lighthouse. There are also views back to Port Ellen and south to the sea. Depending on how high the river is here, you may have to walk down to the shoreline to cross it.

### Viewpoint 2 – Carraig Fhada Lighthouse ♿
Follow the beach south and head up onto the tarmac road at the end. This then leads you to the lighthouse itself. There are some small sandy bays which offer a foreground for the lighthouse. As you approach the lighthouse there are some great jagged rocks around its base which the waves break upon at high tide. This is a great spot for some long exposure images especially if you time your visit to coincide with a high tide as it breaks over the rocks around the lighthouse.

### Viewpoint 3 – The Singing Sands
From the lighthouse ascend the track to the left of the cottages and follow across some undulating and sometimes boggy land down to Tràigh Bhan also

*Singing Sands with Carraig Fhada peaking over the headland (VP2). Fujifilm X–T2, 18–55mm f/2.8–f/4, ISO 200, 1/340s at f/11. Mar.*

known as 'Singing Sands'. This beautiful white sand beach is interspersed with rocky features which the sea breaks upon creating wonderful patterns in the water. There is potential to spend a good while here and the view back to the lighthouse and Port Ellen is particularity special.

### Viewpoint 4 – The American Monument

Above the rugged cliffs of the Oa peninsula, this 131m tall monument serves as a lasting reminder of the loss experienced when two troop ships sank off the coast of Islay in 1918. On the 5th of February, the SS Tuscania, was torpedoed 7 miles offshore claiming the lives of 200 American soldiers and 60 British crew members.

Later that year, The H.M.S. Otranto sank off Machir Bay, with 351 US servicemen and 80 British crew members lost. It is certainly situated in an evocative and dramatic location and it is worth exploring the cliffs to the east, which provide the best views back to the monument as well as long distance views to the coast of Northern Ireland.

**Top**: *the winding path to the American Monument (VP4).*
*Fujifilm X–T2, 35mm f/2.8–f/4, ISO 200 1/40s at f/4. Mar.*
**Above**: *wild goats at Kilnaughton Bay (VP1). Fujifilm X–T2,*
*55–200 f/3.5–f/4.8, ISO 200, 1/170s at f/4. Mar.*

*Top*: the American Monument and the rugged cliffs of The Oa (VP4). Fujifilm X–T2, 35mm /2.8–f/4, ISO 200, 1/40s at f/5.6. Mar.
*Above*: The welcoming party at Kilnaughton Bay (VP1). Fujifilm X–T2, 55–200 f/3.5–f/4.8, ISO 200, 1/170s at f/4. Mar.

*Left*: wild goats visiting the The American Monument (VP4). Fujifilm X–T2, 55–200 f/3.5–f/4.8, ISO 200, 1/500s at f/5.6. Mar.

## How to get here

### Viewpoints 1–3

Head north from Port Ellen and take the road on the left at Port Ellen Maltings. Follow this road through the woodland and keep left at the sign for the Mull of Oa. As you pass the cemetery turn left and park in the car park.

| | | |
|---|---|---|
| | **Lat/Long**: | 55.627610, -6.2209583 |
| | **what3words**: | ///bronzes.misted.screaming |
| | **Grid Ref**: | NR344452 |
| | **Postcode**: | PA42 7AZ |

### Viewpoint 4

For Viewpoint 4, instead of turning left at the cemetery head straight on across the Mull of Oa. Follow the minor road for 15 minutes before taking the left fork at the sign for Lower Killeyan. There is a small parking area and sign boards for the RSPB Reserve. To reach the monument head west along the waymarked track and proceed through the gate on the right which leads to another gate and gives access to an open field. Follow the track around the edge of the field and the monument will come into view.

| | | |
|---|---|---|
| | **Lat/Long**: | 55.597602, -6.317171 |
| | **what3words**: | ///goose.spine.puns |
| | **Grid Ref**: | NR281422 |
| | **Postcode**: | PA42 7AU |

## Accessibility

Kilnaughton Bay is easily accessed along tracks and across the dunes. There may be some difficulty crossing the stream depending on the tide or the level of the river. However, it is wadable with wellies on. The rocks at the lighthouse can be slippery, but good images can be obtained without any rock hopping if so desired. The path to Sining Sands can be boggy, but most of these areas can be avoided.

## Best time of year/day

Kilnaughton Bay works well at sunrise with the sun picking out the lighthouse but can also work at sunset as well. The lighthouse is best at high tide and ideally with some big waves breaking over the rocks to create a dramatic foreground. Singing Sands is an ideal sunrise location with some low sun picking out the rocks and illuminating the lighthouse.

*Above*: *Snow falls on Kilnaughton Bay (VP1). Fujifilm X–T2, 10–24mm f/4, ISO 200, 1/160s at f/8. Mar.*

*Opposite*: *Carraig Fhada Lighthouse (VP2). Fujifilm X–T2, 18–55mm f/2.8–f/4, ISO 200, 8.5s at f/11. Mar.*

# ⟦2⟧ PORT CHARLOTTE

Known as 'The Queen of The Rhinns', the pretty village of Port Charlotte is located mid way between Bruichladdich and Portnahaven on the Rhinns of Islay. Its rows of whitewashed terraced houses cluster around a small harbour and sandy beach with views across the loch to Bowmore. Port Charlotte was a planned village, founded in the 1820s by Walter Frederick Campbell to provide housing for workers in the Lochindaal Distillery.

## What to shoot and viewpoints

The village itself is very interesting with a number of attractive split level buildings with bridges and small courtyards and is definitely worth spending some time in. However if you are pressed for time, the key viewpoints are along the shoreline, either looking towards the lighthouse or back towards the village. Follow the beach around to the pier to the south or north to the rocks where you can gain a view back to the village.

### Viewpoint 1 – The beach

From the parking area at the park, head across the grass and drop down onto the beach below the Port Charlotte hotel. A small sandy cove interspersed with jagged rock formations, it is quite a calm spot, sheltered by the pier to the west. The key view here is towards the Loch Indaal (Rubh' an Duin) lighthouse, perched on a promontory leading down to the sea. The pier offers opportunity for some macro work in amongst the stacks of creels and coiled ropes and also affords a great view across Loch Indaal with the Paps of Jura and the American Monument on the Mull of Oa visible on the horizon.

### Viewpoint 2 – South of the beach ♿

The best view of the village in my opinion is from the north end of the beach looking back towards the Port Charlotte hotel. From the pier head along the shoreline to the end of the beach and up onto a grassy area above the rocks. The village seems to perch right on the shoreline and lends itself to being shot against dark clouds with the white houses providing a pop of contrast. It also works well as a late evening shot with the lights of the buildings reflected in the water. The rocks along the shoreline provide an interesting foreground which works well at a high tide.

*Loch Indaal Ligthouse from the rocky beach at Port Charlotte (VP1). Fujifilm X–T2, 18–55mm f/2.8–f/4, ISO 200, 1/35s at f/16. Mar.*

## How to get here

Port Charlotte is on the A847, 10 miles from Bowmore. As you approach the village from the north you will pass the Loch Indaal (Rubh' an Duin) lighthouse on the left before the village comes into view. There are areas to park throughout the village but be careful not to block access to the houses. North of the Port Charlotte hotel there is on street parking adjacent a park.

| 🅿 **Lat/Long**: | 55.740703, -6.378654 |
| 🅿 **what3words**: | ///blogs.secures.shorts |
| 🅿 **Grid Ref**: | NR252583 |
| 🅿 **Postcode**: | PA48 7TU |

## Accessibility

Sandy shoreline and rocky foreshore. Not fully accessible to those in a wheelchair.

## Best time of year/day

Dusk and dawn are the ideal times for Port Charlotte. At dawn the lighthouse can provide a useful foil for the sun rising over Jura. At sunset the village looks excellent against the darkening sky, however, this view would also work well against a stormy sky or even in bright sunshine. Stormy conditions would also work well with the village huddled down away from the waves.

*Above*: evening sun catches the Loch Indaal lighthouse. Fujifilm X–T2, 10–24mm f/4, ISO 200, 1/420s at f/7.1. Mar.
*Below*: the main street, Port Charlotte. Fujifilm X–T2, 10–24mm f/4, ISO 200, 1/320s at f/8. Mar.

The villages of Portnahaven and Port Wemyss are located at the westernmost edge of the island at the southern tip of the Rhinns of Islay. Built to house people cleared from the interior of the island in the 1800s the two villages have a sense of being a remote outpost on Islay, the last stop before the Atlantic. Portnahaven and Port Wemyss share a church, located in Portnahaven, however, there are separate doors for the residents of each village!

## What to shoot and viewpoints

The two villages and the coastline around them offer a great variety of photographic opportunities from rugged coastal vistas, pretty villages and even the chance to encounter seals on the bay.

### Viewpoint 1 – Portnahaven ♿

The village of Portnahaven sits around a natural harbour, with rows of pretty whitewashed houses and narrow streets perched along the shoreline. It is sheltered by the islands of Orsay and Eilean Mhic Coinnich which protect the bay from the worst of the Atlantic swell, however, in winter the waves crash over the islands which can make for some very dramatic images. The sheltered cove also is home to a large and very vocal seal population so it is worth bringing a long lens to photograph these creatures as they catch fish in the bay and lie out in the sun. The best view of the village is from the rocks on the side of the bay, where these formations can provide a linear foreground interest, however, it is very picturesque village and numerous compositions can be found within it. »

*Below*: A wander around Portnahaven provides plenty of interest.

*Below*: high tide at Portnahaven. Fujifilm X–T2, 18–55mm f/2.8–f/4, ISO 200, 1/1000s at f/8. Mar.

*A seal basks on the rocks at Portnahaven. Fujifilm X–T2, 18–55mm f/2.8–f/4, ISO 200, 1/200s at f/8. Mar.*

*The rugged pebble shore north of Portnahaven (VP2). Fujifilm X–T2, 18–55mm f/2.8–f/4, ISO 200, 27s at f/8. Mar.*

## How to get here

From Port Charlotte follow the A847 southwest for 7 miles . At the 30mph signs either head straight on for Portnahaven or turn left for Port Wemyss. As you head down through Portnahaven there is parking on the street, but be careful not to park across access points. There are a number of spots all around the village for images so it is best to have walk around and explore. To reach the shore from Portnahaven, walk up High Street from the bus turning area and turn left onto Church Street at the church. Follow this road for 2 minutes and take the track on the left. Before reaching the house a gate on the right gives access to a field which slopes down to the shoreline. In Port Wemyss there is parking on the street, but again be careful not to park across access points or in front of peoples houses. The best location to park is at the southern end of the village. From there head back through the village either along Bayview Street or along the Millennium Path until you reach the stream which flows down from the farmland to the west.

## Viewpoint 1 & 2 parking

- **P** **Lat/Long**: 55.680100, -6.509122
- **P** **what3words**: ///tolls.imparts.rivals
- **P** **Grid Ref**: NR166521
- **P** **Postcode**: PA47 7SN

## Viewpoint 3 parking

- **P** **Lat/Long**: 55.675393, -6.504224
- **P** **what3words**: ///tickets.unsettled.sneezed
- **P** **Grid Ref**: NR169516
- **P** **Postcode**: PA47 7SX

### Accessibility

The viewpoints in Portnahaven and Port Wemyss are all accessible from the road or good paths and should present no access issues. The pebble shoreline described in Viewpoint 2 can be steep and unstable in places and is not suitable for those who have limited mobility.

### Best time of year/day

Portnahaven looks great in the sun, especially in the summer with the water in the sandy cove a lovely turquoise colour against the white houses. It's also good at sunset with the houses picking up the low sun. The lighthouse is best photographed at sunset, however, sunrise could also work. The shore in VP2 is best photographed on a day with a big swell where you can capture the waves as they crash into the rocks and pebbles. It works best at sunset.

*The Rhinns of Islay lighthouse peeking out above the cliffs (VP2). Fujifilm X–T2, 18–55mm f/2.8–f/4, ISO 200, 25s at f/8. Mar.*

*A hazy sunset over the The Rhinns of Islay lighthouse from Portnahaven (VP1). Fujifilm X–T2, 18–55mm f/2.8–f/4, ISO 200, 1s at f/11. Mar*

### Viewpoint 2 – The shore

To the north of Portnahaven the coastline gets increasingly rugged with pebble beaches and rocky coves lashed by the Atlantic ocean. It receives such a battering that it was chosen as the location for the first (and now decommissioned) commercial wave power device in the world, the Islay LIMPET. This stretch of steeply sloping pebble beach offers a number of interesting rock formations and outcrops and is certainly a dramatic place in stormy weather. It works best at high tide when the sea reaches the rocky outcrops. As you head north along the shoreline, views will open up to the Rhinns of Islay lighthouse.

### Viewpoint 3 – Isle Orsay and the Rhinns of Islay Lighthouse ♿

The village of Port Wemyss is ten minutes walk from Portnahaven and the views here are mainly dominated by the Rhinns of Islay Lighthouse. Founded in 1825 by Robert Stevenson this 29m structure stands on the Isle of Orsay and wards ships away from the rugged reefs and rocks around the southwest tip of the island. There are a number of good spots for images along the Port Wemyss millennium path which hugs the shoreline, however, the best location for images of the lighthouse is near to the edge of the village where a small burn flows down to the sea. It flows over some interesting rocks and provides a good lead in line to the lighthouse.

*Opposite top: a glimpse of the hills of Ireland on the horizon beyond the The Rhinns of Islay lighthouse. Fujifilm X–T2, 55–200 f/3.5–f/4.8, ISO 200, 1/9000s at f/5.6. Mar. **Bottom**: a young deer poses in front of The Rhinns of Islay lighthouse. Fujifilm X–T2, 55–200 f/3.5–f/4.8, ISO 200, 1/2000s at f/7.1. Mar.*

Machir Bay is a wide, open bay which is backed by dunes with rugged cliffs to the south. It feels like a much calmer beach than Saligo Bay to the north, however, the same could not be said of the sea as Machir Bay has been the site of numerous shipwrecks. The most deadly was in October 1918 when during an autumnal storm the HMS Otranto collided with the HMS Kashmir and the ship drifted onto 'Old Women Reef' 1.2 km offshore resulting in the deaths of approximately 470 men. The American Monument on the Mull of Oa was built to commemorate the men lost aboard the Otranto and the Tuscania which was torpedoed off the southern coast of Islay.

## What to shoot and viewpoints

Machir Bay offers a good variety of opportunities from high marram grass covered dunes to shipwrecks and big waves.

### Viewpoint 1 – Dunes

The beach is entered through the dunes from the car park and they get steadily higher the further south you go. It is worth scaling them in a few places and exploring compositions of the beach from elevation. In spring and summer the lower lying areas behind the dunes are carpeted with machair, a rare habitat which is unique to north west Scotland and parts of Ireland. A combination of shell sand blown inland, grazing animals and rainfall results in an incredible profusion of wildflowers in spring and summer. »

*Opposite: a skim of water across the sand provides great reflections. Fujifilm X–T2, 10–24mm f/4, ISO 200, 1/1000s at f/8. Mar.*

*The shipwreck at low tide (VP2). Fujifilm X–T2, 18–55mm f/2.8–f/4, ISO 200, 1/280s at f/11. Mar.*

*Wind-blown marram grass at the edge of the beach (VP1). Fujifilm X–T2, 18–55mm f/2.8–f/4, ISO 200, 1/105s at f/11. Mar.*

### Viewpoint 2 – Shipwreck

Directly west from where you have entered the beach lie the ruins of a shipwreck. There are some doubts as to whether this is the remains of Patti a steamship from the 1840s or whether it is the Mary Anne of Greenock which is said to have run aground in the 1850s carrying two-hundred cases of whisky, with much of its cargo deposited on the beach. There were scenes of disgraceful looting and drunkenness: Islay's own Whisky Galore. The wreck is best seen at low tide, and affords some possibility for macro studies, however, it is best photographed as the tide recedes. Ideally this would coincide with a sunset and would provide a fantastic long exposure opportunity with the waves rushing past the wreck.

### Viewpoint 3 – Southern end of the beach

At the southern point of the beach the rocks provide some good macro potential and there are number of pools here which can provide some interest. Climbing up the dunes here gives a fantastic view back along the full length of the beach to the farm at Coul Point.

*Opposite top: a dog walker struggles against the wind (VP1). Fujifilm X–T2, 18–55mm f/2.8–f/4, ISO 200, 1/450s at f/11. Mar. Middle: sand patterns. Fujifilm X–T2, 18–55mm f/2.8–f/4, ISO 200, 1/180s at f/11. Mar. Bottom: bits of boats. Fujifilm X–T2, 18–55mm f/2.8–f/4, ISO 200, 1/240s at f/11. Mar.*

## How to get here

Machir Bay is located on the west coast of Islay. Follow the A847 from Bridgend along the shore of Loch Indaal and take the B8018 signposted to Kilchoman. Once past the distillery, at a group of houses take the track where the road turns left and follow down to a parking area.

- **Lat/Long**: 55.783711, -6.453540
- **what3words**: ///princely.than.morphing
- **Grid Ref**: NR208634
- **Postcode**: PA49 7UX

### Accessibility

Easy walking along path to the beach — very accessible.

### Best time of year/day

Machir Bay is at its best in the spring and summer when the machair is in bloom, however, it has much to offer throughout the year. Winter can be particularly dramatic. The beach is west facing so it makes a great location for sunset. It varies greatly on the tide as well so it is worth checking beforehand depending on how you want to experience it and whether you want to photograph the shipwreck.

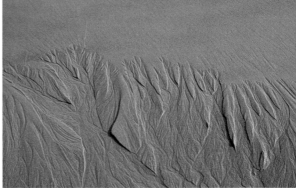

Of all the beaches on Islay's wild Atlantic coast, Saligo Bay is probably the most dramatic. A rugged, rock strewn sandy shore lashed by the sea and dominated by the cliffs of Dun Bheiolain to the north. This prominent feature is the site of an ancient hill fort, with a commanding view of the Atlantic – an ideal location for spotting Viking raiders. It is now known locally as 'The Sleeping Giant' or 'The Sydney Opera House Rocks'. The beach itself is a mixture of wave sculpted rock and sandy coves all of which combine to offer a wealth of opportunity for the photographer. It is a beach which seems to attract wild weather and the waves can be very powerful – be careful on the slippery rocks, swimming is not recommended.

## What to shoot and viewpoints

Saligo Bay is accessed from the minor road which runs in a loop around Loch Gorm. Approached from the south you will pass a row of small cottages by a bend in the road where it turns away from the coast. Park at the corner, making sure you do not block the gate. As you head through the gate and across the dunes you will see the remains of a number of World War Two buildings, which can make for an interesting study in bleak decay. A track to the left leads you down through the dunes to the beach. »

*On the dunes at the southern end of the beach (VP1). Fujifilm X–T2, 18–55mm f/2.8–f/4, ISO 200, 1/40s at f/11. Mar.*

## How to get here

Saligo Bay is located on the west coast of Islay. Follow the A847 from Bridgend which hugs the shore of Loch Indaal and take the B8018 signposted to Kilchoman. Once past the distillery take the minor road on the right and follow for 1.5 miles. The parking area is just past the row of houses on the right. Be sure not to block the gate.

- **Lat/Long:**     55.810175, -6.4523828
- **what3words:** ///lectures.tangling.perfumes
- **Grid Ref:**    NR211664
- **Postcode:**   PA44 7PU

## Accessibility

Easy walking down to the beach with some rougher walking at the northern end. Be careful of the tide, there are powerful undercurrents and the rocks can be slippery.

## Best time of year/day

Saligo Bay is a great location at all times of the year, but can be especially dramatic at high tide with a big swell. As the beach is west facing, it makes a great location for sunset.

*Above: in amongst the rocks and waves (VP2). Fujifilm X–T2, 18–55mm f/2.8–f/4, ISO 200, 1/3s at f/16. Mar.*

*Surf's Up! Fujifilm X–T2, 18–55mm f/2.8–f/4, ISO 200, 1/4s at f/16. Mar.*

### Viewpoint 1 – Dunes

The first stop along the beach is actually above it, climb up the dunes and onto a broad grassy area. Here there is a fantastic view north along the beach to Dun Bheiolain with the Atlantic sweeping in from the west. If you do this first, you won't have to clone out your footprints from the beach! Marram grasses can provide a great foreground, especially on windy days.

*Above: waves rush by a sheltered pool. Fujifilm X–T2, 18–55mm f/2.8–f/4, ISO 200, 10s at f/8. Mar.*

*Opposite: looking north along the beach from the dunes. Fujifilm X–T2, 18–55mm f/2.8–f/4, ISO 200, 1/40s at f/11. Mar.*

### Viewpoint 2 – Rocks at shore

Once you have enjoyed the view from the dunes it's time head down to the shoreline. The rocks here are fantastic; wave sculpted, smoothed and polished they can provide an excellent foreground as well as being subjects in their own right. Keep a look out for any rocks whose form echoes that of Dun Bheiolain, this always help to link your foreground and background. There are numerous compositions to be made here, depending on the level of the tide with views to the south and north. My preference is for high tide and on a day with a big swell, this can result in some fantastic conditions especially with the waves softened with a slow shutter speed. This viewpoint is also good for wave portraits – looking straight to west to the Atlantic.

### Viewpoint 3 – North along the beach

It is worth exploring the rest of the beach, as there are many opportunities along it, depending on the tide. As you head north the beach becomes rockier and the cliffs of cliffs of Dun Bheiolain become more prominent.

Located at the northern end of The Rhinns, Sanaigmore beach is reached by a long and lonely single track road across undulating farmland and bleak moorland. At the end of the road the views open up to reveal a wild and windswept stretch of coastline and a cairn which commemorates the 241 victims of the Exmouth disaster. The emigrant ship Exmouth Castle from Derry was bound for North America and foundered in stormy weather off the coast of Sanaigmore, tragically resulting in the loss of life of all except three people; a stark reminder of the Atlantic's dangerous power.

## What to shoot and viewpoints

The beach at Sanaigmore is fascinating, an enclosed north facing sandy bay with views reaching to Mull on a clear day.

### Viewpoint 1 – Sanaigmore Beach
There are a number of of large rock formations which stand out against the sand and these are worth exploring, especially for those who love studies in geological pattern and form. An overcast day will work the best for these type of shots. The beach looks fantastic on a sunny summer day with the machair in bloom against the turquoise waters of the bay.

### Viewpoint 2 – Rocks at north of beach
Following the beach to the east, around the headland it becomes less sandy and more rugged. At the northern tip, there is a rocky foreshore which is fantastic for wave photography and can be very dramatic at high tide. There are many compositions to be picked out here, with the rocks offering some great lines and contrasts as well as providing foreground for the waves.

*Opposite: waves pound the shores to the east of Sanaigmore. Fujifilm X–T2, 18–55mm f/2.8–f/4, ISO 200, 1/320s at f/8. Mar.*

*Below: breaking waves on the rocky shoreline (VP2). Fujifilm X–T2, 18–55mm f/2.8–f/4, ISO 200, 1/320s at f/8. Mar.*
*Bottom: the savage rocky coastline to the east. Fujifilm X–T2, 18–55mm f/2.8–f/4, ISO 200, 1/30s at f/11. Mar.*

## How to get here

Take the A847 from Bridgend and head west towards Bruichladdich. Take the B8018 which is signposted to Sanaigmore and continue on for 6.3 miles. There is a small parking area at the road end for 3 or 4 cars. Walk past the buildings and take a left turn via a gap in the dry stone wall. A faint path runs down to a gate and from there onto a sandy bay. This is grazing land so all dogs should be on leads and be careful if the cows are with calves.

| | |
|---|---|
| 🅿 **Lat/Long**: | 55.849823, -6.417246 |
| 🅿 **what3words**: | ///scam.seemingly.boarded |
| 🅿 **Grid Ref**: | NR236706 |
| 🅿 **Postcode**: | PA44 7PT |

## Accessibility

The sandy beach is easily accessed along tracks and across the grass. There is a tight squeeze through the opening in the dry stone wall to reach the beach which would preclude access to those in a wheelchair. The rocks to the east are a bit more difficult to access, requiring some sure-footedness especially at high tide when they can become slippery and would pose problems to the who have mobility issues.

## Best time of year/day

These locations would work at most times as the sea always provides an interesting focal point. However, as it is north facing summer sunset and sunrise are best. The rock formations are great photographed under cloudy skies. Visit at high tide for the best wave action, or at low tide to capture more of the sandy beach.

*Oystercatchers perch on the rocks at the eastern end of the beach. Fujifilm X–T2, 18–55mm f/2.8–f/4, ISO 200, 1/80s at f/11. Mar.*

In Gaelic, whisky is known as *Uisge Beatha*, the Water of Life, and from illicit stills hidden across the island to world famous distilleries, the production of whisky on Islay has been a vital component of life for centuries.

The island seems almost designed for the perfect production of malt whisky. Its temperate climate ideally suited to growing barley, the high rainfall providing a steady water supply and the peat, laid down over millennia both filtering the water and bequeathing the Islay whisky with its distinctive smoky quality. The imported bourbon and sherry barrels impart the freshly distilled spirit with flavours and colour from afar and the coastal location for maturation of the whisky imbibes it with a salty tang. The result is a spirit which is both a product of its immediate environment and one of integration with the wider world.

There are nine distilleries on the island with devotees across the world, each producing their own distinctive malt whisky. Which distilleries you choose to visit may be more influenced by your choice of favoured dram. However, some have a more photogenic setting than others. All offer tours (many with tasting) although some have restrictions on photography. The distilleries provide a wealth of interest aside from their scenic locations with the copper stills within the still houses, the distinctive pagodas and chimneys and the weathered barrels situated either outside or in darkened maturing rooms all providing great opportunities for creative compositions.

## What to shoot and viewpoints

### Viewpoint 1 – The southern distilleries: Laphroaig, Lagavulin and Ardbeg ♿

*Ardbeg courtyard. Fujifilm X–T2, 18–55mm f/2.8–f/4, ISO 200, 1/680s at f/10. Mar.*

If you have sailed into Port Ellen on the ferry from the mainland you will no doubt have noticed the three distilleries along the southern coast of Islay with their whitewashed walls bearing the name of the distillery spelt out in huge black letters. These three, Laphroaig, Lagavulin and Ardbeg are the big beasts of Islay. Peaty, smoky monsters which are politely referred to as 'an acquired taste' by some. Each distillery is worthy of a visit for photography even if you are not a fan of the whisky itself! Approaching from Port Ellen, Laphroaig is the first distillery you reach. They offer an excellent tour and are one of the few distilleries which malt their own barley, if you are interested in the distillery process this is the tour to go on. Next is Lagavulin, with its distinctive red chimney. A great view of the distillery can be had from the headland to the east near the ruin of Dunyvaig castle (itself a fine subject). A view to Ardbeg distillery from the coastline is trickier, however, there are many great opportunities here for abstract studies of the whisky barrels in the courtyard. If time permits, it is also worth continuing east to visit Kildalton Cross and Claggan Bay. »

*Whisky barrel at Kilchoman Distillery. Fujifilm X–T2, 18–55mm f/2.8–f/4, ISO 200, 1/60s at f/8. Mar.*

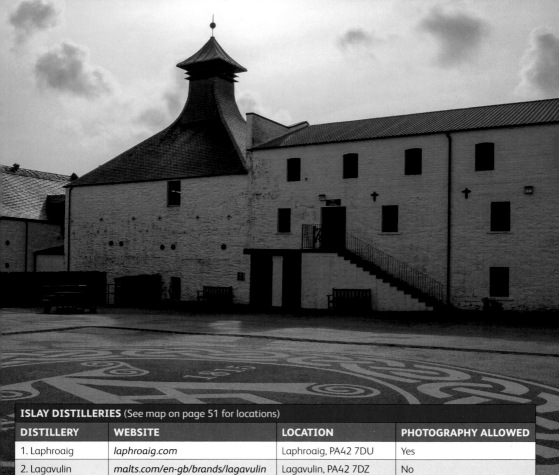

| ISLAY DISTILLERIES (See map on page 51 for locations) | | | |
|---|---|---|---|
| DISTILLERY | WEBSITE | LOCATION | PHOTOGRAPHY ALLOWED |
| 1. Laphroaig | *laphroaig.com* | Laphroaig, PA42 7DU | Yes |
| 2. Lagavulin | *malts.com/en-gb/brands/lagavulin* | Lagavulin, PA42 7DZ | No |
| 3. Ardbeg | *ardbeg.com* | Port Ellen, PA42 7EA | Yes, but not in still house |
| 4. Caol Ila | *malts.com/en-row/brands/caol-ila* | Port Askaig, PA46 7RL | No |
| 5. Ardnahoe | *ardnahoedistillery.com* | Port Askaig, PA46 7RN | Yes |
| 6. Bunnahabhain | *bunnahabhain.com* | Port Askaig, PA46 7RP | Yes, but not in still house |
| 7. Bowmore | *bowmore.com* | Bowmore, PA43 7JS | Yes |
| 8. Bruichladdich | *uk.bruichladdich.com* | Bruichladdich, PA49 7UN | Yes |
| 9. Kilchoman | *kilchomandistillery.com* | Bruichladdich, PA49 7UT | Yes |

## How to get here

The southern distilleries are located along the A846 east from Port Ellen and are all visible and with parking areas signposted from the road. The north eastern distilleries are accessed from the single track road which branches off the A846 northwards at Persabs, just to the west of Port Askaig. They are all signposted from the road. Bowmore is located in the centre of the town and is signposted from the main street. Kilchoman is signposted from the A847 as it swings around the head of Loch Indaal and Bruichladdich is a just a few minutes further on along the lochside.

## Accessibility

All have good access with car parks provided for visitors.

### Best time of year/day

The time of your visit may well be determined by the opening hours of the distillery, particularly if you are partaking in a tour. However, if photographing the exterior you can generally visit at any time. The southern stills are best photographed in the winter with the low sun of the golden hour illuminating the huge white facades. The north-eastern distilleries are also good in winter when a touch of snow on the Paps adds to their already grand appearance.

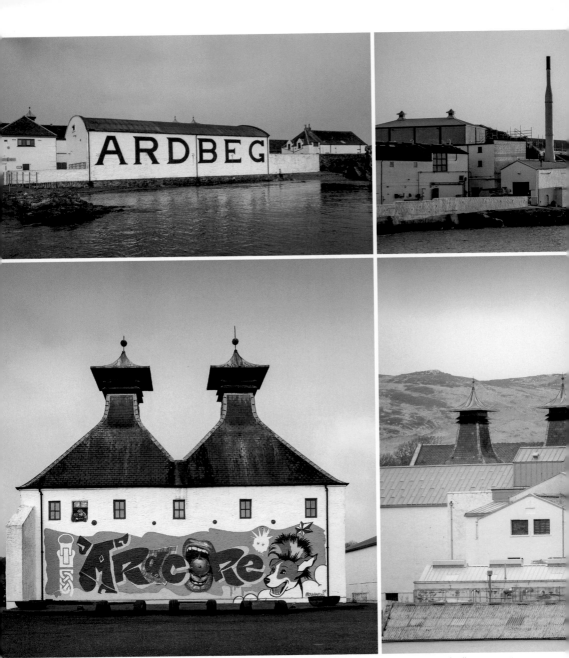

*Top left*: Ardbeg distillery. Fujifilm X–T2, 10–24mm f/4, ISO 200, 1/1000s at f/5.6. Mar. **Top middle**: Bowmore distillery at sunset. Fujifilm X–T2, 55–200 f/3.5–f/4.8, ISO 200, 1/600s at f/5.6. Mar. **Above left**: Ardbeg distillery 'Ardcore' graffiti. Fujifilm X–T2, 10–24mm f/4, ISO 200, 1/900s at f/5.6. Mar. **Above middle**: the distinctive red chimney of Lagavulin distillery. Fujifilm X–T2, 55–200 f/3.5–f/4.8, ISO 200, 1/170s at f/8. Mar.

*Top*: Lagavulin distillery. Fujifilm X–T2, 55–200 f/3.5–f/4.8, ISO 200, 1/180s at f/8. Mar.
*Above*: Bunnahabhain distillery from the rocks to the north. Fujifilm X–T2, 18–55mm f/2.8–f/4, ISO 200, 1/340s at f/8. Mar.

## Viewpoint 2 – North eastern distilleries: Caol Ila, Bunnahabhain, and Ardnahoe ♿

The eastern distilleries of Caol Ila and Bunnahabhain are a little more shy and retiring than the southern stills, tucked away up in the north eastern corner of Islay overlooking the Sound of Jura. They are now joined by Ardnahoe, the newest distillery on Islay. Caol Ila and Bunnahabhain are not the typical whitewashed distilleries and are quite industrial in appearance, however, they do benefit from fantastic views across the Sound of Jura. Caol Ila in particular looks directly onto the Paps of Jura.

## Viewpoint 3 – Central and western distilleries: Bowmore, Bruichladdich and Kilchoman ♿

Bowmore distillery is in the centre of the town of Bowmore and like most distilleries is located on the waters edge. Whilst not as pretty as some of the southern distilleries it does have a certain industrial grandeur and can be photographed well from the pier. Across the loch is Bruichladdich which is difficult to photograph from the outside but offers an informative and entertaining tour which allows photography. They also produce gin, if you fancy a change from whisky! Kilchoman is unusual in that it is located inland, 2km inland from Machir Bay. It is well worth a visit, with a great cafe and can easily be combined with a trip to Machir or Saligo Bay.

*Top*: the Paps of Jura from the road to Caol Ila distillery. Fujifilm X–T2, 18–55mm f/2.8–f/4, ISO 200, 1/300s at f/8. Mar.

*Middle*: casks maturing at Bruichladdich distillery. Fujifilm X–T2, 18–55mm f/2.8–f/4, ISO 200, 1/30s at f/4. Mar.

*Left*: old whisky barrels at Ardbeg. Fujifilm X–T2, 18–55mm f/2.8–f/4, ISO 200, 1/55s at f/8. Mar.

*Left*: the reflection of Ardbeg distillery in a whisky barrel. Fujifilm X–T2, 55–200 f/3.5–f/4.8, ISO 200, 1/750s at f/3.5. Mar.

*Above*: *Laphroaig, perhaps the finest Islay whisky? Fujifilm X–T2, 18–55mm f/2.8–f/4, ISO 200, 1/200s at f/11. Mar.*
*Below*: *the Paps of Jura from Bunnahabhain distillery. Fujifilm X–T2, 18–55mm f/2.8–f/4, ISO 200, 1/200s at f/5.6. Mar.*

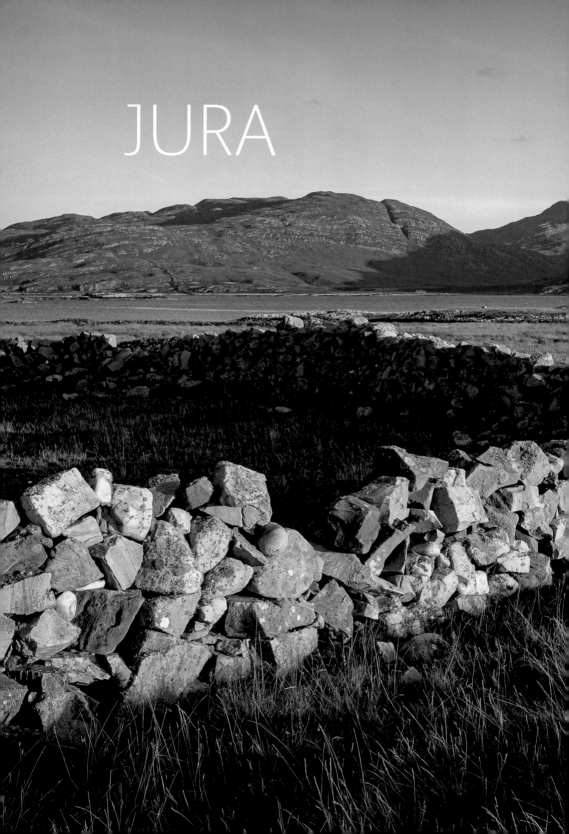

JURA

**Any visitor to the Southern Hebrides will be familiar with the island of Jura and its three distinctive Paps, the conical scree-covered hills which appear in the view from many surrounding islands. It is a rugged island where the deer outnumber the people thirty-five to one. Quite fitting for a place whose name is believed to be derived from the Norse Dýrøy meaning Deer Island.**

Jura lies between the coast of mainland Argyll and Islay yet sits in stark contrast to its island neighbour. Whilst Islay has its share of wild land, Jura certainly takes it up a level with its only road a single track which runs along the south and east coast linking the scattered houses and the main settlement of Craighouse. Beyond that the island is a true wilderness, comprising peat bogs, dense heather clad slopes, rocky beaches, scree covered hills and a few wind blasted trees which survive long enough not to be eaten by deer. For the wildlife photographer it is a paradise, beyond the eponymous deer there are golden eagles, buzzards, hen harriers, seals, wild goats and the west coast is a favoured haunt of sea otters.

Geologically Jura is truly remarkable. The dramatic Paps of Jura were once nunataks, hills that protruded through the ice sheet during the last ice age, their exposed quartzite screes the result of frost shattering which reduced rocks to rubble and today gives them their distinctive silvery hue (as well as their challenging terrain for walking!). There are volcanic dykes which run across the island, remnants of lava flow from the eruption of a volcano on Mull, which can be traced as far as North Yorkshire. However, the most incredible geological features are the raised beaches which are most apparent on the west coast of the island and were formed by a process called 'glacio-isostatic uplift'.

During glacial periods the land was compressed by the weight of the ice sheet and sea levels dropped as water became stored within the ice. As the glaciers melted, sea levels rose again and, free of the excess weight, the land began to lift. However, the land rebounded more slowly resulting in beaches forming which eventually rose far higher than the current high water mark. These incredible beaches, made up of countless wave smoothed pebbles and boulders are stranded high up above the water line and are a distinctive feature in the landscape along the north west coast of Jura.

Adding to the drama of Jura is the Corryvreckan, the third largest whirlpool in the world. Strong currents race through the narrow strait between Jura and Scarba and combine with an underwater pinnacle to produce a thrashing maelstrom of water with standing waves and whirlpools forming on the surface. On a stormy day it is quite a sight, and one which you would not be keen on getting too close to.

Culturally Jura is known for its famous resident George Orwell who lived at Barnhill in the north of the island where he wrote his novel 1984. Orwell had his own run-in with the Corryvreckan, when returning from Glengarrisdale with his son, his boat lost power and capsized. They survived by scrambling onto a skerry and lighting a fire which fortunately was seen by a passing lobster fishermen. The island was also the location where the KLF (a British electronic band) burned £1,000,000 in 1994.

## Maps

- Map: OS Landranger Map 61 (1:50 000)
  Jura and Colonsay

*Previous spread: the walled garden at Ruantallain in the golden hour (VP3). Fujifilm X–T2, 18–55mm f/2.8–f/4, ISO 200, 1/170s at f/8. Sep.*

*Opposite: Ruantallain bothy nestled against the cliffs (VP3). Fujifilm X–T2, 18–55mm f/2.8–f/4, ISO 200, 1/160s at f/10. Sep.*

| JURA | |
|---|---|
| **Scottish Gaelic** | Diùra (Deer island) |
| **Area** | 142 sq. miles (366 sq. km). |
| **Length/breadth** | 24 × 7 miles. |
| **Highest Elevation** | Beinn an Òir, 785m (2,575ft). |
| **Owned by** | Multiple |
| **Population** | 212 |
| **Largest settlement(s)** | Craighouse |
| **Vehicles allowed** | Yes |
| **Car/Bike rental** | Gerry's Cycles. |
| **Public transport** | Garelochhead Coaches. Catch the 456 that travels from Feolin Ferry to Craighouse and onwards to Inverlussa on the 'Long Road'. |
| **Day trips from mainland?** | Yes. Passenger ferry from Tayvallich. |
| **Internet/mobile phone coverage** | Broadband. 3G/4G dependent on carrier. Wifi at Jura Hotel and Jura Service Point. |
| **Power** | Grid |
| **Island website(s)** | *welcometojura.com • juradevelopment.co.uk • jurawhisky.com juracommunityshop.co.uk • isleofjura.scot • southernhebrides.com visitsscotland.com • scotland.org.uk* |
| **Festivals/Events** | Jura fell race, *isleofjurafellrace.co.uk* (May). The Craft Fair in the Village Hall is on every Wednesday in July and August. |
| **Accommodation** | There is one hotel on the island, The Jura Hotel (*jurahotel.co.uk*) and a handful of B&Bs with plenty of self-catering accommodation. Just make sure you order your supplies before you get here. Book at *juradevelopment.co.uk* or *welcometojura.com/plan-your-trip/where-to-stay* |
| **Provisions/Eating Out** | The Jura Community Shop in Craighouse and the Jura Hotel for meals. |
| **Wildlife** | Red deer (6,000 of them), otters, seals, golden eagles, sea eagles, hen harriers, buzzards, shags, arctic terns, oyster catchers, gannets and guillemots. |
| **Night Sky Bortle Scale** | Class 2 |

## What to shoot and viewpoints

### Viewpoint 1 – Craighouse

The village of Craighouse is the main settlement on Jura and is home to a shop, a hotel and the Jura Whisky distillery. The distillery offers tours and the hotel can be a welcome relief after roughing it on the west coast. It is a pretty wee village with a sheltered sandy harbour.

To reach the next two viewpoints you can either undertake a long, and often pathless walk-in from the main road which is not for the in-experienced walker or ideally charter a boat. Crinan Classic Charters (crinanclassiccharters.co.uk) offer the chance to experience the rugged west coast of Jura on Sgarbh, a beautifully restored teak motor vessel.

### Viewpoint 2 – Glengarrisdale

Sailing around from the north of Jura there are a number of bays which are visible from the sea in between towering cliffs. One of the most inviting of these is Glengarrisdale with its white-washed bothy sporting a cheery red roof which pops out against the jungle of green bracken in summer. The bothy is owned by the Ardlussa Estate (for permission to stay call Ardlussa Estate, 01496 820 323), but is maintained by the Mountain Bothy Association. Comprising two small rooms downstairs and a sleeping area in the loft it is a wonderful place to spend a few days soaking up the peace and tranquility of this remote glen. Once the site of Aros Castle, Glengarrisdale was the seat of the Clan Maclean who owned the north of the island until 1745. It was the site of a battle between Campbells and Macleans and a skull said to belong to one Maclean soldiers sat on a shelf in a cave nearby. Maclean's Skull, as it came to be known, vanished in 1976. The bothy makes a fine base to explore the surrounding coastline and also provides a lovely point of interest in the view across to Scarba from the hills to the south west. »

*Glengarrisdale bothy and the island of Scarba (VP2). Fujifilm X–100S, 23mm f/2.8, ISO 200, 1/800s at f/8. May.*

## How to get here

Jura's most famous resident, George Orwell once said that the island is "extremely un-getable". Like many of his statements it holds true today and Jura is still not directly accessible by car from the mainland. To reach the island you must first catch a ferry to Islay and then take a smaller ferry from Port Askaig to Feolin on Jura. In summer a passenger ferry runs from Tayvallich in Knapdale. To reach the viewpoints you can either undertake a long, and often pathless walk-in from the main road which is not for the in-experienced walker or ideally charter a boat. Crinan Classic Charters (crinanclassiccharters.co.uk) offer the chance to experience the rugged west coast of Jura on Sgarbh, a beautifully restored teak motor vessel. The Skipper, Ross Ryan, has extensive knowledge of the area and can tailor a trip to Jura to suit your requirements, whether that is heading through the Corryvreckan and down the wild west coast or just sailing across to Craighouse to visit the Jura Distillery. The boat departs from Crinan Basin.

### Viewpoint 1 – Craighouse

- **Lat/Long**: 55.833247, -5.9503861
- **what3words**: ///quoted.imposes.rolled
- **Grid Ref**: NR527670
- **Postcode**: PA60 7XU

### Viewpoint 2 & 3 – Crinan boat depart

- **Lat/Long**: 56.089981, -5.5567611
- **what3words**: ///station.fools.massaging
- **Grid Ref**: NR788942
- **Postcode**: PA31 8SW

## Accessibility

The west coast of Jura is incredibly rugged and generally pathless. It is remote and visitors need to be confident in their skills in map reading and negotiating wild terrain. It is possible to reach the west coast from the road on the east coast with estate tracks leading some of the way to the bothies, however, these routes are beyond the scope of this guidebook. It is far easier to reach the west coast by sea.

## Best time of year/day

Late September / early October is a special time on Jura. The bracken has turned to a lovely golden russet and the stags are rutting in the hills. Hearing the stags bellow and roar whilst you are tucked up in a cosy bothy will either scare you or delight you. If you are walking during the deer stalking season (August to October) it is prudent to check with the local estate gamekeepers to avoid any potential disruption. Ruantallain is a special location for sunset and sunrise at any time of the year, with the quartzite of the Paps picking up the low light beautifully.

*Above: the Paps of Jura from Ruantallain. Fujifilm X–T2, 18–55mm f/2.8–f/4, ISO 200, 1/80s at f/8. Sep.*

*Top left*: the Sgarbh in the Sound of Jura. Fujifilm X–T2, 18–55mm f/2.8–f/4, ISO 200, 1/1500s at f/5.6. Sep. **Top right**: juvenile Kittiwake. Fujifilm X–T2, 18–55mm f/2.8–f/4, ISO 200, 1/750s at f/8. Sep. **Above left**: cormorants on rock, West Loch Tarbert. Fujifilm X–T2, 18–55mm f/2.8–f/4, ISO 200, 1/160s at f/8. Sep. **Above right middle**: bothy stories at Ruantallain. Fujifilm X–T2, 18–55mm f/2.8–f/4, ISO 200, 1/180s at f/4. Sep. **Above right**: bothy books at Ruantallain. Fujifilm X–T2, 18–55mm f/2.8–f/4, ISO 200, 1/180s at f/4. Sep.

**Opposite top**: Craighouse from the sea (VP1). Fujifilm X–T2, 18–55mm f/2.8–f/4, ISO 200, 1/300s at f/10. Sep. **Bottom**: Jura Distillery in Craighouse. Fujifilm X–T2, 18–55mm f/2.8–f/4, ISO 200, 1/480s at f/8. Sep.

*The Paps of Jura from Ruantallain in the blue hour. Fujifilm X–T2, 18–55mm f/2.8–f/4, ISO 200, 0.6s at f/11. Sep.*

## Viewpoint 3 – Ruantallain

The wild west coast continues south past Glengarrisdale, becoming more and more exposed until the mouth of Loch Tarbert is reached. The Loch bites deep into Jura, almost severing it into two islands. The name Tarbert is found throughout Scotland and describes an isthmus or a narrow area of land between two waterbodies. It is similar to portage, being the place where the boats are hauled across land. If travelling by boat it is fantastic journey up the loch, taking in raised beaches and a wonderful narrow gorge . On the southern shore is Glenbatrick Lodge, an idyllic house nestled at the foot of the Paps of Jura in front of a golden sandy beach. The lodge is reputed to be owned by Viscount Astor and is apparently a favoured holiday destination of David Cameron. A more realistic location to spend a night is at Ruantallain bothy on the northern side of Loch Tarbert. Maintained by the Ruantallain Estate, the bothy provides simple accommodation in one of the most remote locations in Jura. It is also one of the most beautiful, with its fantastic situation affording views out to Colonsay and Islay and south across Loch Tarbert to the Paps of Jura. There is much to explore in the vicinity – a freshwater loch, caves, volcanic dykes and raised beaches are all a stones throw from the bothy. If you have arrived by foot you will want to make the most of your long walk and spend a few days in this location, it really is stunning.

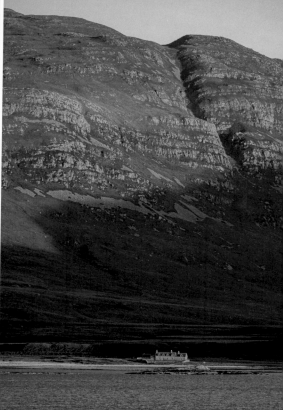

*Top left*: Ruvaal lighouse on Islay from Ruantallain. Fujifilm X–T2, 18–55mm f/2.8–f/4, ISO 200, 1/4s at f/8. Sep.
*Top right*: Glenbatrick Lodge. West Loch Tarbert, Fujifilm X–T2, 55–200 f/3.5–f/4.8, ISO 200, 1/170s at f/4.8. Sep. **Middle**: Craighouse harbour. Fujifilm X–T2, 18–55mm f/2.8–f/4, ISO 200, 1/300s at f/10. Sep. **Left**: waterfalls on the wild west coast, Fujifilm X–T2, 55–200 f/3.5–f/4.8, ISO 200, 1/450s at f/5.6. Sep.
**Above**: a fitting dram for a Jura bothy, Fujifilm X–T2 18–55mm f/2.8–f/4, ISO 200, 1/180s at f/4. Sep.

COLONSAY

# COLONSAY – INTRODUCTION

Colonsay is the most northerly of the Southern Hebrides islands and is located 8 miles north of Islay and 9 miles west of Jura. To the west, the island is open to the wild Atlantic ocean. It is joined at low tide to the even smaller isle of Oronsay and the walk across the strand is definitely one of the highlights of a trip to Colonsay. In the north of the island is Kilmory Bay, one of the finest beaches in Scotland and one which has all the ingredients you need for photographing the ideal Hebridean beach; wild waves, dunes, sculpted rocks and fine white sand; just perfect. There are many other excellent locations on the island and it is a fantastic island to explore. it is small enough to cycle round in a day on its quiet roads, but large enough to provide a great level of variety.

The main settlement of Scalasaig provides a sheltered harbour (most of the time!) for the Calmac service from the mainland which is six times a week in the summer and three days a week in the winter. In Scalasaig you will find a well stocked shop and Post Office, a cafe and a bookshop as well as the islands hotel. The island also has two gin distilleries and a brewery. There are a number of holiday cottages on the island, however, there is no provision for campervans.

There are plenty of historical sites to visit, with the most dramatic being Oronsay Priory which is though to have been in existence since the 14th century. The priory buildings are remarkably well preserved and they enjoy an idyllic setting looking out across to Islay and Jura. On the east coast of Colonsay, to the north of Scalasaig, another historical site is the abandoned settlement of Riasg Bhuidhe. Occupied until 1918, these houses are now gradually weathering away but they possess a haunting air and make a fine photographic study with an excellent view back to the mainland.

*Previous spread*: *stormy sea at Kiloran Bay. Fujifilm X–T2, 18–55mm f/2.8–f/4, ISO 200, 3.2s at f/11. Nov.*

The island is home to the popular Colonsay Book Festival, a celebration of literature which is held annually in the summer and attracts many authors, poets and artists. There is also the fantastic Ceòl Cholasa, the annual folk music festival. These two festivals are undoubtedly the highlight of the island's cultural calendar. For those who like a challenge, why not try climbing all the MacPhies (the name given to a hill over 300ft on Colonsay or Oronsay). There are 22 official MacPhies and the challenge is to climb them all in a day which equates to roughly 32km of walking across some fantastic island scenery.

## How to get to Colonsay

### Ferry

The Caledonian MacBrayne car ferry service from the port of Oban takes two and a quarter hours and runs every day from March to late October. You can reach Oban from Glasgow by car (2+ hours), train (Scotrail, 3+ hours) and bus (Citylink, 3+ hours). On Wednesdays and Saturdays there are sailings from Kennacraig and Islay to and from Colonsay. In winter there are ferries on Monday, Wednesday and Friday.

### Air

Hebridean air operates from/to Oban (Connel airport) via Islay making return flights every week on a Tuesday and, during term time in the winter, at the weekend (bookable three weeks in advance). Details from *hebrideanair.co.uk*. Booking line: **0845 805 7465** and Oban office: **01631 572909**.

### Day Trips

On Wednesdays and Saturdays you can take a day trip to Colonsay by CalMac ferry from Port Askaig, Islay. You will have about 6hrs to explore Colonsay, and bicycles travel free.

| COLONSAY | |
|---|---|
| Scottish Gaelic | Colbhasa (Columba's island). |
| Area | 15.75 sq. miles (41 sq. km). |
| Length/breadth | 10 × 2 miles. |
| Highest Elevation | 143m (469ft). |
| Owned by | The Strathcona family. |
| Population | 124 |
| Largest settlement(s) | Scalasaig |
| Vehicles allowed | Cars yes but camper vans are only allowed if you have booked accommodation in advance. Roads are narrow and are not suitable for large camper vans. No overnight parking. |
| Car/Bike rental | colonsaybikesandboards.co.uk |
| Public transport | No |
| Day trips from mainland? | Day trips to Colonsay are best on Wednesdays and Saturdays by CalMac ferry from Port Askaig, Islay. You will have about 6hrs to explore Colonsay, and bicycles travel free. |
| Internet/mobile phone coverage | Broadband. 3G/4G dependent on carrier. There is free Wi-Fi access available at The Colonsay and the Council Service Point at the far end of the village hall. |
| Power | Grid, coal, oil. |
| Island website(s) | visitcolonsay.co.uk • colonsay.org.uk |
| Festivals/Events | Colonsay International Golf Open (August). Colonsay Festival Of Spring (April). Colonsay Book Festival (April). Ceol Cholasa (September). Autumn Food & Drink Festival (October). |
| Accommodation | 40 self-catering holiday cottages, an award winning hotel, a backpackers' lodge and a guesthouse that offers specialised weekend breaks and wild camping. Book online at visitcolonsay.co.uk/accommodation |
| Provisions/Eating Out | Colonsay Shop (colonsayshop.net/Colonsay restaurant and bar, the Colonsay House Gardens Café, the Pantry, Wild Thyme Spirits. See: visitcolonsay.co.uk/about/eating |
| Wildlife | Grey and common seals, wild goats, otters, black-legged kittiwakes, cormorants, guillemots, corncrakes and golden eagles. 50 colonies of the European dark bee. |
| Night Sky Bortle Scale | Class 2 |

## LOCATIONS

## Maps

• OS Landranger 61: Jura & Colonsay: 1:50 000

For such a small island, Colonsay offers a great diversity of landscape photography opportunities. In this location there is a reed-fringed loch, a ruined village with a fascinating history and excellent views to Jura.

## What to shoot and viewpoints

### Viewpoint 1 – Loch Fada ♿

Loch Fada bites deeply into the island, extending in a north easterly direction from the Atlantic. The loch is actually three waterbodies joined together by streams and is crossed by the main B8087. It is at this point where the best photographic opportunities are located. The obvious vista is to the south west, reaching down the loch to the houses at the far end, with the hills on the left forming a good balance to the frame. This works particularly well at sunset where the hill, reeds and houses can be silhouetted against a bright sky. However, the big vista isn't the only opportunity here; the reeds themselves provide wonderful forms for some detail studies. »

*The ruined buildings of Riasg Bhuidhe (VP2). Fujifilm X–T2, 18–55mm f/2.8–f/4, ISO 200, 1/300s at f/8. Nov.*

*Abandoned building above Loch Fada (VP1). Fujifilm X–T2, 18–55mm f/2.8–f/4, ISO 200, 1/350s at f/8. Nov.*

## How to get here

From Scalasaig head north on the B8086. After 5 minutes follow the switchback road around the corner. At this next corner, a track extends in a loop from the road and it is possible to park here. To reach Viewpoint 1, walk down the hill along the roadside. To reach Viewpoint 2, head back up the road until you reach the recycling depot on the left hand side. Pass by the fence on the left, of the fence following the faint path and make your way down the hill. It can be quite boggy but keep to the heather-clad higher points and your feet should remain dry. The gables of Riasg Bhuidhe come into view after about 20 minutes of walking.

- **Lat/Long:** 56.080445, -6.1942284
- **what3words:** ///coverings.laptops.spreading
- **Grid Ref:** NR391954
- **Postcode:** PA61 7YN

### Accessibility

Loch Fada is essentially road side and is easily accessible to everyone. Riasg Bhuidhe requires some route finding and the route can be boggy, but it should be within the capabilities of most walkers.

### Best time of year/day

Loch Fada is a great spot for a winter sunset with the potential for silhouetting the reeds and hills against a bright sky. However, it also works well on overcast still days where details of the reeds can provide some wonderful opportunities for some studies in zen-like simplicity. Riasg Bhuide works at all times, but to take in the view at its best requires a day of good visibility.

*Above*: the gables of a house at Riasg Bhuidhe (VP2). Fujifilm X–T2, 18–55mm f/2.8–f/4, ISO 200, 1/125s at f/10. Nov.
*Below*: a stormy sunset over Loch Fada (VP1). Fujifilm X–T2, Fujifilm X–T2, 55–200 f/3.5–f/4.8, ISO 200, 1/420s at f/5. Nov.

*The snowy hills of the mainland beyond Riasg Bhuidhe. Fujifilm X–T2, Fujifilm X–T2, 55–200 f/3.5–f/4.8, ISO 200, 1/300s at f/8. Nov.*

## Viewpoint 2 – Riasg Bhuidhe

The abandoned village of Riasg Bhuidhe, sits in an isolated position on the east coast of Colonsay and is reached by a boggy and somewhat pathless route. As you walk down the hill towards the sea, passing an abandoned house at Bonaveh, the walls and remaining gables of Riasg Bhuidhe come into view against the backdrop of the sea and the isle of Jura. It's a wonderfully isolated place, however, you can't help but wonder at how difficult life would have been here for the occupants. Formerly an agricultural village, it became a herring fishing village in the late 19th century, and was occupied until 1918 when new houses at Glassard on the outskirts of Scalasaig were built for the residents. The site had been occupied for over a thousand years, with evidence of a ruined chapel and a well to the south of the village. An intricately carved cross once sat beside this well, and it can now be seen in the gardens of Colonsay House. Photographically the houses and the street which they form are a fascinating subject both in terms of their situation in the wider view and in the details found amongst the tumbledown walls and overgrown remains.

*__Top right__: chimney detail (VP2). Fujifilm X–T2, Fujifilm X–T2, 55–200 f/3.5–f/4.8, ISO 200, 1/100s at f/8. Nov. __Middle__: roofless houses at Riasg Bhuidhe. Fujifilm X–T2, 18–55mm f/2.8–f/4, ISO 200, 1/300s at f/8. Nov. __Bottom__: Loch Fada. Fujifilm X–T2, 18–55mm f/2.8–f/4, ISO 200, 1/100s at f/8. Nov.*

*Top*: *looking across to Jura from the slopes above Riasg Bhuidhe (VP2). Fujifilm X–T2, 18–55mm f/2.8–f/4, ISO 200, 1/240s at f/8. Nov.*
**Above left**: *Reeds detail at Loch Fada. Fujifilm X–T2, 55–200 f/3.5–f/4.8, ISO 200, 1/210s at f/4.8. Nov.* **Above middle**: *reeds at sunset on Loch Fada (VP1). Fujifilm X–T2, 55–200 f/3.5–f/4.8, ISO 200, 1/220s at f/4.8. Nov.* **Above right**: *a triangle of sea between the gables. Fujifilm X–T2, 55–200 f/3.5–f/4.8, ISO 200, 1/250s at f/8. Nov.*

Kiloran Bay is the crowning jewel of the many fine beaches on Colonsay and to my mind the finest beach in the Southern Hebrides. A golden crescent of sand, overlooked by a craggy peak, lashed by the open Atlantic Ocean: you really couldn't ask for more! It's a magical place to spend time and one whose character can vary greatly on the conditions from an idyllic holiday beach in summer to a savage wave strewn strand in winter. However, it's not just beach at Kiloran, there are hills, standing stones and even whales to be found in the vicinity.

## What to shoot and viewpoints

### Viewpoint 1 – Overlooking the beach ♿

One of the best spots to view the beach from is at the parking area; a path leads down to a kissing gate and gives access to a close cropped sward of grass punctuated with wind and rain smoothed rocky outcrops. From here the full majesty of the beach is revealed and the inclusion of a bench makes it a particularly fine place to sit and wait for the light!. The peak of Carnan Eoin dominates the view and wide shots are necessary if you wish to include this and the whole of the beach. There are also some interesting opportunities looking to the beach from the road past the parking area, with gorse bushes providing a good foreground to the view. There are some interesting rock formations which get more dramatic as you move towards the west with some water sculpted rock making a great foil for the breaking waves.

### Viewpoint 2 – The beach

The beach itself offers many opportunities, far more than can be photographed on a single trip. The burn which flows along the southern edge provides excellent macro opportunities as its shifting course creates miniature landscapes amongst the sand and boulders. Towards the northern end of the beach there is a fascinating rocky outcrop with wonderfully folded rocks which seem to replicate the wave forms of the ocean. It is a great spot for long exposure work, especially on an incoming tide. **>>**

*Rocky outcrops at the northern end of the beach (VP2). Fujifilm X–T2, 18–55mm f/2.8–f/4, ISO 200, 27s at f/8. Nov.*

## How to get here

As you will likely to have arrived by ferry you will be familiar with the main settlement, Scalasaig. From here head north on the B8086. After ten minutes of wonderful scenery you will reach Colonsay House. Follow the dog leg road round through the trees and head on through the farmland. After a sharp left turn head straight on until you reach a car park on the right. This also functions as a turning area so please make sure you park considerately. If it is full, turn back and park just off the track which leads to Balnhard farm. This is just before the sharp turn.

🄿 **Lat/Long**:     56.100874, -6.1865568
🄿 **what3words**: ///outbursts.gestures.star
🄿 **Grid Ref**:     NR397976
🄿 **Postcode**:     PA61 7YT

*Above*: *the wide sweep of Kiloran Bay from the rocks at the southern end (VP1). Fujifilm X–T2, 14mm f/2.8, ISO 200, 6s at f/11. Nov.*

## Accessibility

Very simple and easily accessed, it is a short walk down to the beach. However, if the burn is high after heavy rainfall, wellies would be useful. Alternatively, head back down the road and take the track on the left before heading across the dunes after the cattle grid. The walk to Meall na Suiridhe is steep but nothing too strenuous.

## Best time of year/day

Kiloran Bay faces north west, so if you are wanting to get a shot of the sun setting you will need to be there in summer. However, it is great at all times offering many opportunities whatever the weather. A wild winter day can offer some fantastic conditions and on a high tide, with the waves crashing on the rock its a really dramatic place. Likewise, a low tide in summer with blue skies and the sun glinting off the shallow pools of water left on the sand can also be a photographers dream. It's simply one of the finest beaches in the Hebrides and should be number one on the list when visiting Colonsay.

*The gate to the beach (VP1). Fujifilm X–T2, 18–55mm f/2.8–f/4, ISO 200,1/160s at f/11. Nov.*

### Viewpoint 3 – Hills, stones and whales

From the rocks to at the northern end of Kiloran Bay (currently home to a decomposing whale) a path leads up from the burn onto the dunes. A gate gives access onto the grazing land and a faint path leads across to the concrete road which snakes up the shoulder of Carnan Eoin. There are some good views from here back to Kiloran bay, but nothing too fantastic photographically. Heading on along the track, it descends down to the rocky beach of Port Sgibnish, a Viking port over which the jagged cliffs of Meall na Suiridhe loom. From the beach, faint paths lead up to a single standing stone, perched in a wonderful (but precarious) position on top of the cliffs. It was erected in 2003 to commemorate the 50th birthday of a local resident. No matter its lack of ancient history it still makes a fine subject. Looking north from the stone, the huge partially filled outline of a whale can be discerned on the grass. This is an evolving stone sculpture by the artist Julian Meredith which is gradually being filled in by visitors.

*Top*: *the 50th Birthday Stone (VP3). Fujifilm X–T2, 18–55mm f/2.8–f/4, ISO 200, 1/180s at f/11. Nov.*
*Above*: *studies of sand and water on Kiloran Bay.*

*Opposite*: *a sheep keeps watch on Meall na Suiridhe (VP3). Fujifilm X–T2, 18–55mm f/2.8–f/4, ISO 200, 1/220s at f/5. Nov.*

At the southwestern end of Colonsay is a fascinating stretch of coastline. Rocky raised beaches and gentle sandy bays provide a wonderful contrast and offer a wealth of opportunity for seascape photography. A ruined fort provides a fantastic elevated viewpoint over the south west of the island and also across to Oronsay. If you visit on a clear day you may even see the Dubh Artach lighthouse 15 miles to the west.

## What to shoot and viewpoints

### Viewpoint 1 – The raised beaches

The raised beaches along the west coast of Scotland are the result of a fascinating geological process called glacial isostatic uplift. As the glaciers which once covered Scotland melted, the force which depressed the land was removed, resulting in the land rising and leaving the beaches high and dry. The raised beaches extend north to Port Mòr and this pebble shoreline, interspersed with jagged rocks is ideal for long exposures on a wild day. To access the raised beaches head west from the parking area at the golf course along a faint path in the grass passing a rusting structure and a lookout structure on the hill to the right.

### Viewpoint 2 – Tràigh an Tobair Fhuair (beach) and Dùn Ghallain (hill fort)

From the parking area, Dùn Ghallain is noticeable to the south, rising up above the surrounding beaches and low-lying areas. It is easy to see why it was chosen to be the site of the Iron Age hill fort as it provides a perfect vantage point for the surrounding area. To reach Dùn Ghallain head down the grassy slope to the crescent of beach called Tràigh an Tobair Fhuair (Beach of the Cold Well). The beach provides a useful foreground for the hill with a graceful curve of sand which draws the eye through the scene. From here make your way along the rocky shoreline past more raised beaches and head towards the hill. There aren't any paths but it's quite easy to pick a route up the grassy slope. The top of the hill is crowned with the remains of the hill fort which must have been quite a large structure judging by the amount of rock. The views from the fort are excellent, with interest in all directions; over to Oronsay, to Jura and up the rugged west coast of Colonsay. Definitely a great spot to set up and wait for sunset. From here you can either retrace your steps north along the coast or head back across the golf course.

*Looking down from Dùn Ghallain (VP1). Fujifilm X–T2, 18–55mm f/2.8–f/4, ISO 200, 1/180s at f/8. Nov.*

## How to get here

From Scalasaig head inland from the ferry terminal on the B8086 passing the hotel on your right. After 5 minutes you will pass a farmhouse on the left and the sea comes into view. As you follow the road on, you pass a turnoff on the left to Colonsay Airfield and Golf Course. Past this the road rises up to a crest and there is an area which you can pull off onto on the left.

| | | |
|---|---|---|
| 🅿 **Lat/Long:** | 56.065678, -6.2446316 |
| 🅿 **what3words:** | ///plan.fork.cookbooks |
| 🅿 **Grid Ref:** | NR359939 |
| 🅿 **Postcode:** | PA61 7YR |

## Accessibility

Both viewpoints are accessible to walkers, but they may be unsuitable to those with restricted mobility. The raised pebble beaches can also be very slippery when wet and there isn't a clear path up Dùn Ghallain from the beach, however, it is not too tricky.

## Best time of year/day

As this viewpoint is on the west coast of Colonsay with a clear view out to the Atlantic it makes the ideal location for sunset. However, both locations offer opportunities outside the golden hour and can be spectacular in stormy conditions.

*Top left: Towards Tràigh an Tobair Fhuair and Dùn Ghallain from the road. Fujifilm X–T2, 18–55mm f/2.8–f/4, ISO 200, 1/75s at f/8. Nov.* **Middle**: *The lookout structure above the raised beach (VP2). Fujifilm X–T2, 18–55mm f/2.8–f/4, ISO 200, 1/480s at f/8. Nov.* **Right**: *Rusty remains on the raised beach. Fujifilm X–T2, 18–55mm f/2.8–f/4, ISO 200, 1/480s at f/8. Nov.*

**Above left**: *a sheep poses. Fujifilm X–T2, 55–200 f/3.5–f/4.8, ISO 200, 1/900s at f/4.8. Nov.* **Right**: *the pebbles of the raised beach. Fujifilm X–T2, 18–55mm f/2.8–f/4, ISO 200, 1/350s at f/8. Nov.*

Getting to an island is always special. Whether it is by ferry or canoe or via a bridge, there is always a thrill passing over water to get to your destination. However, for some reason it feels even more special to be able to walk across to an island at low tide, knowing that you will be cut off when the sea rushes back in. Oronsay, a small island at the southern tip of Colonsay is one of these islands. Not only is it a tidal island, it also has a historic priory, a farm, plentiful wildlife and fantastic white sand beaches. It really isn't to be missed.

## What to shoot and viewpoints

### Viewpoint 1 – Crossing The Strand

Getting to Oronsay is part of the fun. Ideally you want to maximise the amount of time you can spend on the island so it is best to cross as the tide is on its way out, making sure you return before it comes in again. Tide times are available online, however, the best place to find out when you should cross is at the Post Office where you can get detailed information. Once you have determined when to go to Oronsay you have to cross the Strand. At low tide, this is a 1km walk across firm sand following the vehicle tracks made by island residents. It can be quite wet underfoot, so wellies are advisable. It's a nice stroll across and the pools, and patterns in the sand can make for some interesting images. The view back to Beinne Eibhne on Colonsay is also rather special in the morning light. Once you reach the far shore follow the track inland.

### Viewpoint 2 – The eastern beaches

After 15 minutes of walking the track slopes down and meets a dry stone wall on the left hand side. Head through the first gate and make your way across the grazing land towards the beach. The views from here are stunning, with the distinctive outline of Jura laid out along the horizon. Keep your eyes peeled for local wildlife, the whole island is managed by the RSPB using low-intensity farming methods and is home to many birds. You might be lucky enough to see the distinctive chough, with its bright red beak or hear the elusive corncrake with its rasping call. You are very likely to see some sheep, and these can provide a lovely foreground to the view. As you walk towards the beach look out for the gable end of Seal Cottage, a house which is perched in the most idyllic spot and head towards it. The beaches here are beautiful with incredibly white sand and a fantastic outlook to Jura. A really incredible view. **»**

*Below left: the Paps of Jura from the road to the Priory. Fujifilm X–T2, 55–200 f/3.5–f/4.8, ISO 200, 1/2000s at f/8. Nov.*

## How to get here

Getting to Oronsay does need a bit of planning. Once you have established your tide times and calculated your time on the island head inland from the ferry terminal on the B8086 passing the hotel on your right. After a cattle grid look for a narrow road on the left hand side. Follow this winding road for 5 minutes until you reach a small parking area on the left at the roads end. After that, follow (on foot) the vehicle tracks across The Strand. Make sure you leave enough time to return before the tide turns.

| | |
|---|---|
| **Lat/Long**: | 56.040211, -6.2208234 |
| **what3words**: | ///playroom.roaming.debater |
| **Grid Ref**: | NR372910 |
| **Postcode**: | PA61 7YS is 3.159 km from NR372910 |

### Accessibility

The island is quite tricky to reach and may be unsuitable for those of limited mobility. Be very careful to plan your visit according to the tides, and most importantly leave time to get back to Colonsay before the tide turns.

### Best time of year/day

Unless you plan your trip very carefully, the time of day when you visit will be decided by the tide. Ideally you would be able to experience the sun rising over Jura or the late sun catching the walls of the priory, but that may not be likely. In reality it doesn't matter, it is a special island and is fantastic in all conditions. However, it would be best to experience it on a clear day with good visibility.

The view to Jura from the sandy eastern shore. Fujifilm X–T2, 18–55mm f/2.8–f/4, ISO 200, 1/80s at f/11. Nov.

Celtic Cross at Oronsay Priory. Fujifilm X–T2, 18–55mm f/2.8–f/4, ISO 200, 1/100s at f/2.8. Nov.

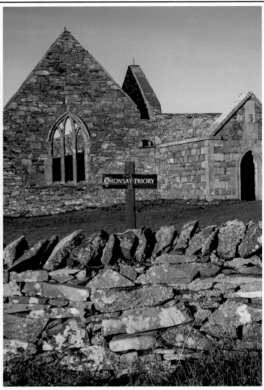

*Above*: *Oronsay Priory. Fujifilm X–T2, 18–55mm f/2.8–f/4, ISO 200, 1/350s at f/8. Nov.* **Opposite**: *an exploration of the Priory (VP3).*

## Viewpoint 3 – The Priory

It is possible to walk south along the coastline eventually arriving at the priory via the western beaches, however, depending on how long you have on the island it may be best to retrace your steps back to the main track and head along to the Priory. As you reach the end of the track you will pass the very pretty Oronsay farm on your right, before a timber gate gives access to the Priory grounds. The Priory was established in the 14th century, however, it is rumoured that it stands on a much older site, said to be founded by St Columba on his way to Iona. It is quite an awe-inspiring collection of buildings and ruins, especially in this remote setting. Luckily most have been well preserved and you can walk through the cloisters and get a good feel for how the space was in the 14th century. Within the grounds are two Celtic crosses and the view across the priory from the hillock to the north is really special.

*Top*: *crossing the Strand to Oronsay (VP1). Fujifilm X–T2, 18–55mm f/2.8–f/4, ISO 200, 1/200s at f/10. Nov.*

*Middle*: *the sandy beaches on the eastern shore (VP2), Fujifilm X–T2, 18–55mm f/2.8–f/4, ISO 200, 1/80s at f/11. Nov.*

*Bottom*: *the road to the Priory. Fujifilm X–T2, 18–55mm f/2.8–f/4, ISO 200, 1/125s at f/8. Nov.*

# GIGHA

Sunset over Jura from Port Mòr, Fujifilm X-T2, 18-55mm f/2.8-f/4, ISO 200, 0.5s at f/11, May

The short crossing to Gigha on the ferry from Tayinloan is always a lovely experience. In summer, under a blue sky it is incredibly idyllic, with the sandy bays along the east coast lapped by a shallow turquoise sea looking particularly inviting; as does the Boathouse restaurant which sits just behind one of the beaches. However, before that, there are some pleasant short walks nearby which offer a variety of photographic opportunities as well as giving a great vantage point over the area. The northern end of Gigha is a particularly special landscape, a peaceful mix of farmland, sheltered sandy bays and small hills with an outlook across the sea to Jura and its distinctive Paps. The main attraction of the area are the Twin Beaches, a combo of beautiful sandy bays, however, there are also some other great spots to be found in this small area and it's worth spending some time exploring the hillocks and hidden coves.

## How to get to Gigha

### Ferry

Gigha is accessed by the Caledonian MacBrayne ferry from Tayinloan on the Kintyre coast. The ferry runs year-round and the crossing takes 20 minutes landing at Ardminish. Tayinloan is 2.5 hours drive from Glasgow with the train taking 3+ hours (Scotrail to Arrochar then a bus) and the Citylink bus taking 4 hours. You are encouraged to leave your car at Tayinloan, parking is free, to reduce congestion on the narrow Gigha roads. Caravans are not permitted on the island or the ferry. Campervans and motorhomes are permitted. You can hire bikes in Tayinloan.

### Air

You can fly (Loganair) from Glasgow Airport to Campbeltown Airport 17 miles south of Tayinloan on Kintyre peninsula.

### Maps

• OS Landranger 62: North Kintyre & Tarbert: 1:50 000

*Sunrise at Port Mòr looking to Jura (VP4). Fujifilm X–T2, 18–55mm f/2.8–f/4, ISO 200, 1/9s at f/10. May.*

| GIGHA | |
|---|---|
| Scottish Gaelic | Giogha (God's island). |
| Area | 5.3 sq. miles (14 sq. km). |
| Length/breadth | 7 × 1.5 miles. |
| Highest Elevation | Creag Bhàn 100m (330ft). |
| Owned by | Community-owned (Isle of Gigha Heritage Trust). |
| Population | 163 |
| Largest settlement(s) | Ardminish |
| Vehicles allowed | Yes |
| Car/Bike rental | Gigha bikes and boats. Gigha Boats & Activity centre (bike hire) 07549 682 700. |
| Public transport | No |
| Day trips from mainland? | Yes, easily. |
| Internet/mobile phone coverage | Broadband. 3G/4G dependent on carrier. |
| Power | Wind turbines. Gigha Renewable Energy Ltd. |
| Island website(s) | visitgigha.co.uk • gigha.org.uk • southernhebrides.com visitscotland.com • scotland.org.uk |
| Festivals/Events | Sound of Gigha (music) Weekend in June. |
| Accommodation | Gigha Hotel, a camp and motorhome site. Self Catering and Bed & Breakfast. More info at visitgigha.co.uk/Places-To-Stay |
| Provisions/Eating Out | Gigha Resaurant & Pub, The Boathouse, The Nook, Ardminish Stores And Post Office. Local produce including Gigha Halibut. More info at: visitgigha.co.uk/Places-To-Eat-And-Drink |
| Wildlife | Guillemots and eiders, mallards, teal, wigeons and pochards can be found along with herons, snipes, pheasants and red grouse. There are no red deer, stoats, weasels, red foxes or hares. |
| Night Sky Bortle Scale | Class 2 (Dark Sky Discovery Site ). |

## What to shoot and viewpoints

### Viewpoint 1 – The bays ♿

As you disembark the ferry, the first of a series of sheltered sandy bays appears on the left hand side. The colours here are breathtaking, with picture postcard white sands and almost luminous blue seas. A stroll along the road allows you to take in these small bays and in summer the yachts in the bay provide an interesting backdrop. As you pass the Boathouse, the coast becomes rockier and the path weaves its way alongside the shore and through dense thickets of gorse. In spring and summer this is a riot of yellow flowers with an intoxicating scent of coconut. A sheltered sandy bay is reached with a small building above it, where you can follow the path which returns to the main road. Or retrace your steps back to the Boathouse restaurant. »

*Turquoise water on the eastern coast (VP1). Fujifilm X–T2, 18–55mm f/2.8–f/4, ISO 200, 1/800s at f/8. May.*

### How to get here

Gigha is accessed via the Caledonian MacBrayne ferry from Tayinloan on the Kintyre coast.

### Viewpoint 1 – The bays

There is a parking area to the right as you disembark the ferry. From here, follow the road along the coast taking in the bays, at low tide it is possible to walk along the sand most of the way along to the Boathouse. From there a path leads along the bays to the south.

### Viewpoint 2 – Creag Bhàn

To reach Creag Bhàn head back to the main road and follow it inland to the shop. Turn right and follow the long straight road which runs between farmland and the golf course. Upon reaching a farm on the right, take the track on the left passing some rusting tractors. The track continues on for a further 10 minutes before the Water Treatment Works are reached on the right. Follow the track towards this structure before a path branches off to the summit of Creag Bhan, weaving through dense thickets of gorse. The walk from the car park to Creag Bhàn takes around 45 minutes.

### Viewpoint 1 & 2 parking

- **P Lat/Long**: 55.678664, -5.7339278
- **P what3words**: ///september.vesting.insolvent
- **P Grid Ref**: NR653491
- **P Postcode**: PA41 7AA

### Viewpoint 3 – The Twin Beaches & Viewpoint 4 – Port Mòr and Palm Tree Beach

To reach the north of the island head inland and take a right at the T junction next to the shop. From here proceed north for 15 minutes. There is a parking area on the left in a field (through a gate) for motorhome parking which provides access for the walk down to the Twin Beaches. There is also a turning area further north at Port Mòr.

### Viewpoint 3 & 4 parking

- **P Lat/Long**: 55.721958, -5.7272944
- **P what3words**: ///dunk.easels.assemble
- **P Grid Ref**: NR660539
- **P Postcode**: PA41 7AA

## Accessibility

The beaches are all accessible to walkers, past the boathouse there are a few rocks to hop over but nothing too challenging. Creag Bhan is a leisurely stroll along a quiet road with a steep slope at the end. There are good paths throughout. Much of the island is very flat and exploring by bike is a fine way to experience it. The twin beaches are reached via a signposted track which runs down to the beach through some dense scrubby woodland. It can be very muddy after rainfall. However, there are usually some from of stepping stones across the worst of the quagmire. It is possible to head northeast along the coast from the twin beaches to the smaller sandy bay. However, it is a bit of a rocky scramble and in summer can be very overgrown. There is a path which runs from the road (follow the black and white striped posts) which runs alongside a field boundary before diving off into the undergrowth and appearing on the shore. Palm Tree Beach is best accessed at low tide when it is possible to nip across the bay. Alternatively just follow the high tide line where it is relatively dry. The hillocks can be accessed via small tracks from the roadside.

## Best time of year/day

Gigha is one of those places which look fantastic under a bright summer sky. The combination of white sand and shallow sea creating that wonderful, typically Hebridean combination. The beaches along the east are probably best experienced on a sunny day, and actually are at their finest outside of the golden hour. Creag Bhan is a great spot on a day of clear visibility and also works well for summer sunsets. Sunset over Jura from the northern end of the island is beautiful. In fact, The Paps of Jura are probably best photographed from the surrounding islands rather than Jura itself. The distinctive skyline is best experienced from the hillocks, however, the lack of potential foregrounds makes the lower areas at Port Mòr or the Twin Beaches more desirable. Port Mòr is also a fantastic dawn location.

*Atop Creag Bhàn looking north to the twin beaches (VP2). Fujifilm X–T2, 18–55mm f/2.8–f/4, ISO 200, 1/480s at f/8. May.*

## Viewpoint 2 – Creag Bhàn

The highest point of Gigha, Creag Bhàn, is only 100m above sea level but it gives a fantastic panoramic view of Gigha and further afield. Islay, Jura, Kintyre, Arran and on a clear day, the hills of Northern Ireland are visible on the southern horizon. The top of the hill is mix of smooth rock outcrops, dense heather and gorse and these contrasting ground covers can provide a some great foreground opportunities. Of particular interest in the view north are the Twin Beaches which join Gigha to Eilean Garbh, with the white sands standing out against the sea. In late spring the route up the hill passes through large swathes of bluebells.

*Rocky shoreline along the bays. Fujifilm X–T2, 18–55mm f/2.8–f/4, ISO 200, 1/1250s at f/8. May.*

*Windblown grasses on the twin beaches (VP3). Fujifilm X–T2, 14mm f/2.8, ISO 200, 67s at f/5.6. Jul.*

## Viewpoint 3 – The Twin Beaches

The Twin Beaches is the name given to the tombolo which connects Gigha with Eilean Garbh. It is formed of two beaches backed by marram grass with Bagh Rubha Ruaidh to the south and Bagh na Doirlinne to the north. Bagh na Doirlinne is the more photogenic of the twins, with a perfect arc of bright white sand and turquoise waters. It features a delightful combination of rock outcrops and marram grass on the beach which provides a great foreground to the view north east. There is also another smaller bay which brings the Paps of Jura fully into view locate further along the rocky coastline to the north east. **»**

***Left above**: looking down on the twin beaches from the north east. Fujifilm X–T2, 18–55mm f/2.8–f/4, ISO 120, 1/9s at f/11. May.*
***Left**: high tide at the northern side of the twin beaches (VP3). Fujifilm X–T2, 18–55mm f/2.8–f/4, ISO 200, 1/340s at f/5.6. May.*

*Anchored off Palm Tree Beach (VP4). Fujifilm X–T2, 18–55mm f/2.8–f/4, ISO 200, 1/8s at f/11. May.*

## Viewpoint 4 – Port Mòr and Palm Tree Beach

At Port Mòr the road ends and a track runs out to the remains of a ruined pier. From the end of the track there is a fantastic view across to Jura with some shapely rocks providing an interesting foreground. In spring the sea pinks provide a delightful pop of colour on the rocks. However, the local cow population also seem to be fond of them! To the east is Palm Tree Beach, so called because of the single palm tree growing on the dunes above the sand. Comparing a Hebridean island with the Caribbean is a well worn trope, however, at Palm Tree Beach you may be forgiven for saying "this could be the Caribbean, if it wasn't so cold"! The bay provides a sheltered anchorage and in summer it is popular spot for yachts. The small hills to the west also provide some good vantage points, particularly across to Jura.

*The palm of Palm Tree Beach, Fujifilm X–T2, 18–55mm f/2.8–f/4, ISO 200, 1/1250s at f/5.6. May.*

***Opposite**: a huge variety of photographic opportunities for such a small island.*

# THE CENTRAL HEBRIDES

# THE CENTRAL HEBRIDES – INTRODUCTION

**In this guide we have grouped the islands of Mull, Iona, Staffa, Coll and Tiree together as the Central Hebrides. They are served by Caledonian MacBrayne ferries from the port town of Oban on the west coast, with Iona connected to Mull via the small ferry from Fionnphort.**

The largest of the islands is Mull, a vast island with a multitude of fascinating sites for photography. There are fine beaches in the north and south, wild hills in the centre and dramatic volcanic landscapes throughout the island. The busy town of Tobermory with its brightly-painted buildings along the harbour is definitely highlight.

Just offshore from Mull is the Isle of Iona. A hugely important site in the development of Christianity in Scotland, it has been a site of pilgrimage since St Columba landed there in 4AD. Today Iona is a popular island, particularly in summer but it still exudes a sense of peace and tranquility particularly on the beautiful beaches along the north and west coasts.

To the north is the Isle of Staffa. An island steeped in Celtic myths and legend, inspiration to artists and composers and home to some of the most dramatic basalt landscapes you can find anywhere. The booming of waves inside Fingal's Cave is an experience you won't forget. In the summer months the island is home to puffins and you can experience these magical wee birds up close along the cliffs on the eastern side of the island. Boat trips depart for Staffa from Tobermory and Fionnphort on Mull and also from Iona throughout the spring and summer.

To the west are Coll and Tiree. Tiree is the more popular of the two with its stunning sandy beaches and relaxing ambience drawing visitors from far and wide. Coll is a bit more shy and retiring, but also has some stunning beaches and is a wonderful place for peace and solitude.

*Tráigh Chornaig from the dunes. Fujifilm X–T2, 18–55mm f/2.8–f/4, ISO 200, 1/80s at f/8. Jul.*

***Previous spread**: the Old Pier at Salen. Fujifilm X–T2, 55–200mm f/3.5–f/4.8, ISO 200, 20s at f/8. Apr.*

SEA OF THE
HEBRIDES

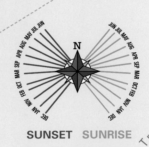

**3** The Western Beaches
VP1: Tràigh Thorastain
& Tràigh Garbh
VP2: Bagh an Trailleich
VP1: Cliad Bay

**2** Cliad & Hogh Bay
VP2: Hogh Bay
Ballyhaugh
RSPB Coll
Ben Hogh 104m

VP1: Tràigh Bousd
**4** The North
VP2: Tràigh Tuath
Bousd   Sorisdale
Sorisdale Bay
Toraston Farm
B8072
B8071

**COLL**
Arinagour
B8070

**1** The South
VP2: Feall Bay
Arileod
Garden Ho.
VP1: Breachacha
& Crossapol Bay   Castles

Calgary Point
**4** VP4 Village &
Machair
Gunna
Gunna Sound

Gott Bay, Vaul
& Caolas **4**
VP3: Tràigh Chornaig
VP2 Vaul
Balephetrish Bay
Caoles
VP3 Caolas Beach
B8069
VP1 Gott Bay
Milton

**1** Balevullin
VP1/2
Clachan Mór
Balephetrish
Tiree Airport
B8068
B8065
Crossapol
Scarinish

**2** Hough Bay
Balevullin
VP1: Ben Hough
Kilkenneth
VP1: The 'Maze' Beach
B8065
B8067
Soroby Bay
Crossapol Bay
**TIREE**

VP1 Tràigh nan Gilean
**3** Ceann a'Mhara
VP2 Tràigh Bhi
B8068
Balephuil Bay
Hynish
Lighthouse Museum

N
SUNSET   SUNRISE
0                    5
miles

Treshnish Pt
Treshnish Isles
Flade
Lunga

**STAFFA**
Scotland's National Nature Reserves
VP2 & 3
VP1

**IONA**
VP3
VP2
Baile Mòr
VP1
VP4
Fionnph
Fidde
VP2
Erraid
VP3
**7**
Fionnphort Fidden & Erraid

MULL

**Mull is the largest island in what we have termed the Central Hebrides and is located approximately 10 miles west of the mainland port town of Oban.** It is a fantastically varied place and from the hustle and bustle of Tobermory's colourful harbour to the secluded beaches on the Ross of Mull there are a wealth of attractions just waiting for you to discover throughout the island.

The island is connected to the mainland by three ferry services all of which are run by Caledonian MacBrayne. The most popular crossing is from Oban to Craignure, with a number of crossings every day. It's a particularly lovely route, which skirts past the northern tip of the island of Kerrera, and the southern point of the isle of Lismore with a grand view of the hills on both the mainland and on Mull. It even provides a great opportunity to photograph Duart Castle. There are also crossings between Fishnish and Lochaline (Morvern peninsula), and between Tobermory to Kilchoan (Ardnamurchan peninsula) which do not require pre-booking.

The main settlement on Mull is the town of Tobermory; famous as Balamory, from the children's TV programme, its brightly-painted buildings along the harbour front will delight all who visit. On a sunny day it is a lovely spot to enjoy some fish and chips and watch the comings and goings of the boats. There is a good supermarket in Tobermory and a number of hotels and restaurants. Whilst there are smaller grocery shops throughout the island, it is definitely worth stocking up on essentials in Tobermory.

Mulls attractions are spread out across the island and whilst the distances in terms of mileage don't appear to that great, the windy single track roads can take longer than you would expect. As such, it may be best to spend a few days in different locations across the island to allow time to explore them thoroughly.

Alongside Tobermory, Calgary Bay is one of the highlights in the north of Mull. A wonderful sandy beach, it is fantastic under blue skies but even under grey clouds the sea has a beautiful turquoise hue. For more beaches head to the Ross of Mull, the narrow peninsula that reaches west along the southern edge of the island towards the magical isle of Iona. Together with Erraid (the island featured in Robert Louis Stevensons classic 'Kidnapped') these two islands off the coast of Mull make for some incredible day trips and should definitely be on your list. For those seeking further island adventures, the island of Staffa with its hexagonal basalt columns and famous Fingal's Cave is also reached from Mull with boat trips departing from Fionnphort and Tobermory.

Geologically, Mull is fascinating. The island centres around Ben More, the highest peak on Mull and the only island Munro (a mountain above 3000ft) outside of Skye. It is the remnant of an extinct volcano which erupted approximately 60 million years ago and throughout the area you can see the evidence of the lava flows; the basalt columns on Staffa or the stepped terraces and fossilised tree on the Ardmeanach Peninsula almost appear to show a freeze frame of intense geological activity.

With so many uninhabited and wild open areas, Mull is a fantastic island for wildlife spotting. Golden and white-tailed Eagles patrol the skies. Otters and seals abound on the shoreline. Puffins chortle and squabble on Staffa. Out to sea whales, dolphins and basking sharks can be seen in the crystal clear waters.

## How to get to Mull

Caledonian MacBrayne operate three ferry routes to Mull, Oban to Craignure, Lochaline to Fishnish and Kilchoan on the Ardnamurchan Peninsula to Tobermory. It is a 45 minute ferry ride from Oban to Craignure. This is the main ferry route if coming from the south.

Oban is 98 miles from Glasgow (2hrs 18 mins drive) and 124 miles (3hr 6 mins drive) from Edinburgh. Buses (Citylink – 3 to 4 hours) and trains (Scotrail – 3 to 5 hours)) are available from both cities.

| MULL | |
|---|---|
| **Scottish Gaelic** | Muil (An t-Eilean Muileach). |
| **Area** | 337 sq. miles (875 sq. km). |
| **Length/breadth** | 30 × 25 miles. |
| **Highest Elevation** | Ben More, 966m (3,169ft). |
| **Owned by** | Mixed, including the Forestry Commission and Argyll Estates. |
| **Population** | 3000 |
| **Largest settlement(s)** | Tobermory |
| **Vehicles allowed** | Yes |
| **Car/Bike rental** | On Yer Bike Hire, Salen: **01680 300 501**. Mull Car Hire: *mullcarhire.co.uk* Harbour Garage: **01688 302 103**. |
| **Public transport** | Yes, operated by West Coast Motors linking towns and villages. |
| **Day trips from mainland?** | Yes. Several ferries a day from Lochaline, Kilchoan and Oban to Mull and back, all take less than an hour. |
| **Internet/mobile phone coverage** | Broadband. 3G/4G dependent on carrier. |
| **Power** | Grid |
| **Island website(s)** | *isle-of-mull.net* • *visitmullandiona.co.uk* • PDF guide at: *isle-of-mull.net/ wp-content/uploads/2021/05/Explore-Mull-and-Iona-Guide-2021.pdf mulleaglewatch.com* • Hebridean Whale & Dolphin Trust: *hwdt.org southernhebrides.com* • *visitscotland.com* • *scotland.org.uk* |
| **Festivals/Events** | Mull Music Festival, Mull and Iona Open Studios (April). Clan Maclean International Gathering (June). Mull Rally (October). |
| **Accommodation** | Mull has a diverse selection of accommodation from wild camping to hotels. See a comprehensive selection at: *isle-of-mull.net/accommodation* |
| **Provisions/Eating Out** | There is a list of many great restaurants and pubs at: *isle-of-mull.net/attractions/food-drink* |
| **Wildlife** | 261 different bird species including the white-tailed eagle. Basking sharks, minke whales, porpoises, dolphins, otters, pine martens, red deer and red squirrels. |
| **Night Sky Bortle Scale** | Class 1 & 2. |

## LOCATIONS

## Maps

- OS Explorer 375: Isle of Mull East: 1:25 000
- OS Explorer 373: Iona, Staffa & Ross of Mull: 1:25 000
- OS Landranger 48: Iona & West Mull: 1:50 000
- OS Landranger 49: Oban & East Mull: 1:50 000

*Previous spread: Tobermory Harbour. Fujifilm X–T2, 18–55mm f/2.8–f/4, ISO 200, 1/250s at f/11. Apr.*

However you arrive at Tobermory, whether by the small ferry which sails across from Kilchoan, Ardnamurchan or via the steep road down to the harbour, the brightly coloured buildings clustered around the harbour are guaranteed to put a smile on your face. It is a thriving, bustling little town with great shops, pubs and restaurants and it makes an ideal base for exploring the island of Mull. Anyone with children will know it better as Balamory from the popular TV show of the early 2000s and it retains its popularity to this day with young people who will seek out the cheerfully painted houses of their favourite characters. For those a little older there is a fine distillery as well!

## What to shoot and viewpoints

### Viewpoint 1 – The harbour ♿

At the southern end of the bay, as you enter the town there is a large car park adjacent to the Tobermory distillery where you are likely to find a space. Along the seaward side of the car park there are some great opportunities to photograph the sweep of the bay with some handily sited nautical relics providing foreground interest. As you head to the main street, a slipway gives access to the stony beach and you may find some boats on the shore which can be used to draw the eye along the harbour. Further on, at the excellent fish and chip van, it is worth exploring the pier which juts out into the harbour. This is a particularly good vantage point at high tide, when the colourful buildings are reflected in the blue water of the bay. The view from the far end of the street back along the harbour is attractive, but perhaps not as fine as the previous views. >>

*Tobermory Distillery. Fujifilm X–T2, 10–24mm f/4, ISO 200, 1/1250s at f/7.1. Apr.*

## How to get here

Tobermory is usually reached via the A848 which runs up the east coast of Mull from Craignure to Tobermory. Alternatively a small ferry runs from Kilchoan in Ardnamurchan.

| | | |
|---|---|---|
| **P Lat/Long**: | 56.62078, -6.0688850 |
| **P what3words**: | ///punters.beak.severe |
| **P Grid Ref**: | NM504550 |
| **P Postcode**: | PA75 6NR is 0.056 km from NM504550 |

## Accessibility

The viewpoints along the harbour are all readily accessible and are essentially roadside. It is possible to drive to Argyll Terrace, should you not wish to attempt the steep path up from the harbour. The walk to Rubha nan Gall Lighthouse is relatively flat on a good path although there is a steep drop off down to the water.

## Best time of year/day

Tobermory is an ideal sunrise location. Facing roughly south east, the brightly painted buildings along the harbour pick up the morning sun fantastically. At sunset the buildings fall into shadow. It is best photographed at high tide where the potential for colourful reflections is maximised. Rubha nan Gall Lighthouse makes a good sunrise or sunset location but is worth the walk at anytime.

*Above*: Tobermory Harbour. Fujifilm X–T2, 10–24mm f/4, ISO 200, 1/640s at f/7.1. Apr.

*The colours of Tobermory.*

### Viewpoint 2 – Argyll Terrace

From the car park take the small path which leads up to Argyll terrace. From here there are couple of good vantage points to obtain an aerial view of the harbour.

*Opposite: an anchor on the quayside. Fujifilm X–T2, 10–24mm f/4, ISO 200, 1/480s at f/7.1. Apr.*

### Viewpoint 3 – Rubha nan Gall Lighthouse

If the hustle and bustle of Tobermory is too much you for then the peaceful walk to Rubha nan Gall Lighthouse might be just the ticket. The 2km walk starts behind the ferry terminal and winds its way through lovely woodland above steep drops down to the sea. After a short walk the lighthouse comes into view and there is a fantastic outlook north to Ardnamurchan with the Rum Cuillin peeking over the peninsula.

## [2] CALGARY BAY

Situated on the north west tip of Mull, Calgary Bay is an idyllic location. A broad sweep of pure white sand, backed with low dunes and colourful machair, it is an archetypal Hebridean paradise. Sheltered by hills on either side, it is a calm, relaxing place and in summer its crystal clear waters are both tempting for photography and for a swim. The woodland to the north also provides an attractive area for a walk as well as giving an excellent elevated view over the beach.

## What to shoot and viewpoints

### Viewpoint 1 – The southern headland

There are two car parks at Calgary Bay, the smaller of which is located at the the southern end. This also has a toilet block and a small area for informal camping. From this car park you can easily access the beach across the small stream or alternatively head out along the road where you can make your way along the rocky edge of the beach. This provides a great spot to photograph the grand sweep of the beach and the rocks provide an interesting counterpoint to the soft white sand. Particularly appealing is the way that the sweeping curves of the tide, beach and hills seem to intersect. A lovely spot during the golden hour at sunset.

### Viewpoint 2 – The beach and dunes

The beach itself can be accessed from either car park and offers plenty of interest at both high and low tide. At low tide, the wide expanse of sand is revealed with the corrugated patterns left by the receding tide providing some wonderful textures and patterns. These are particularly good after sunset when they pick up the last glow of light from the sky, creating some wonderful abstract shapes. The dunes themselves are quite low, but get down amongst them and they can provide a great foil to the hard edges of the hills and cliffs, especially at sunset. Behind the dunes is a large area of machair which is a riot of colour and texture in the summer months. The top car park offers an elevated view of the beach and also good access to the beach itself down a grassy path as well as an ice cream and snack shop fashioned from an upturned boat; a vital stop on a hot summer day. >>

*Sunset stroll (VP1). Fujifilm X–T2, 10–24mm f/4, ISO 200, 1/300s at f/8. Apr.*

## How to get here

Calgary Bay is on the north west coast of Mull, 12 miles from Tobermory along the A8073. It's a windy little road and will take roughly 30-40 minutes to drive, particularly in summer when it can be busy.

P **Lat/Long**:        56.576353 , -6.2779133
P **what3words**: ///cork.painters.dividers
P **Grid Ref**:        NM373509
P **Postcode**:        PA75 6QT

### Accessibility

The beach can be easily accessed from the main car park down a grassy path. From the smaller car park adjacent to the toilet a small stream bars the way, however, there are stepping stones to hop across onto the sand.

## Best time of year/day

Calgary Bay is an ideal sunset location. During the golden hour, it catches the light beautifully and once the sun has dipped behind the northern hills, their distinctive silhouette makes a wonderful shape against a post-sunset sky. The turquoise waters and white sand obviously look fabulous on a sunny day, but they also work well on cloudy days, as does the machair within the summer months.

*Above: a sunny summer day on Calgary Bay. Fujifilm X–T2, 10–24mm f/4, ISO 200, 1/1250s at f/8. Apr.*

*Top*: looking down onto the beach from Calgary Art and Nature (VP4). Fujifilm X–T1, 18–55mm f/2.8–f/4, ISO 200, 1/350s at f/8. Jul. *Above*: the Ice Cream Boat (VP2). Fujifilm X–T2, 10–24mm f/4, ISO 200, 1/850s at f/8. Apr.

*Top*: pink sunset at Calgary Bay. Fujifilm X–T1, 18–55mm f/2.8–f/4, ISO 200, 1/4s at f/8. Jul. *Above*: rabbits on the dunes. Fujifilm X–T1, 55–200mm f/3.5–f/4.8, ISO 200, 1/500s at f/4.8. Jul.

## Viewpoint 3 – The north shore

The crumbling pier on the north shore which is seen from the beach can be accessed by a track which runs along the northern shoreline. The pier itself is in a state of disrepair but does offer a good outlook towards the beach and to the southern headland.

*Opposite*: the dunes at dusk. Fujifilm X–T2, 10–24mm f/4, ISO 200, 1/20s at f/9. Apr.

## Viewpoint4 – Art in nature trails

The Calgary Art and Nature trails wind through the forest to the north of Calgary Bay. There are numerous excellent sculpture, and environmental art pieces together with seating areas and some fantastic elevated views south to the beach and out towards Tiree. The cafe is also a great spot for lunch.

Like many names in the Hebrides, Eas Fors is a combination of Gaelic (Eas: Waterfall) and Norse (Fors: Waterfall). So Waterfall Waterfall Waterfall. In fact, there are three main waterfalls, so maybe it has all worked out for the best. The three waterfalls all have different characters and are located in a dramatic part of Mull, perched high up above the shore of Loch Tuath with views across to Ulva. There is also a fantastic outlook to Ben More and the cliffs of Gribun over Loch na Keal from the scenic road along the coast.

## What to shoot and viewpoints

### Viewpoint 1 – The upper falls
There is a small car park on the main road and the upper falls are located immediately adjacent. The lovely woodland through which the water cascades provides plenty of interest, and the trees help to frame the waterfalls as they cascade over the cliffs above.

### Viewpoint 2 – The mid falls
On the other side of the road, a short and steep path leads down the eastern side of the waterfall. This leads to a lovely shaded pool with a gnarled tree growing across across the water. The tree itself makes fine study and the wider view back up to the road bridge is also worth exploring. The river continues its flow south to the edge of the cliff, where it disappears from view.

### Viewpoint 3 – The lower falls
The most dramatic waterfall is a lot harder to reach. From the car park, head east along the road. At the bottom of the hill, look out for a track on the right hand side, this doubles back on the road and leads down through fields to the shore. Head through the gate at the bottom of the field and make your way along the bouldery shore. After roughly 15 minutes you should gain your first view of the lower falls. It's a fine sight – the waterfall plunges over the cliff in a single drop into a deep, dark pool before winding its way across the rocky beach to the sea. There is plenty of variety to be explored here, from wide shots using the river as a lead in to the falls, to detailed studies of the water as it cascades across the rocks. >>

*The upper falls (VP1). Fujifilm X–T2, 10–24mm f/4, ISO 200, 7.5s at f/8. Apr.*

*The mid falls (VP2). Fujifilm X–T2, 10–24mm f/4, ISO 200, 5s at f/8. Apr.*

***Opposite**: the lower falls from the beach. Fujifilm X–T2, 10–24mm f/4, ISO 200, 5s at f/8. Apr.*

## How to get here

The Loch na Keal viewpoint is located on the B8073, 8 miles west from Salen. It is a very narrow single-track road and will take roughly 20 minutes from Salen depending on how much traffic you meet on the way. As the road reaches its high point look out for a small track on the right hand side of the road, there is space here to park a car. From here walk back along the road and choose your spot. Don't be tempted to park in the passing places. Eas Fors is a further 3 miles along the B8073 and there is a dedicated car park at the roadside.

### Viewpoint 1 to 3 – Eas Fors Waterfalls

- **Lat/Long**: 56.503203, -6.1524993
- **what3words**: ///tame.arranges.clots
- **Grid Ref**: NM445422
- **Postcode**: PA73 6LT

### Viewpoint 4 – Loch na Keal viewpoint

- **Lat/Long**: 56.480342, -6.1106083
- **what3words**: ///poems.compress.taller
- **Grid Ref**: NM469396
- **Postcode**: PA73 6LY

## Accessibility

The upper falls are roadside, the mid-falls require a short walk down a steep path. Don't be tempted to try and look over the cliff above the lower falls, the ground here is dangerous and slip would be fatal. The lower falls are more tricky to reach. The bouldery shore is treacherous underfoot with slippery seaweed making it harder than it appears to reach the falls. At the falls themselves, you will require waterproof boots to cross the river in order to get close to the plunge pool.

## Best time of year/day

The falls are at their best after a period of heavy rainfall. They all face south, so will pick up the light throughout the day. They are an ideal autumn location with the deciduous woodlands adding wonderful colour to the scene. The view across Loch na Keal can be photographed at any time, although being directly south facing it will be best at sunrise or sunset.

## Viewpoint 4 – Loch na Keal viewpoint ♿

A further 3 miles to the east is an excellent roadside spot to take in the view across Loch na Keal. It's a fantastic scene, and cries out for a panorama taking in Ben More, the island of Eorsa at the cliffs of Gribun and even the northern end of Iona on the far horizon. Alternatively, use a longer lens and home in on individual elements in the view.

*Above*: *panorama looking south across Loch na Keal, Iona visible on the western horizon. Fujifilm X–T1, 18–55mm f/2.8–f/4, ISO 200, 1/500s at f/8. Jul.*

*A brooding Ben More. Fujifilm X-T1, 18–55mm f/2.8–f/4, ISO 200, 1/200s at f/8. Sep.*

The little village of Salen sits half way up the east coast of Mull between Craignure and Tobermory. Photographically the village itself is charming enough but the real draw are the remains of its past along the seashore. The wrecks of three old fishing boats, drawn up on the shoreline to the north of the village and the ruins of its old pier are fascinating subjects and worthy of a visit.

## What to shoot and viewpoints

### Viewpoint 1 – The boats

The three old fishing boats, long drawn up on the beach and scuttled have been weathering gracefully for over twenty years now. Clustered together just below the roadside and leaning on each other for support they make a melancholy scene and one which is immediately appealing to photograph. It's a popular spot, and most visitors slow down to take a look. Together, the boats make an interesting composition, forming the foreground to a lovely view up the Sound of Mull but perhaps the most fun is to be had in homing in on the textures of the weathered paintwork, rusted ironmongery or their graceful curves. The colours and forms are truly fascinating. There is a lot to shoot here and it is easy to spend a while lost in the intricate patterns. »

*The road to Salen. Fujifilm X–T2, 18–55mm f/2.8–f/4, ISO 200, 1/60s at f/11. Apr.*

## How to get here

Salen is located mid way between Craignure and Tobermory on the A849. The boats are located just to the north of the village and there is a parking area at the roadside. To get to the old pier take the first right as you enter the village, signposted to the campsite. Follow the road until you pass the campsite and the old pier is on the left.

### Viewpoint 1 – The boats

- **Lat/Long:** 56.520031, -5.9532778
- **what3words:** ///remaining.mailing.caring
- **Grid Ref:** NM569434
- **Postcode:** PA72 6JG

### Viewpoint 2 – The Old Pier

- **Lat/Long:** 56.524441, -5.9409529
- **what3words:** ///vandalism.rave.backlog
- **Grid Ref:** NM577438
- **Postcode:** PA72 6JJ

## Accessibility

The boats themselves are easily accessible at low tide, although it is damp underfoot. The small path to the best view of the pier is narrow and can be muddy.

## Best time of year/day

The boats work well in most conditions. Under bright sun the colours in the weathered paint really pop out and overcast conditions lend a melancholy atmosphere to the ruins. At high tide it is not possible to get up close to the boats. The old pier is a great sunset location.

*Opposite: the boats. Fujifilm X–T2, 18–55mm f/2.8–f/4, ISO 200, 1/420s at f/8. Apr.*

*Looking up the Sound of Mull past the two old boats. 18–55mm f/2.8–f/4, ISO 200, 1/420s at f/8. Apr.*

### Viewpoint 2 – The Old Pier

Another relic of a bygone seafaring age are the skeletal remains of the Old Pier located to the east of the village. The pier itself has long slipped into the sea, but the uprights still remain, providing a lookout perch for seabirds. The best view of the pier is to be had from the small path which leads out onto a headland from opposite the campsite entrance . From this spot (with a handy picnic bench) you can set them against the backdrop of the Sound of Mull. There are plenty of options for composition here, so explore different focal lengths. You may opt for wide angle, taking in all the uprights, or perhaps zoom in on groupings of two or three. They make a fine subject for a long exposure, the smooth water contrasting with the hard uprights can make a powerful image.

*Sunset at the Old Pier.18–55mm f/2.8–f/4, ISO 200, 60s at f/8. Apr.*

*Plenty of opportunities for studies in amongst the old boats.*

With its strategic position overlooking the mouth of Loch Linnhe it comes as no surprise that Duart Castle was an important fortress. Situated up on top of cliffs with a commanding view all the way up the loch the castle has been occupied for over 800 years and is the ancestral seat of Clan Maclean. Currently undergoing an extensive renovation, the castle is now being restored to its former glory.

## What to shoot and viewpoints

### Viewpoint 1 – From the ferry ♿

The 45 minute crossing from Oban to Carignure is a delight. As it slips out of the bustling port town, it skirts past the northern tip of Kerrera before heading across to Mull. The long green island of Lismore is visible to the north and the ferry passes the fine lighthouse on its southern tip. Excellent views abound in all directions with the mountains of Argyll on the eastern seaboard. As the ferry draws nearer to Mull you will get your first glimpse of Duart Castle, sitting aloft on the cliffs. It's a fine setting with the hills towering beyond.

### Viewpoint 2 – The road to the castle ♿

The narrow road from the A849 branches off to the left just after leaving Craignure in a southerly direction. It is from this road that you gain some excellent views of the castle sitting on its perch across Duart Bay. Unfortunately there aren't many suitable places to park until you reach the graveyard, however, it is no real hardship to walk back along the road. From the graveyard itself there is an excellent view of the castle which works particularly well with a long lens, drawing the mountains on the mainland into the scene. »

*Lighthouse on Eilean Musdile just off Lismore. Fujifilm X–T2, 55–200mm f/3.5–f/4.8, ISO 200, 1/5000s at f/4.4. Apr.*

## How to get here

Duart Castle is located 3 miles south of Craignure. Head south on the A849 and take the signposted road on the left. The graveyard is located midway between the turn off and the castle.

### Viewpoint 2 – The road to the castle

| | | |
|---|---|---|
| 🅿 **Lat/Long:** | 56.446981, -5.6668833 |
| 🅿 **what3words:** | ///detriment.hurls.boils |
| 🅿 **Grid Ref:** | NM741343 |
| 🅿 **Postcode:** | PA64 6AP |

### Viewpoint 3 – The castle

| | | |
|---|---|---|
| 🅿 **Lat/Long:** | 56.454925, -5.6538944 |
| 🅿 **what3words:** | ///lookout.gathering.escaping |
| 🅿 **Grid Ref:** | NM749351 |
| 🅿 **Postcode:** | PA64 6AP |

## Accessibility

All viewpoints are accessible. There is a steep grassy path down to the foreshore at the castle.

## Best time of year/day

The castle works well at sunrise where it can be silhouetted against the mountains of the mainland. During the golden hour the sun illuminates the stonework beautifully.

*Above*: *Duart Castle and the mountains of the mainland (VP2). Fujifilm X–T2, 55–200mm f/3.5–f/4.8, ISO 200, 1/5000s at f/4.4. Apr.*

### Viewpoint 3 – The castle

There is a large car park at the castle and from here you are free to explore the grounds. A steep grassy track leads down to the foreshore where a number of good compositions can be found with the castle towering up above. It's worth walking a little further south, where a good view towards Lismore lighthouse can be obtained.

*Duart Castle from beside the graveyard on the road to the castle. Fujifilm X–T2, 18–55mm f/2.8–f/4, ISO 200, 1/420s at f/8. Apr.*

**Below**: *the castle from lower ground to the south (VP3). Fujifilm X–T2, 18–55mm f/2.8–f/4, ISO 200, 1/250s at f/8. Apr.*

**Below**: *the castle from the flat grass by the car park. Fujifilm X–T2, 18–55mm f/2.8–f/4, ISO 200, 1/350s at f/8. Apr.*

*Duart Castle from the ferry from Oban to Craignure (VP1).*
*Fujifilm X–T2, 55–200mm f/3.5–f/4.8, ISO 200, 1/640s at f/8. Apr.*

The Ross of Mull extends westward from the mountainous centre of the island towards Iona and the Atlantic Ocean. The main road runs along the northern coast, passing through the village of Bunessan and enjoys fine views across to the Ardmeanach peninsula. On the southern coast there are many excellent beaches all with a fine outlook across to Colonsay and Jura and each is an absolute joy to explore. These three beaches all have their charms and are all worth visiting offering a wealth of opportunities for seascape photography.

## What to shoot and viewpoints

### Viewpoint 1 – Uisken ♿

A narrow road from Bunessan runs south to the beach of Uisken, where there is a parking area at the road end. It is possible to camp here, with a small payment payable at the crofthouse. It's a fine beach, a lovely sweep of white sand and at hight tide numerous offshore skerries punctuate the water, leading the eye across to Jura. At the eastern side it is possible to scramble along the rocky shoreline above the shallow sea which is a fantastic turquoise against the white sand. The calm, shallow waters make it a popular spot in summer for paddleboarding and sailing. »

*Looking across from Bunessan to Ardmeanach. Fujifilm X–T2, 18–55mm f/2.8–f/4, ISO 200, 1/500s at f/5.6. Apr.*

### How to get here

Uisken and Ardlanish are accessed from the minor road which heads south, just beyond Bunessan, it signposted to Uisken. To reach Kilvickeon Beach take the minor road to the east of Bunessan along the side of Loch Assapol. This deteriorates into a very bumpy and rocky track and is not recommended if you have a car with low suspension. As you pass the ruined church on the right there is a small parking area on the left.

### Viewpoint 1 – Uisken

| 🅿 Lat/Long: | 56.289310, -6.2190484 |
| 🅿 what3words: | ///aliens.earlobes.ribs |
| 🅿 Grid Ref: | NM390187 |
| 🅿 Postcode: | PA67 6D |

### Viewpoint 2 – Ardlanish

| 🅿 Lat/Long: | 56.293375, -6.2474177 |
| 🅿 what3words: | ///reefs.hails.tablet |
| 🅿 Grid Ref: | NM372193 |
| 🅿 Postcode: | PA67 6DR |

### Viewpoint 3 – Kilvickeon

| 🅿 Lat/Long: | 56.297580, -6.1808713 |
| 🅿 what3words: | ///opposites.connects.flatten |
| 🅿 Grid Ref: | NM414195 |
| 🅿 Postcode: | PA67 6DW |

## Viewpoint 4 – Bunessan

- **Lat/Long:** 56.316159 , -6.2352070
- **what3words:** ///whistle.sheepish.smiling
- **Grid Ref:** NM382218
- **Postcode:** PA67 6DP

## Accessibility

Uisken and Ardlanish are easily accessible with just a short walk from the parking areas. Kilvickeon requires a short walk through farmland. There are usually cows in the field beside the beach and it's not advisable to walk through them when they have young calves in spring.

## Best time of year/day

All the beaches are south facing so can be tricky to shoot in the middle of the day. All work well at sunset or sunrise, however, the sun sets or rises over the land in summer. At high tide the island on Kilvickeon is cut off.

*Kilvickeon Beach from the track down to the shore. Fujifilm X–T2, 18–55mm f/2.8–f/4, ISO 200, 1/640s at f/8. Apr.*

### Viewpoint 2 – Ardlanish

Ardlanish is accessed from the same road as Uisken. Take the minor road signposted to Ardlanish weavers and park in the small car park on the left hand side of the road just before the house. From here it is a 10 minute walk down a good path to the beach. The beach itself is very different to Uisken. A large expanse of sand, backed by low dunes with an uninterrupted view of Colonsay and Jura. There is much to explore depending on the level of the tide, with a fine rocky outcrop in the middle of the beach making for an interesting foreground.

### Viewpoint 3 – Kilvickeon

Kilvickeon beach may be the best of the three. Or perhaps that's just the relief of surviving the Scoor Road. This minor road to the east of Bunessan eventually peters out past the last house and a sign warns you of the bumpy nature of the following track. In truth it's not too bad, you just need to drive very, very slowly. Once you have negotiated the road, park at the old church and follow the track down to the beach. The finest views are from above where an old wall and wind blasted trees make a fine foreground to the beach with its distinctive tidal island. The beach is grazed by cattle, who often wander out across the sand adding further colour to the scene. »

*Above*: scenes from the dunes at Ardlanish
with Jura on the horizon

*The sign for The Scoor Road. Fujifilm X–T2,*
*18–55mm f/2.8–f/4, ISO 200,*
*1/500s at f/8. Apr.*

### Viewpoint 4 – Bunessan ♿

The village of Bunessan is on the north coast of the Ross of Mull and sits in a sheltered position overlooking the water. There is an excellent view to be had from the shoreline along the main street or alternatively head up to the houses above, for a wide view which takes in the natural harbour, the loch and the fine outlook across to the Ardmeanach Peninsula. The dramatic rock formations of the cliffs are particularly striking in the golden hour at sunset where the low sun picks out them out beautifully.

### Nearby – Carsaig Bay, the red phone box and Carsaig Arches

Carsaig Bay is a beautiful and remote cove to the east Kilvickeon (VP3) known for its dramatic cliffs, wildlife and is the start of the walk to the Carsaig arches. The coastal walk (8-miles round trip) to the arches is challenging and is only suitable for the agile and those confident walking by steep drops. There is a full description of this walk at *walkhighlands.co.uk*. On the road to Carsaig Bay, look out for the red phone box that featured in the 1945 film 'I Know Where I'm Going', the phone box is Category B Listed by Historic Scotland. In the area around the bay look out for wild goats and golden eagles.

*Top*: the distinctive outline of Jura from Ardlanish. Fujifilm X–E3, 55–200mm f/3.5–f/4.8, ISO 200, 1/1000s at f/8. Apr.

*Middle*: rocky shoreline at Uisken. Fujifilm X–T2, 18–55mm f/2.8–f/4, ISO 200, 1/350s at f/8. Apr.

*Left*: rock outcrop in the centre of Ardlanish beach. Fujifilm X–T2, 18–55mm f/2.8–f/4, ISO 200, 1/640s at f/8. Apr.

*Left*: a red boat at Bunessan. Fujifilm X–T2, 18–55mm f/2.8–f/4, ISO 200, 1/350s at f/8. Apr.

*Above*: looking back to Uisken from the coastline to the east. Fujifilm X–T2, 18–55mm f/2.8–f/4, ISO 200, 1/250s at f/8. Apr.
*Below*: swimming at Uisken. Fujifilm X–T2, 18–55mm f/2.8–f/4, ISO 200, 1/350s at f/8. Apr.

# 7 FIONNPHORT, FIDDEN AND ERRAID

After driving the long and winding single track road to the end of the Ross of Mull, the pretty village of Fionnphort comes as a relief to some. Most visitors rush through Fionnphort to get the ferry across to Iona but there is much to offer the photographer in this location. Wonderful sandy beaches, roaming highland cows and a tidal island with a famous literary backstory – there is something for everyone in this wonderful corner of Mull. The campsite at Fidden Farm makes the perfect base to explore this area as well as providing a great view across to Iona and Erraid.

## What to shoot and viewpoints

### Viewpoint 1 – Fionnphort ♿

The small sandy beach at Fionnphort is a great place to spend some time especially at sunset when the low sun intensifies the colour of the pink granite. Situated in the centre of the bay is a single large boulder, split in two as if cleaved by a giant sword. Rumours abound about this rock, either it was dropped and smashed by Fingal on his way to Staffa or was shattered with explosives by a local looking for suitable building materials. Either way, it makes a fascinating element in the view. The local highland cows graze freely around the beach and will happily pose for photos. At low tide it is worth exploring the far side of the beach where a great view to Iona can be found amongst the smoothed granite rocks. »

## How to get here

Fionnphort is at the end of the A849, there is parking in the village with a free car park located at The Columba Centre. To reach Fidden Farm, take the first left as you enter the village, the campsite is located at the sharp left turn. Knockvologan and the start of the Erraid walk is a further 5 minutes along the road. There is a parking area on the left hand side of the road as you pass the first house on the right. From here follow the farm track down to the shore.

### Viewpoint 1 – Fionnphort

- 🅿 **Lat/Long**: 56.323933, -6.3653688
- 🅿 **what3words**: ///pickup.estimates.inversion
- 🅿 **Grid Ref**: NM302231
- 🅿 **Postcode**: PA66 6BH

### Viewpoint 2 – Fidden Farm

- 🅿 **Lat/Long**: 56.308068, -6.3633433
- 🅿 **what3words**: ///thunder.probing.glimmers
- 🅿 **Grid Ref**: NM302214
- 🅿 **Postcode**: PA66 6BN

### Viewpoint 3 – Erraid

- 🅿 **Lat/Long**: 56.299772, -6.3426944
- 🅿 **what3words**: ///tucked.owners.likes
- 🅿 **Grid Ref**: NM314204
- 🅿 **Postcode**: PA66 6BN is c.1 km from NM314204

## Accessibility

Fionnphort and Fidden Farm are roadside and the beaches at each can be easily accessed. Erraid is slightly trickier but with a bit of planing you should be able to time your visit to coincide with the tides which can be checked at the notice posted on the pier at Fionnphort. The northern area of the island including the walk up to the viewpoint are usually achievable within the time. The walk down to Tráigh Gheal requires route-finding ability as the path is indistinct and it can also be difficult underfoot.

## Best time of year/day

The local pink granite glows an intense red at sunset and the small beach at Fionnphort is a great spot to appreciate this, especially coupled with the view across to Iona. The beach at Fidden Farm can be busy at sunset, but at sunrise you are likely to have it alll to yourself. Your time on Erraid will be somewhat determined by the tide.

*Above*: *Highland cows on the beach at Fionnphort. Fujifilm X–T2, 18–55mm f/2.8–f/4, ISO 200, 1/250s at f/8. Apr.*

### Viewpoint 2 – Fidden Farm ♿
Fidden Farm is located a short drive from Fionnphort and is one of the most idyllic campsites you can visit. There is a sandy beach along its western edge with numerous offshore skerries and rocks adding to the view to Iona. To the south of the campsite there is an excellent view across to the island of Erraid with distinctive granite rocks popping out of the smooth grassy sward.

### Viewpoint 3 – Erraid
The tidal island of Erraid situated just off the southern shore of Mull has a fascinating history. It is most famous for its role in Robert Louis Stevenson's Kidnapped where the protagonist David Balfour becomes stranded after his ship runs aground on Torran Rocks to the south the of the island. Balfour walks around the island, convinced that he is stranded until locals in a passing boat reveal to him that he can simply walk across at low tide. That is not the only Stevenson connection to Erraid, the lighthouses of Skerryvore and Dubh Artach were designed by his father Thomas Stevenson and can be seen out in the Atlantic to the west on clear days. A signal station on Cnoc Mor was used to communicate with the two lighthouses, and the keepers were housed in the row of pretty cottages on the northern side of the island when not off-shore. Today, Erraid is owned by The Findhorn Foundation, an intentional community which lives sustainably and spiritually on this wonderfully peaceful island. The island is cut off at high tide but can be reached (with dry feet) at low tide across a sandy beach. To access the island head past

Knockvologan Farm and follow the path to the beach. It is best to time your visit an hour after the tide goes out to give yourself the most time on the island. Cross the sandy bay and head north following the western shore and at the northeast corner pick up the path which heads west along the northern shore of the island. As you pass the walled gardens, turn left up the hill towards the row of cottages. The path continues on past the old quarry and some land art sculptures before you arrive at the small white bothy building (a former lighthouse signal station). The view across to Iona is fantastic, as is the view back over Mull to Ben More, and out to sea where the southern tip of Iona and the western tip of Mull fracture into myriad tiny islands. South from here the island slopes down to the lovely hidden bay of Tráigh Gheal. There is a small and sometimes indistinct path which leads down to the lovely white sandy beach which is enclosed with pink granite cliffs. It's easy to spend time relaxing in this peaceful place, but don't forget you need to return before the tide cuts off the island!

*Sunset from the tent at Fidden Farm. Fujifilm X–T1, 18–55mm f/2.8–f/4, ISO 200, 1/4s at f/8. Jul.*

*The rugged landscape and sheltered coves of Erraid. Fujifilm X–T1, 18–55mm f/2.8–f/4, ISO 200, 1/250s at f/8. Jul.*

*A wander around Fionnphort will usually involve meeting some of the local characters.*

***Overleaf****: Looking across to Erraid from Fidden Farm.*
*Fujifilm X–T1, 18–55mm f/2.8–f/4,*
*ISO 200, 1/80s at f/8. Jul.*

*The dark and dramatic cliffs of Gribun (VP2). Fujifilm X–T2, 18–55mm f/2.8–f/4, ISO 200, 1/200s at f/8. Apr.*

As you drive through the wild interior of Mull you eventually reach Loch Beg, a smaller loch at the head of Loch Scridain. This large, sea loch reaches deep into the island, separating the Ross of Mull in the south to the Ardmeanach peninsula in the north. Here you have the option of continuing along the Ross or looping back north, over the pass and down through the rugged cliffs of Gribun. It's one of the great scenic drives on Mull and there are a number of moments where you will be desperate to stop the car and absorb the breathtaking landscapes.

## What to shoot and viewpoints

### Viewpoint 1 – Loch Scridain and Loch Beg ♿

The shoreline of Loch Scridain is rocky and indented with a number of small pebbly coves. On the southern side of

the loch, particularly beside Pennyghael Stores where the forlorn shell of a wrecked boat sits on the shore, there is a great view back to the mountains with Ben More dominating the view. On the northern side of the loch, there are more great little coves to explore with some windblown trees providing a lovely pop of intrigue agains the dark waters of the loch. Otters are often sighted along this shoreline, particularly at dusk and dawn so keep your eyes peeled for movement in the shallows. The old stone bridge over the river at Loch Beg is worth a stop if the lighting conditions are right as it provides some nice foreground interest in the view towards the hills. Often there are highland cattle in the fields nearby who tend to be happy to pose for photos. Just adjacent to the main road there there are opportunities looking upstream towards the hills, or downstream towards the loch with the old bridge as the focal point.

## How to get here

The viewpoints are all accessed from the A849 or the B8035.
From Craignure head south on the A849, after 17 miles the B8035
branches off to the right and is signposted Salen Scenic Route.
It is approximately 8 miles from here to Viewpoint 2 where
you can then continue on to Salen.

### Viewpoint 1 – Loch Scridain

- **Lat/Long**: 56.383508, -6.049270
- **what3words**: ///badminton.harnessed.rave
- **Grid Ref**: NM501286
- **Postcode**: PA69 6ER

### Viewpoint 1 – Pennyghael Stores

- **Lat/Long**: 56.382791, -5.996143
- **what3words**: ///scratches.deck.decorated
- **Grid Ref**: NM534283
- **Postcode**: PA70 6HB

### Viewpoint 1 – Loch Beg Bridge

- **Lat/Long**: 56.390923, -5.979159
- **what3words**: ///horseshoe.plank.builds
- **Grid Ref**: NM545291
- **Postcode**: PA70 6HG

### Viewpoint 2 – Above Balmeanach

- **Lat/Long**: 56.419975, -6.129283
- **what3words**: ///weeps.squeaking.obviously
- **Grid Ref**: NM454329
- **Postcode**: PA68 6EH

## Accessibility

All the viewpoints are essentially roadside and are easily accessed.
However, the most tricky aspect of this location is finding suitable
parking areas. There are some larger passing places along the road
which can be used for a quick stop, however, as always be mindful
of other road users. It's quite a narrow and windy road in places
so make sure you are confident reversing. In summer it can be
quite busy. The short grassy scramble described in Viewpoint 2
is relatively simple although can be slippery after rain.

## Best time of year/day

Loch Scridain and Loch Beg can be photographed at any time,
although the river looks best after some rainfall. In dry spells it can
be very low. The cliffs of the Gribun can be tricky to photograph,
in early morning the cliffs tend to be in shadows, and are best
photographed either in overcast weather or at sunset. The rocky
shoreline along Loch na Keal is a grand sunset location in summer,
particlaury the view west along the cliffs.

*Above right: the road sandwiched between cliff and shore.
Fujifilm X–T2, 18–55mm f/2.8–f/4, ISO 200,
1/200s at f/5.6. Apr.*

## Viewpoint 2 – The cliffs of Gribun

The Ardmeanach peninsula is a tricky environment for
most people to get to, but a taster of the dramatic
wilderness at its western end can be had from the road
which descends down to the shore of Loch na Keal. As it
switchbacks down from the pass look out for larger passing
place on the right roughly 300m before you reach the
small white house on the left hand side off the road. From
here you can scramble up the grassy terraces to a small
lookout point which gives a fantastic view west along the
cliffs with the beaches at northern end of Iona visible the
horizon. The view back down the road is also quite
dramatic and provides a nice outlook to Inchkenneth in
Loch na Keal and across to Ulva. It is also worth walking
down the road, past the house to the next corner where
more of the towering cliffs are revealed to the west. From
this point the road continues on down to sea level at Loch
na Keal and there are a number of lay-bys where it is
possible to pull off the road and photograph the views
back along the cliffs, or even of the road itself as it clings
to the narrow space between the cliffs and the loch.

## Nearby – MacCulloch's Fossil Tree

At the western tip of the Ardmeanach peninsula is a
geological wonder, MacCulloch's Fossil Tree, which stands
12 metres high, 1.5 metres in diameter and was discovered
by geologist John MacCulloch in 1819. This spectacular
walk to the tree is amongst the 'lost world of Mull' is only
for the adventurous and is a real wilderness. It is a 12-mile
round trip and involves some scrambling and a descent
down a ladder. A full description of this walk can be found
at: *walkhighlands.co.uk*

IONA

**Iona is magical place which exudes a sense of calm and tranquility. It is most well known as the birthplace of Christianity in Scotland which was brought to the island by St Columba in AD563. St Columba was exiled from Ireland and sailed north to Iona with twelve companions and would go on to have a huge influence on life in Scotland. The monastery he founded was hugely significant, and emissaries spread the word of Christianity across the western seaboard of Scotland and further afield.**

Whilst today, Iona may appear remote; a small island, off the coast of another island, itself located off the west coast of Scotland, in Columba's day it was at the centre of Christianity in the Middle Ages, with sea routes connecting it to Ireland, the inner and outer Hebrides and the mainland of Scotland. Today it is still a place of pilgrimage with thousands of visitors a year, and yet despite the huge influx of visitors it never loses its calming spiritual atmosphere. Whether you are a believer or not, Iona is a very special place. It is also a place of stunning natural beauty with fine beaches all around the coast, and is even home to that most elusive of Hebridean birds; the corncrake.

## How to get to Iona

Iona is reached via the small ferry which crosses the Sound of Iona from Fionnphort on Mull. Cars are not allowed on Iona unless you are a resident or a blue badge holder in which case you need a permit from *argyll-bute.gov.uk*. The ferry runs every half hour or so in summer – less regularly in winter – and the crossing takes around 10 mins.

*Iona Post Office and the ferry heading back to Mull. Fujifilm X–T2, 10–24mm f/4, ISO 200, 1/850s at f/5.6. Apr.*

| IONA | |
|---|---|
| **Scottish Gaelic** | Ì Chaluim Chille. |
| **Area** | 3.5 sq. miles (9 sq. km). |
| **Length/breadth** | 3 × 1 miles. |
| **Highest Elevation** | Dùn Ì, 101m (331ft). |
| **Owned by** | National Trust for Scotland. |
| **Population** | 120 |
| **Largest settlement(s)** | Baile Mor. |
| **Vehicles allowed** | No |
| **Car/Bike rental** | Bikes can be hired from Iona Craft Shop: *ionacraftshop.com* (*info@ionacraftshop.com*). Iona Taxi: *ionataxi.co.uk* |
| **Public transport** | No |
| **Day trips from mainland?** | Yes, from Mull or if sailing from Oban you will have 2/3 hours on the island. |
| **Internet/mobile phone coverage** | Broadband. 3G/4G dependent on carrier. |
| **Power** | Grid |
| **Island website(s)** | *welcometoiona.com • visitmullandiona.co.uk • southernhebrides.com visitscotland.com • scotland.org.uk* |
| **Festivals/Events** | See latest listing at *iona.org.uk/events* |
| **Accommodation** | Iona Campsite: *ionacampsite.co.uk* • Iona Pods: *ionapods.com* Iona Hostel: *greenshediona.co.uk* • B&Bs: *welcometoiona.com* Argyll Hotel: *argyllhoteliona.co.uk* • St Columba Hotel: *stcolumba-hotel.co.uk* Self-catering: *welcometoiona.com* |
| **Provisions/Eating Out** | Meals at Heritage Centre Garden Café, Argyll Hotel and St Columba Hotel. There is a spar, a post office, several craft shops and galleries, and Iona Seafood selling freshly caught fish, crab, lobster and langoustine. |
| **Wildlife** | Terns, kittiwakes, bottlenosed dolphins, common dolphins, minke whales, killer whales, pilot whales, basking sharks, seals and otters. |
| **Night Sky Bortle Scale** | Class 1 |

## LOCATIONS

## Maps

• OS Explorer 373: Iona, Staffa & Ross of Mull: 1:25 000

*Previous spread*: Looking across to Mull from Dùn Ì. Fujifilm X–T2, 10–24mm f/4, ISO 200, 1/850s at f/7.1. Apr.

## What to shoot and viewpoints

### Viewpoint 1 – The abbey and nunnery ♿
On arrival from the ferry, there is an immediate opportunity to the right of the landing slip. A lovely white sandy beach (St Ronan's Bay) lapped by turquoise water which provides an excellent foreground to the view of the main street and the abbey behind. To reach the abbey head west up the hill where you can take a short walk through the ruined nunnery. Returning to the road, the route heads north towards the abbey. The abbey itself makes a fine subject, it's ancient stone walls particularly appealing in the low light and it is worth venturing inside and exploring the cloisters with their intricate stone carvings and gravestones. The best views of the abbey are to be found from the west, where it can be set in its coastal context. It is also possible to scramble up the grassy bank on the opposite side of the road, the extra elevation helps to provide some separation although the telegraph wires are slightly tricky to avoid. It is certainly worth paying the fee to walk around the grounds.

### Viewpoint 2 – Dùn Ì
Continuing north up the spine of the island, fine views north east across to Mull are revealed. To obtain an even better view, cross the field just after the Iona Pods and head up the muddy track to the top of Dùn Ì. At 100m it scarcely even qualifies as a hillock but the view from its rocky summit is incredible: east towards Ardmeanach on Mull, north to Rum, west to Coll and Tiree. Perhaps south is the finest view though, with the Abbey in the foreground, then Mull, Erraid, Kiloran Bay on Colonsay and the Paps of Jura on the far horizon. If you are blessed with a day of outstanding visibility you may even see the distant hills of Ireland. Perhaps St Columba would have climbed the hill to catch a glimpse of his homeland. »

*Above*: the view to the abbey from the pier (VP1). Fujifilm X–T2, 18–55mm f/2.8–f/4, ISO 200, 1/600s at f/8. Apr.

*Looking towards Ardmeanach on Mull from Dùn Ì. Fujifilm X–T2, 55–200mm f/3.5–f/4.8, ISO 200, 1/800s at f/8. Apr.*

## How to get here

The Abbey is only ten minutes' walk from the Fionnphort pier. Bikes can be hired on the island and there is a local taxi available. Plus, many accommodation providers offer a pick-up from the pier if they know when visitors are arriving.

### Fionnphort ferry

| | | |
|---|---|---|
| P | Lat/Long: | 56.323933, -6.3653688 |
| w | what3words: | ///pickup.estimates.inversion |
| P | Grid Ref: | NM302231 |
| P | Postcode: | PA66 6BH |

## Accessibility

Visitor cars are not permitted Iona but it is lovely place to walk around and is also excellent to explore by bike (bike hire is available at Iona Craft Shop). The beaches are all accessed by good tracks and the abbey is just off the main road. The walk up Dùn Ì is via a short but steep and sometimes muddy path.

## Best time of year/day

In summer it is a busy place but you are still likely to find peace and quiet on the beaches. If you want to visit and photograph in the golden hours or at sunset you will either have to go in winter or stay on the island as during the summer hours the first and last sailings of the ferry are during daylight.

*Jura, Colonsay, Erraid, Mull and Iona from Dùn Ì (VP2). Fujifilm X–T2, 18–55mm f/2.8–f/4, ISO 200, 1/600s at f/7.1. Apr.*

*Above*: Tráigh an t-Suidhe on the west coast of Iona (VP3). Fujifilm X–T1, 18–55mm f/2.8–f/4, ISO 200, 1/1250s at f/5.6. Jul.
*Below*: the village of Baile Mòr and the abbey (VP1). Fujifilm X–T2, 18–55mm f/2.8–f/4, ISO 200, 1/400s at f/7.1. Apr.

*The Bay at The Back of The Ocean. Fujifilm X–T2, 10–24mm f/4, ISO 200, 3.2s at f/8. Apr.*

### Viewpoint 3 – The northern beaches

Returning from Dùn Ì to the main road, it is just a short walk to the beaches at the northern end of the island. A gate gives access into the farmland and you have the choice of heading north east to Tráigh Bhán or north west to Tráigh an t-Suidhe. Both beaches are beautiful with the classic Hebridean combination of rugged rocky outcrops and bright white sand. It is worth walking around the headland and connecting the two, they both deserve your time. The dunes at Tráigh an t-Suidhe are particularly attractive.

### Viewpoint 4 – The Bay at The Back of The Ocean

The romantically named Bay at The Back of The Ocean is located on the western side of Iona. To reach it, head left from the ferry slipway and follow the road along the coast which deviates inland past the campsite and eventually stops at the golf course. From here, walk across the course and down to the beach. It is a cracker. A wide expanse of shingle banks, sandy bays and offshore rocks there are images to be made up and down this beach and it is a seascapers paradise. The local granite is particularly splendid with rich seams of red rock contrasting with darker, blueish shades and you may even find some smooth pebbles of Iona marble amongst the shingle.

*Opposite: the abbey is a fascinating site to explore.*

*The Bay at The Back of The Ocean. Fujifilm X–T2, 10–24mm f/4, ISO 200, 2.5s at f/8. Apr.*

STAFFA

**Staffa is a small, uninhabited island off the coast of Mull which is only accessible by local tour boats. Staffa is 7 miles west of central Mull and 6 miles north-east of Iona. It is an island which has been famed throughout history for its dramatic landscape inspiring royalty, poets, authors and composers. Its distinctive columnar basalt pillars thrust upwards from the sea, the remnants of an ancient volcanic eruption which shaped much of the landscape of the west coast of Scotland. The name Staffa is believed to be derived from the Norse "Stave" as the basalt column which make up the island reminded the Vikings of the staves or pillars which formed their houses.**

This hexagonal basalt is also similar to that found on the Giants Causeway in Northern Ireland and this similarity was mythologised in the story of Fionn MacCumhaill, the legendary Irish warrior giant. Intent on challenging a Scottish giant, Fionn (AKA Finn MacCool), built a causeway to connect this home in Ireland with Staffa. Fleeing in defeat, the Scottish giant broke up the causeway and all that remains now are the columns at either end. One of Staffa's main attractions, Fingal's Cave, was named after Fionn MacCumhaill. However, its Gaelic name is Uamh Bhinn the "Melodious Cave", an apt description as it provided the inspiration for composer Felix Mendelssohn's Hebrides Overture.

## How to get to Staffa

There are several local companies who provide boat tours of Staffa departing from Fionnphort, Iona, Tobermory, Ulva Ferry, Oban and Kilchoan, ranging in price from £30 to over £100 depending on the extent of the tour and where you depart from. Some tours include visiting the puffin paradise of the Treshnish Isles. The three main operators are:

*staffatours.com • staffatrips.co.uk • turusmara.com*

If you are visiting the Ross of Mull it makes a fantastic day out and can be combined with a trip to Iona. Boats leave from Fhionnphort throughout the day from April to October with timetables available at the pier and online. It is worth booking in summer as the tours are very popular. The crossing can be quite choppy and if it is windy at the pier it will be even windier out at sea. Landing on Staffa is dependant on the sea conditions; if it is too rough the boats cannot dock so it is worth checking with the skipper prior to departing.

**Fhionnphort**

| | | |
|---|---|---|
| 📍 **Lat/Long:** | 56.32522, -6.3663639 |
| 📍 **what3words:** | ///cyber.digested.soothing |
| 📍 **Grid Ref:** | NM301233 |
| 📍 **Postcode:** | PA66 6BL |

### LOCATIONS

*Opposite: Staffa on the approach from the south. Fujifilm X–T2, 18–55mm f/2.8–f/4, ISO 200, 1/850s at f/5.6. Apr.*

*Previous spread: Staffa on a calm day. Fujifilm X–T1, 18–55mm f/2.8–f/4, ISO 200, 1/400s at f/8. Jul.*

| STAFFA | |
|---|---|
| Scottish Gaelic | Stafa (Stave or Pillar island). |
| Area | 0.13 sq. miles (0.3 sq. km). |
| Length/breadth | 0.5 × 0.25 miles. |
| Highest Elevation | 42m (138ft). |
| Owned by | National Trust for Scotland. |
| Population | 0 |
| Largest settlement(s) | None and no facilities. |
| Vehicles allowed | No |
| Day trips from mainland? | Yes |
| Internet/mobile phone coverage | No |
| Island website(s) | nts.org.uk/visit/places/staffa |
| Accommodation | No |
| Wildlife | Whales, dolphins, harbour porpoises, basking sharks, seals, fulmars, common shags, puffins, great skuas and gulls. |
| Night Sky Bortle Scale | Class 1. |

## What to shoot and viewpoints

### Viewpoint 1 – Approach by sea

Travelling north from Mull and Iona, Staffa gradually appears on the horizon, its great southern face rearing up like a ships prow. Fingal's Cave and the colonnade of basalt columns are clearly visible form the boat and depending on how choppy the sea is, you should be able to make some interesting compositions. Once ashore, the small landing stage and the nearby areas provide a good outlook to Am Buachaille (the shepherd), the name given to the small islet a few meters off the coast of Staffa. Of particular interest are the curved basalt colours of various colours in stark contrast to the vertical black basalt. The sea races between the two islands here, with some good opportunities for long exposure images. >>

*Rough seas crash in to the basalt columns. Fujifilm X–T2, 18–55mm f/2.8–f/4, ISO 200, 1/850s at f/5.6. Apr.*

### Accessibility

The route to Fingal's Cave is across the tops of collapsed and wave-worn basalt columns and they can be quite slippery when wet. However, there is a chain installed as a handrail along the colonnade which helps, especially if you are still on sea legs! Inside Fingal's cave there are some steep drops above water and it can be busy with people going to and fro so be aware. The steps up from the landing stage are steep and there are high cliffs around the island topped with grass which can be very slippery.

### Best time of year/day

As you are on a boat trip with a fixed time period on the island the conditions you get are somewhat determined by luck. However, leaving on the early morning boat should provide the best light as the main attractions of the island are south easterly facing. In reality though, you should go with the mindset that you are there to enjoy and experience the unique landscape of the island and if the stars align and you get some fantastic conditions it's a bonus. If you are wising to observe the puffins at close quarters then visit during the breeding season which runs from May to August.

## Viewpoint 2 – Fingal's Cave

Fingal's cave extends deeply into the great southern face of Staffa, a line of weakness which has been exploited by the ocean and gradually expanded into a large cavern where the sea booms against the walls and echoes around the chamber. There are great opportunities here for long exposures with a lovely contrast between the hard black basalt and the flowing sea. You are somewhat constrained by the terrain in terms of producing any particularly original compositions, however, it is still a fascinating and atmospheric location. You are unlikely to have the cave to yourself so there are two potential strategies to minimise the number of people you share the scene with; either get off the boat first and quickly walk along to the cave whilst others are deciding where to go, or wait until the end of your time on the island when people may have gone in search of the puffins leaving you with a bit of peace in the cave!

## Viewpoint 3 – The puffins

During the summer months Staffa is home to a large colony of puffins. These characterful little birds are an absolute delight and nest in burrows on the clifftops at the north west of the island. Completely unafraid of humans it is possible to get quite close to the birds, and photograph them in their natural habitat as they fly out to sea and return with with fish for their young. They are a fascinating subject and it is easy to spend a long time in their company.

*Top*: *a distant view of The Dutchman's Cap. Fujifilm X–T2, 18–55mm f/2.8–f/4, ISO 200, 1/1000s at f/5.6. Apr.*

*Middle*: *Fingals Cave. Fujifilm X–T2, 18–55mm f/2.8–f/4, ISO 200, 1/400s at f/5.6. Apr.*

*Bottom*: *the entrance to Fingals Cave. Fujifilm X–E3, 55–200mm f/3.5–f/4.8, ISO 200, 1/200s at f/5.6. Apr.*

*Next spread*: *birds and Basalt – two of the highlights on Staffa.*

*Above*: the dramatic southern face of Staffa. Fujifilm X–T2, 18–55mm f/2.8–f/4, ISO 200, 1/200s at f/8. Apr.
*Below*: the eastern coast of Staffa with Ulva and Mull on the horizon. Fujifilm X–T1, 18–55mm f/2.8–f/4, ISO 200, 1/420s at f/8. Jul.

COLL

**Coll tends to be much less visited than its neighbour Tiree, even though the two islands are on the same ferry route.** Coll's charms are perhaps less immediately apparent than Tiree, the beaches are harder to reach and the land is more rugged. But it's also these elements which make Coll such a special island. It's a quiet, peaceful place with empty beaches where the only sound you will hear is that of the waves and the plaintive call of the oystercatcher.

The usual way to reach Coll is by the Caledonian MacBrayne. ferry from Oban. This fantastic route heads across to Mull, past Tobermory and out into open seas west of Ardnamurchan. On a calm day, you will no doubt spend the whole journey on deck with a front row seat to some of the finest scenery in Scotland. As well as the potential for close up encounters with sealife it is a good crossing for island spotting with so many Hebridean islands visible over the course of the 3.5 hour crossing. You can also fly to Coll from Oban, but flights are less frequent, however, the view from the plane would be quite spectacular .

Clustered around the harbour are the white-washed cottages of Arinagour, the islands main settlement and parents may notice the similarity to the fictional island of Struay from the popular Katie Morag stories. Home to two shops, a bunkhouse, a post office and a fantastic hotel and restaurant, Arinagour will provide all you need for your time on the island. There is a campsite located in the south of the island and self-catering accommodation is available in various locations. Coll has also been officially designated a Dark-sky Community by the International Dark-sky Association. This means that in the winter months you

are guaranteed a clear view of the night sky without any light pollution. Of course this is weather dependant, however, Coll enjoys a favourable situation as the clouds tend to build up over the mountains to the north on Rum, or on the mainland, making Coll an excellent choice for astro photographers and for those hunting the elusive northern lights.

Colls beaches are truly impressive, even by Hebridean standards. There are the expansive sandy bays at Feall and Crossapol, separated by a vast dune system, the wave-lashed strands of Cliad and Hogh Bay and to the north a string of idyllic sandy coves which punctuate the rocky western shoreline like jewels on a necklace. All of these offer a wealth of opportunity to the seascape photographer and there is scope here to make some really original images, away from the more popular Hebridean locations.

Coll is a hugely important island for birdlife, and the large RSPB reserve 6 miles west of Arinagour is must visit for birdwatchers. It is an important site in the Corncrake Recovery Programme and you may be lucky enough to see one these shy and elusive birds, although it is more likely that the only sign of them will be their rasping call!

## How to get to Coll

### Ferry
In the summer there are daily sailings of the Caledonian MacBrayne ferry from Oban, five sailings per week from Tiree and one from Barra. In the winter there are five sailings per week from Oban and Tiree.

### Air
Flights are operated by Hebridean Air Services Ltd. with services from Oban (Connel Airport) and Tiree. For the current timetable and to make a reservation, visit: *hebrideanair.co.uk*

| COLL | |
|---|---|
| **Scottish Gaelic** | Cola |
| **Area** | 30 sq. miles (77 sq. km) |
| **Length/breadth** | 13 × 3 miles. |
| **Highest Elevation** | Ben Hogh, 106m (348ft). |
| **Owned by** | RSPB and private owners. |
| **Population** | 195 |
| **Largest settlement(s)** | Arinagour |
| **Vehicles allowed** | Yes |
| **Car/Bike rental** | E Bikes – Coll Bunkhouse: *collbunkhouse.com*<br>Car hire: TORAZ Vehicle Rentals: *toraz.co.uk*<br>IsleGO sea taxi: *islego.co.uk* |
| **Public transport** | No |
| **Day trips from mainland?** | Yes, from 2 to 9 hours depending on the season and ferry timetable. |
| **Internet/mobile phone coverage** | Broadband. 3G/4G dependent on carrier. |
| **Power** | Grid |
| **Island website(s)** | *visitcoll.co.uk* • *southernhebrides.com/isle-of-coll-machairs-and-beaches* *southernhebrides.com* • *visitscotland.com* • *scotland.org.uk* |
| **Festivals/Events** | Easter concert (Easter) • Coll Bird Festival (May) • Fishing Competition (July)<br>Coll Agricultural Show, Coll Half Marathon, East-end Fishing Competition (August).<br>Dark Sky events start (October). |
| **Accommodation** | B & B: *visitcoll.co.uk/BandB* • Coll Bunkhouse: *collbunkhouse.com*<br>Garden House Camping: *visitcoll.co.uk/camping*<br>The Coll Hotel: *visitcoll.co.uk/hotel* • Campervans: *visitcoll.co.uk/motor_homes*<br>20 Self-catering cottages: *visitcoll.co.uk/self_catering* |
| **Provisions/Eating Out** | Coll Hotel Restaurant • The Island Café • Coll Stores<br>• Sat Market – Community Centre • Post Office/An Acarsaid. |
| **Wildlife** | Corncrake, puffins, short-necked oil beetles, sand lizards, seals, otters,<br>brown hares, dolphins, whales. |
| **Night Sky Bortle Scale** | Class 1. Coll is an International Dark-sky Association Dark-sky Community. |

## Maps

• OS Explorer 372: Coll & Tiree: 1:25 000
• OS Landranger 46: Coll & Tiree: 1:50 000

*Previous spread*: *looking across to Rum from Tràigh Bousd.*
*Fujifilm X–T2, 18–55mm f/2.8–f/4, ISO 200, 1/2s at f/11. Oct.*

At the southern end of the island is the vast Coll Nature Reserve which is managed by the RSPB. A mix of dunes, huge sandy beaches and carefully managed farmland it is an ideal place to both photograph and see wildlife. Seasonal visitors to the reserve include barnacle geese, red shanks and even the elusive corncrake, however, it is more likely that you will hear it's call rather than see this shy and retiring bird. Otters are often seen hunting for fish along the shoreline so keep your telephoto lens handy. Also within this location are the two Breachacha Castles, which appear incongruous in this flat coastal landscape.

## What to shoot and viewpoints

### Viewpoint 1 – Breachacha Castles
The two Breachacaha Castles look out across the wide tidal sand flats at the head of Loch Breachaha and provide a strange and slightly eerie presence on the skyline. The old Breachacha Castle was built in the 15th Century by the MacLeans of Coll and stands just above the shoreline, looking across the beach: a fine view. It eventually fell into a dilapidated state until it was restored in the 1960s. The new Breachacha Castle was built in the 18th century and is a grand old house, which is now currently being restored to its former glory. The castles make a fine subject together or individually, and the stone walls picks up the late sun well. Look out for pools of water on the beach which pick up the reflection of the old castle. »

## How to get here

From the main settlement of Arinagour head inland and take the the left fork of the road at the church. Follow this road, the B8070, as it rises up across some lochan studded moorland, before descending and heading round a bend at Uig. Head past Coll Aerodrome on the right and at the next T-junction turn left and follow the road until you reach a cattle grid immediately past a house on the left. At the junction with the access track to the castles, there is space to park a car on the gravel. To reach the castles walk back along the road you have just driven and go through the gate on the right. From here make your way across

the grazing land to the beach. The parking for Feall and Crossapol bay is located at the end of the road on which you have parked for Viewpoint 1.

### Viewpoint 1 – Breachacha Castles

| | |
|---|---|
| **Lat/Long**: | 56.596844, -6.6327760 |
| **what3words**: | ///dose.elsewhere.anchovies |
| **Grid Ref**: | NM157546 |
| **Postcode**: | PA78 6TB |

## Viewpoint 2 – Feall Bay and Crossapol Bay

- **Lat/Long**: 56.589734, -6.6413193
- **what3words**: ///dining.outlast.unsecured
- **Grid Ref**: NM151538
- **Postcode**: PA78 6TB

### Accessibility

The castles are easily accessed across farmlands. The beaches can be accessed on flat ground, however, if you want to combine the two, you will need to climb up some steep dunes, but it is not too taxing.

### Best time of year/day

The castles are best photographed after the tide has receded if you are intending to catch the reflection in the shallow water. Feall Bay is a great sunset location and is definitely one to visit if there is a big swell on a high tide. Crossapol Bay and the view back to Mull works well in the evening light.

*Above*: the two Breachacha Castles from the beach (VP1). Fujifilm X–T2, 18–55mm f/2.8–f/4, ISO 200, 1/240s at f/9. Oct.

*Top*: *a couple walk on Crossapol Bay. Fujifilm X–T2, 18–55mm f/2.8–f/4, ISO 200, 1/80s at f/11. Oct.* **Above left**: *a distant view of Mull from Crossapol Bay. Fujifilm X–T2, 55–200mm f/3.5–f/4.8, ISO 200, 1/240s at f/8. Oct.* **Above Right**: *Feall Bay (VP2). Fujifilm X–T2, 18–55mm f/2.8–f/4, ISO 200, 1/100s at f/11. Oct.*

## Viewpoint 2 – Feall Bay and Crossapol Bay

The twin beaches of Feall Bay and Crossapol Bay are separated by a huge dune system, which offer fantastic elevated views over these sweeping shores. From the car park at the end of the road head north for 2km along a grassy track which eventually swings round through the dunes to the eastern end of Feall Bay. The beach sits below the hill Ben Feall which can provide a fine viewpoint, and the base of this hill has some great stratified rocks which knit into the sand. The beach itself is best appreciated from the dunes, with the gradual curve of the marram grass providing a great lead-in line through the view. It also attracts some big waves and as these rise, the translucent blues of the sea are revealed before dissipating in white foam; a great spot for some wave photography. From the middle of the beach a faint path leads up and across the giant dunes and this can be followed across to the calmer Crossapol Bay. Another huge beach, this feels altogether more relaxed and the pretty farmhouses at its western end provide a great focal point. There are also fantastic views east towards Mull, with Ben More looking tantalisingly close, especially through a long lens. For the more energetic, there are other excellent beaches further to the east, which face out to the Sound of Gunna, Gunna Island and Tiree.

A distant view to the Outer Hebrides from Feall Bay above a breaking wave.
Fujifilm X–E3, 55–200mm f/3.5–f/4.8, ISO 200, 1/280s at f/10. Oct.

These are two classic Hebridean beaches, with wide sandy shores backed by towering dunes. Both are exposed to the full brunt of the Atlantic ocean and wild waves are a common occurrence. Breakers race along the shoreline with a thundering noise that can be heard on the approach, long before the sea comes into view. Although similar in size, each has its own character and it is well worth visiting both beaches.

## What to shoot and viewpoints

### Viewpoint 1 – Cliad Bay

The walk to Cliad Bay follows a good track past the recycling centre and into a huge dune system. Paths undulate across the terrain and the dunes themselves offer good photographic opportunities. On windy days especially, the flowing shapes of marram-covered banks provide scope for some lovely long exposure work. A ruined caravan in the dunes, slowly being reclaimed by the landscape provides a nice spot for a shot of decay and provides a contrast to the picture postcard view of the beach. Arriving at the beach via steep dunes the view along the length of the beach is fantastic especially with sun glinting off the marram grass. on the beach itself, a stream flowing across the sand gives some nice foreground interest. »

*Abandoned caravan in the dunes at Cliad Bay. Fujifilm X–T2, 18–55mm f/2.8–f/4, ISO 200, 1/170s at f/11. Oct.*

*The beach at Cliad Bay. Fujifilm X–T2, 18–55mm f/2.8–f/4, ISO 200, 1/350s at f/10. Oct.*

## How to get here

From the main settlement of Arinagour head inland and take the the right fork of the road at the church. Follow this road, the B8071 for 5 minutes and then turn right at the T– junction. From here drive for a couple of minutes and park beside the access track to the recycling depot. For Hogh Bay, follow the road on for 10 minutes. There is a small parking area outside the Hebridean Centre at Ballyhaugh.

### Viewpoint 1 – Cliad Bay

**Lat/Long:**   56.646773,-6.5584952
**what3words:** ///elections.defensive.handle
**Grid Ref:**   NM206598
**Postcode:**   PA78 6TE

### Viewpoint 2 – Hogh Bay

**Lat/Long:**   56.628715,-6.6078836
**what3words:** ///airbag.dull.pythons
**Grid Ref:**   NM175580
**Postcode:**   PA78 6TB

### Accessibility

Both the beaches are very easy to access, with pleasant walking across farmland or on good tracks through the dunes.

### Best time of year/day

To experience the drama of big waves it's best to go on windy days with a big swell. Both beaches are excellent at sunset where the low sun will pick up the surging waves.

*Above*: Cliad Bay from the dunes. Fujifilm X–T2, 18–55mm f/2.8–f/4, ISO 200, 1/140s at f/11. Oct.
*Below*: Ben Hogh Fujifilm X–T2. 18–55mm f/2.8–f/4, ISO 200, 1/100s at f/8. Oct.

*Hogh Bay presents a great opportunity to get up close and personal with the wild waves.*

### Viewpoint 2 – Hogh Bay

The road winds down the west coast of Coll past a windswept football pitch and into a narrow valley between Beinn Tioraidh and Ben Hogh. It terminates at the edge of reed-fringed loch under the looming hill of Ben Hogh, which looks far higher than its 104m summit suggests. A walk to the summit is tempting if you have time, but the main jewel in this area is Hogh Bay. Head through the gate next to the Hebridean Centre and follow the track across the farmland with the sound of the waves pulling you on. As you enter the beach between the high dunes and steep cliffs the view is stunning. A wide sweep of sand, studded with pebbles and pounded by the ocean. It's a really dramatic spot in stormy conditions with waves crashing over the rocks at the northern end and rushing up the beach. The machair at the southern end of the beach at Totronald is also worth visiting in the summer where a profusion of wildflowers covers the ground.

*Above*: Wild sea at Hogh Bay. Fujifilm X–E3, 55–200mm f/3.5–f/4.8, ISO 200, 1/1000s at f/5.6. Oct.
*Below*: Hogh Bay rocks and dunes. Fujifilm X–E3, 55–200mm f/3.5–f/4.8, ISO 200, 1/1000s at f/4.8. Oct.

The western beaches of Coll are magnificent and can be linked together in a great walk which takes in many of the sights. Access is limited to one or two areas and signposts on Coll are rare so you will need to venture off the beaten track to get the most out of this location. The coast here is varied in character; large sandy beaches with expanses of rippled sand at low tide to small, intimate coves protected by ragged rocky skerries. You are likely to see seals along here, so a long lens would be useful to capture these animals lounging on the rocks. It is also a favoured habitat of otters and you may be lucky enough to see one, or perhaps even just their tracks.

## What to shoot and viewpoints

### Viewpoint 1 – Tràigh Thorastain and Tràigh Garbh

Located just to the north of Cloiche Farm, Tràigh Thorastain is a quiet beach which sits below the small hill of A'Chroich. Beautiful turquoise sea laps at white sand and it is an idyllic spot in summer. Photographically, the graceful sweep of the dunes immediately jumps out and the numerous skerries can be utilised to create some complex seascape images. From here a short but pathless walk around the seaward side A'Chroich leads to Tràigh Garbh, which has some fascinating rock formations which connect back to the shore with strands of yellow sand. The view south west along the coast is excellent, with a rugged and indented shoreline and lovely contrasts between sand and rock. At the southern end of the beach are a series of large boulders which can form a great foreground to the view back up the coast to Rum on the far horizon. >>

## How to get here

From the main settlement of Arinagour head inland and take the the right fork of the road at the church. Follow this road, the B8071 for 5 minutes and then turn right at the T junction. From here drive for 10 minutes until you pass Cloiche Farm on the right. Parking is possible just before the road bridge.

### Cloiche Farm

| | | |
|---|---|---|
| **P** Lat/Long: | 56.675071, -6.5169860 |
| **P** what3words: | ///spotted.pounding.playback |
| **P** Grid Ref: | NM234628 |
| **P** Postcode: | PA78 6TE |

## Accessibility

All the beaches are relatively easy to access if you don't mind some pathless walking across rough ground. Route-finding is not especially tricky, however, it is prudent to take a map and a compass.

## Best time of year/day

As the beaches are west facing, they are great sunset locations, but they can work well in most conditions.

*Above*: the graceful sweep of Tràigh Thorastain. Fujifilm X–T2, 18–55mm f/2.8–f/4, ISO 200, 1/340s at f/8. Oct.

***Top left***: *boulders on Tràigh Garbh. Fujifilm X–T2, 18–55mm f/2.8–f/4, ISO 200, 1/340s at f/11. Oct.* ***Above left***: *the rugged coastline between Tràigh Thorastain and Tràigh Garbh. Fujifilm X–E3, 55–200mm f/3.5–f/4.8, ISO 200, 1/480s at f/8. Oct.* ***Above right***: *the road north looking to Rum. Fujifilm X–T2, 18–55mm f/2.8–f/4, ISO 200, 1/125s at f/8. Oct.*

## Viewpoint 2 – Bagh an Trailleich

Further southwest leads to Bagh an Trailleich, another fine beach. Especially attractive are the dunes and it is a lovely area for macro studies of sand patterns. Rippled and waved, blown into shapes the sand here seems to be a mix of various types and offers a great opportunity to photograph the intimate landscape it creates at the base of the dunes. The wider view is just as enchanting with rocks offshore catching the waves on stormy days and throwing up some big waves. You can either retrace your steps back along the beaches described in Viewpoint 1 or follow the winding single track road back. The road is a lovely walk and reaches a high point which gives a great view north over the island. From the beach, follow the northern side of the stream across the dunes to reach the road via a gate at a sheep shearing pen.

*Opposite: intimate landscapes along the western beaches.*

As you wind your way along north along the single track road, the grass growing through the middle a reminder of how little it is travelled, the land becomes steadily more rugged and dramatic. The beaches, hidden out of sight to the left by dunes, the way ahead obscured by rocky outcrops that push through heather clad slopes until cresting a hill reveals a fantastic panorama. The northern tip of Coll with the islands of Rum, Skye Eigg and Muck all laid out in a shimmering sea. A sight to behold!

## What to shoot and viewpoints

### Viewpoint 1 – Traigh Bousd

Tràigh Bousd is a wonderful beach. Marram grass covered dunes, pure white sand and a view across rocky skerries to Rum and Eigg. From the roadside, a gate gives access to the machair and a faint path leads the way to the western end of the beach. There is a lot to photograph here, with rocky outcrops a perfect foil for rushing waves and interesting sand patterns formed by a stream which bisects the beach. At low tide it is possible to walk out to the two rocky outcrops via a ridge of sand onto which waves break to each side. This feature is best photographed from the dunes and as the tide comes in it gets steadily narrower until the rocks are connected by a golden thread of sand. Further to the east, the view to Eigg across the Cairns of

Coll and the beacon of Sùil Ghorm is very appealing in the golden hour at sunset. A place to linger and return to, Tràigh Bousd is one of those special Hebridean beaches that gets under your skin. »

*The pretty harbour at Arinagour. Fujifilm X–T2, 18–55mm f/2.8–f/4, ISO 200, 1/420s at f/8. Oct.*

## How to get here

It's difficult to get lost on Coll. From the main settlement of Arinagour head inland and take the the left fork of the road at the church. Follow this road, the B8071 for 5 minutes and then take turn right at the T–junction. From here Tràigh Bousd is a 15 minute drive. You pass a rusting piece of farm machinery on the right next to a track and it is possible to park on the verge on the left hand side next to a gate. Tràigh Tuath is another 10 minutes down the road from here.

### Viewpoint 1 – Traigh Bousd

| | | |
|---|---|---|
| **P Lat/Long:** | 56.683956, -6.4852433 |
| **w what3words:** | ///tailing.croutons.revival |
| **P Grid Ref:** | NM254636 |
| **P Postcode:** | PA78 6TE |

### Viewpoint 2 – Tràigh Tuath

| | | |
|---|---|---|
| **P Lat/Long:** | 56.681907, -6.4603232 |
| **P what3words:** | ///trial.patching.belonged |
| **P Grid Ref:** | NM269633 |
| **P Postcode:** | PA78 6TE |

### Accessibility

Tràigh Bousd is easily accessed across flat ground. Tràigh Tuath is more difficult, with pathless walking across boggy ground. It's not far from the road, but is a tricky walk and requires a basic familiarity with map reading.

### Best time of year/day

Both of these locations work well at sunset, however, sunrise can produce some beautiful light on the islands of Rum and Eigg. Walking to Tràigh Tuath in low light could be tricky.

*Dawn on Tràigh Bousd. Fujifilm X–T2, 18–55mm f/2.8–f/4, ISO 200, 0.7s at f/11. Oct.*

### Viewpoint 2 – Tràigh Tuath

The northernmost beach of Coll is a glorious crescent of sand backed by steep dunes through which a herds of cattle graze. From here the view is superb, across to Rum, Eigg and Skye but also north east to the mainland with the mountains of Knoydart etched across the skyline. It feels like a remote beach. This is a wild and wind-swept outpost at the tip of a rugged island and is one that requires a bit of trackless walking to reach. Parking is scarce, however, it is possible to park on the large verge to the south of the turning area. Use your discretion, if the verge looks boggy, do not attempt to park on it. From here head south for a minute until a gate on the right is reached. Head through the gate and make for another one at the top of the field. Note, the field boundaries on the OS map are not accurate. After the second gate, you need to head roughly north east across that classic Hebridean terrain which is simultaneously rocky and boggy. You will should reach the shore in about 10 minutes. After photographing the beach you can either retrace your steps back to the car or follow the dunes and shoreline around to the east where eventually you will reach Sorrisdale Bay and can pick up the track through the village to your car. Sorrisdale Bay also offers a good view back to Mull.

*Right: Golden hour on Tràigh Bousd, Fujifilm X–T2, 18–55mm f/2.8–f/4, ISO 200, 1/13s at f/11. Oct. Below: looking towards the the Cairns of Coll from Tràigh Tuath, Fujifilm X–E3, 55–200mm f/3.5–f/4.8, ISO 200, 1/100s at f/8. Oct. Below middle: Tràigh Tuath dunes, Fujifilm X–T2, 18–55mm f/2.8–f/4, ISO 200, 1/240s at f/8. Oct. Below right: looking across to Rum from Tràigh Bousd, Fujifilm X–T2, 18–55mm f/2.8–f/4, ISO 200, 0.7s at f/11. Oct.*

TIREE

**Tiree is a special island. A low-lying, fertile green isle surrounded by turquoise seas and fringed with huge sandy beaches. On Tiree the sky feels bigger, uninterrupted by forests or hills – save for two small hills on the western side of the island and one the east – and on a summers day the combination of a huge blue sky above and blue seas stretching to the horizon is a sight to behold. The island seems to instil a sense of relaxation, you feel no need to rush along the the roads or dash from location to location. Everything you could need is within reach. Tiree feels different to all other Hebridean islands, even the traditional thatched roof crofthouses have their own unique aesthetic. It's an island which should be high up on your list to visit.**

Tiree is connected to the mainland via the Caledonian MacBrayne ferry which sails from Oban and in summer is also connected one day a week to Barra at the southern tip of the Outer Hebrides. It is also possible to fly to the island, on LoganAir from Glasgow, but most people arrive by boat. This docks at the main settlement Scarinish where you will find the local supermarket, the bank, post office and hotel.

The obvious attraction when looking at a map of Tiree are the beaches and the island is spoilt for choice with the variety on offer around its 46 miles of coastline. There is the large, flat expanse of Gott Bay which is favoured by kite and wind surfers or the sheltered coves of Caolas which look out over Gunna Sound. To the north there is the idyllic Tràigh Cornaig with its croft houses perched out at the end of a perfect shoreline. Then there is Balevullin, a beautiful village on the machair above a fantastic sandy beach beloved by surfers. The west coast has its grand beaches as well, open to the full swell of the Atlantic, wild in winter but in summer an absolute paradise. Behind many of the beaches are swathes of machair, that wonderfully unique wildflower landscape created by windblown shell sand, home to the rare corncrake whose call you will hear throughout summer evenings.

Tiree is blessed with an enviable microclimate and is commonly known as the sunniest place in Scotland. It also can be quite breezy, which is no bad thing in summer as the midge is practically nonexistent!

## How to get to Tiree

### Ferry

The main route to Tiree is by the Caledonian MacBrayne ferry service from Oban which takes 4 hours, in the summer there are daily sailings.

### Air

There are several Hebridean Air Service flights a day from Oban to Tiree's small airport. Flights are also available by Loganair from Glasgow.

*hebrideanair.co.uk • loganair.co.uk*

*Previous spread: looking across Tràigh Chornaig from the dunes. Fujifilm X–T2, 18–55mm f/2.8–f/4, ISO 200, 1/480s at f/11. Jun.*

| TIREE | |
|---|---|
| Scottish Gaelic | Tiriodh (Land of Corn). |
| Area | 30 sq. miles (77 sq. km). |
| Length/breadth | 10 × 5 miles. |
| Highest Elevation | Ben Hynish, 141m (463ft). |
| Owned by | Argyll Estates. |
| Population | 653 |
| Largest settlement(s) | Scarinish |
| Vehicles allowed | Yes. Motorhomes need proof of campsite booking to board the ferry. |
| Car/Bike rental | Tiree Car Hire: 01879 220 555 • TORAZ Car Hire: 07788 810 623 Tiree Fitness Solutions (bikes): *tireefitness.co.uk* • Millhouse Cycles: *tireemillhouse.co.uk* • Blackhouse Bike Rental: *blackhouse-watersports.co.uk* Sea Tours: *tireeseatours.co.uk* |
| Public transport | Ring'n'Ride bus service • Taxi service 01879 220 419 |
| Day trips from mainland? | Yes, from 2 to 9 hours depending on the season and ferry timetable. |
| Internet/mobile phone coverage | Broadband. 3G/4G dependent on carrier. |
| Power | Grid and Wind Turbine. |
| Island website(s) | *isleoftiree.com* • *southernhebrides.com* • *visitscotland.com* • *scotland.org.uk* |
| Festivals/Events | Tiree 10k and Half Marathon (April) • Tiree Music Festival (July) • Tiree Ultramarathon (September) • Sea Change Film Festival • Tiree Wave Classic (October). |
| Accommodation | Hotel, catered accommodation, croft camping, camping and self-catering cottages. *isleoftiree.com/places-to-stay* |
| Provisions/Eating Out | Tiree Lodge Hotel, Kirkapol • Yellow Hare, Gott Pier • Scarinish Beach Hotel, Stoirm Restaurant • Aisling's Kitchen, Crossapol • Farmhouse Cafe, Balemartine Supermarkets • Bùth a' Bhaile, Crossapol • Co-operative Store, Scarinish. |
| Wildlife | Brown hares, seals, basking sharks, barnacle, greylag and Greenland white-fronted geese, harbour porpoises and dolphins. |
| Night Sky Bortle Scale | Class 1. |

## LOCATIONS

## Maps

- OS Explorer 372: Coll & Tiree: 1:25 000
- OS Landranger 46: Coll & Tiree: 1:50 000

You may be forgiven for thinking you have stepped into a painting when you arrive at the township of Balevullin. A ribbon of blacktop flows across impossibly colourful machair, alongside thatched blackhouses and finishes above an arc of white sand fringed by turquoise sea. Sheep and cattle wander between cottages, grazing on buttercups. It's an idyllic place and one of the most beautiful locations in Tiree, if not the entire Hebrides. The name comes from Baile a'Mhuilinn, the Village of the Mill. Both the village and the beach are really special and offer a number of great photographic opportunities.

Amongst many great beaches on Tiree, Tràigh Chornaig is perhaps the finest. On a summer day the combination of white shell sand and turquoise water is hard to beat and it really is an idyllic spot. From the beach you can just make out the isle of Rum to the north east and to the north west the uninhabited islands south of Barra are seen on the horizon. At the western end of the beach a scattering of blackhouses complete this perfect Hebridean scene.

## What to shoot and viewpoints

### Viewpoint 1 – The township ♿

From the parking area head back down the road you have driven through the village. There are a number of blackhouses which make fascinating studies with their setting on the machair and the traditional marram grass thatched roofs weighed down by rocks. Please be mindful that people do live here so make sure you respect their privacy. The sheep and cows roaming around the village make great subjects as they graze on the machair. »

*Cow on the machair (VP2). Fujifilm X–T2, 55–200mm f/3.5–f/4.8, ISO 200, 1/2000s at f/4.8. Jun.*

## How to get here

Head north from Scarinish on the B8068. At Gott Bay carry straight on. After five minutes you will reach the village of Balephetrish with the road skirting along the edge of the beach on the right. Continue straight on to the windsurfing centre on Loch Bhasapol. To get to Balevuillin continue on the road as it heads inland, and after a couple of minutes turn right at the T-junction. The road leads down through the village of Balevullin with a parking area at the end of the road above the beach.

### Viewpoint 1 & 2 – The township and the beach

- **Lat/Long**: 56.519578, -6.955806
- **what3words**: ///eaten.conjured.flaked
- **Grid Ref**: NL953473
- **Postcode**: PA77 6XD

### Viewpoint 3 – Tràigh Chornaig
- **Lat/Long**: 56.521321, -6.9207192
- **what3words**: ///extensive.emotional.blizzard
- **Grid Ref**: NL974474
- **Postcode**: PA77 6XA

## Accessibility

All the viewpoints in and around Balevullin are easily accessible from the car park along single track roads or sandy beaches. Tràigh Chornaig is easily accessed across tracks and grassland, however, the dunes are quite steep and may be difficult for those with limited mobility. As it is grazing land be careful to keep away from cows, especially if they are with calves.

### Best time of year/day

Summer in Balevullin is fantastic, the machair blooms in June and July and really is a sight to behold. It's a great location at any time of the day, but the village looks incredible under bright sun on a summers day. The beach faces north west so is ideal for a summer sunset. Tràigh Chornaig looks fantastic in summer with the blue sea and white sand looking at its best. However, it can be busy at this time with people enjoying the sea, so if it is solitude you are after it might be best to come in spring or autumn. It is suitable for both sunset and sunrise, but it is a location which can work at most times of the day.

*Above*: the distinctive Tiree cottages (VP1). Fujifilm X–T2, 18–55mm f/2.8–f/4, ISO 200, 1/1000s at f/8. Jun.
*Below*: the tracks to the beach at Balevullin. Fujifilm X–T2, 18–55mm f/2.8–f/4, ISO 200, 1/240s at f/8. Jun.

## Viewpoint 2 – The beach

The beach is accessed from the car park on the machair at
the end of the road. The machair offers a great foreground
for the beach, with the yellow of the buttercups contrasting
against the blue of the sea. There are a number of
opportunities on the beach which depend somewhat on
the tide. At low tide there are some great rock formations
at either end of the beach which can be used for
foregrounds and a number of shallow pools and streams
which catch the light. The beach is popular with surfers and
windsurfers and some good actions shots can be had from
the shoreline. >>

*Sheep on the Machair at Balevullin. Fujifilm X–T2, 55–200mm
f/3.5–f/4.8, ISO 200, 1/2000s at f/4.8. Jun.*

***Opposite***: *red accents at Balevullin (VP1).*

*Calm sunset Tràigh Chornaig. Fujifilm X–T2, 18–55mm
f/2.8–f/4, ISO 200, 15s at f/8. Jun.*

### Viewpoint 3 – Tràigh Chornaig

From the parking area at Loch Bhasapol, a favourite spot for those learning to windsurf, head east along the road and take the first left. Follow the road past the school and take the gate on the left hand side. From here a path leads across the machair and dunes to a gate in the fence above the beach. The dunes above the beach are ideal for a sweeping vista of the shore with the marram grass providing an interesting foreground. As it is a north facing beach it works well in summer with opportunities guaranteed throughout the day without the worry of having to shoot into the sun. The beach itself offers a nice variety of opportunities. There are areas of rocky skerries to explore, shallow turquoise pools and of course the white sand itself. The only slight downside is the lack of vertical elements, which can lead to the sky becoming a big part of the view. However, if you choose a day with dramatic clouds you can use this to your advantage.

*Right: Machair and beach at Balevullin (VP1). Fujifilm X–T2, 18–55mm f/2.8–f/4, ISO 200, 1/800s at f/8. Jun. **Below**: surfing at Balevullin (VP1). Fujifilm X–T2, 55–200mm f/3.5–f/4.8, ISO 200, 1/4000s at f/4.8. Jun. **Below middle**: Tràigh Chornaig from the dunes. Fujifilm X–T2, 18–55mm f/2.8–f/4, ISO 200, 1/450s at f/11. Jun. **Below right**: in amongst the pools at Tràigh Chornaig (VP3).Fujifilm X–T2, 18–55mm f/2.8–f/4, ISO 200, 1/1000s at f/8. Jun.*

The west coast of Tiree is exposed to the full brunt of the Atlantic and Tràigh Thodhrasdail (also know as The Maze) has all the hallmarks of a classic Hebridean beach. White sand, wave sculpted rock, marram grass dunes all of which is backed by a fantastic area of machair. It's another favoured spot for windsurfing and on a breezy day it attracts some fair gusts. It is also home to the second highest peak in Tiree, Ben Hough which tops out at a giddy 119m.

## What to shoot and viewpoints

### Viewpoint 1 – The beach, Tràigh Thodhrasdail

There are a real variety of seascapes here – as you enter the beach across a small burn you arrive at a stony shore interspersed with skerries facing roughly south west. This is a tricky area to photograph, as it is difficult to get separation between the areas of rock, however, depending on the tide, it can be possible. Heading north along the top of the beach you reach an area of marram grass with a path that leads down onto the main beach. This has a larger area of sand which is punctuated by a number of shapely rocks – they offer great opportunities, particularly when the tide is high and waves are breaking upon them. A band of higher rocks protrudes onto the beach and with careful scrambling to the top, this position provides a fine vantage to view the beach and the distant headland of Ceannn a M'hara. Further north are some wave worn rocks with a distinctive orange colour. At sunset they catch the sun superbly and provide a real pop of warmth against the blue tones of the sea. The beach continues to the north and it is feasible to carry on to Tràigh Hough, however, there are plenty of opportunities on Tràigh Thodhrasdail. »

## How to get here

Tràigh Thodhrasdail And Ben Hough are located on the west coast of Tiree. From Scarinish take the B8065 west past the airport following the signs for Sandaig. As you begin to head northwards a parking area is signposted to the left, just before a cattle grid. For Viewpoint 1, take this track on the left across the machair and park up above the beach. For Viewpoint 2, follow the road straight on through Kilkenneth. Just at the foot of Ben Hough there is a private road on the left. There is space to park a car at this spot but be careful not to block the access.

### Viewpoint 1 – The Beach, Tràigh Thodhrasdail

| | Lat/Long: | 56.489664, -6.9727995 |
|---|---|---|
| | what3words: | ///foods.aboard.sublet |
| | Grid Ref: | NL940441 |
| | Postcode: | PA77 6XG |

### Viewpoint 2 – Ben Hough

| | Lat/Long: | 56.499359, -6.9632534 |
|---|---|---|
| | what3words: | ///dark.defaults.supposed |
| | Grid Ref: | NL946451 |
| | Postcode: | PA77 6XE |

## Accessibility

The beach is very easily accessed and is relatively flat. There is a small burn to ford, however, it is relatively easy to cross. Ben Hough is a short but steep walk up a tarmac road, well within the capabilities of walkers. Crossing the hill to the northern top is a bit trickier with a steep scramble up and down slippery grass.

## Best time of year/day

As it is west facing, the beaches look fantastic at sunset, particularly when the rocks are illuminated by low sun. Ben Hough would work at most times although a clear day with good visibility is best for obtaining the long views across the island.

*Above*: *golden light on the rocks of Tràigh Thodhrasdail.*
*Fujifilm X–T2, 14mm f/2.8, ISO 200, 1/60s at f/11. Jun.*

*Midsummer skies at Tràigh Thodhrasdail (VP1). Fujifilm X–T2, 14mm f/2.8, ISO 200, 2.3s at f/11. Jun.*

### Viewpoint 2 – Ben Hough

Tiree is a very flat island and as such hills like Ben Hough at just 119m offers fantastic panoramic views across most of the land. From the main road head along the private road and follow the road up to the transmitters on the summit. Even at this modest altitude the views are superb. There are opportunities here for a variety of shots, from taking in the whole vista, to using a long lens to pick out the attractively coloured crofthouses below. The northern point of the hill topped with the ruins of a lookout tower gives a great view down to Balevuillin.

*An abandoned farmhouse from Ben Hough. Fujifilm X–T2, 18–55mm f/2.8–f/4, ISO 200, 1/800s at f/8. Jun.*

*The flat land of Tiree as seen from Ben Hough (VP2). Fujifilm X–T2, 18–55mm f/2.8–f/4, ISO 200, 1/1000s at f/8. Jun.*

## ③ CEANN A' MHARA

Located on the west coast of Tiree the headland Ceann a'Mhara juts out into the Atlantic with rugged cliffs exposed to the pounding surf. On either side of the headland are two beaches: Tràigh nan Gilean and Tràigh Bhi which have quite different characters; one rugged and isolated the other overlooked by pretty houses. The headland itself, whilst interesting for a walk does not provide many great photographic opportunities and is best utilised as a subject, not as a location itself.

## What to shoot and viewpoints

### Viewpoint 1 – Tràigh nan Gilean

Despite being sheltered by Ceann a'Mhara, the beach of Tràigh nan Gilean still attracts its share of big waves and the numerous skerries in the bay create some lovely white water. Using long exposures here can produce some fantastic images. The beach itself is a mixture of sand and shingle and can offer some great macro opportunities, with the wind blown sand creating some fascinating rippled patterns when I was last there. Cows wander freely across the beaches in Tiree and they can make some great subjects on the beach, lending a sense of scale. The rocks at the northern end of the beach provide a good opportunity to get some elevation and look great when illuminated by the setting sun. »

### How to get here

Ceann a'Mhara is on the west coast of Tiree. From Scarinish take the B8065 west past the airport following the signs for Sandaig. The road heads inland after Crossapol until a junction with the B8066. For Viewpoint 1, turn right and then left on the B8065. After Sandaig take the track on the left at the sign for Middleton. Follow this bumpy track down through the machair until the obvious parking area is reached. For Viewpoint 2, head south on the B8067 for Balemartine. Before the village take the B8067 for Balephuil. As you reach the village take the road on the right and follow it on across the fields, past the bird hide at Loch a' Phuill until a parking area is reached.

### Viewpoint 1 – Tràigh nan Gilean

- **Lat/Long**: 56.474253, -6.9756970
- **what3words**: ///gravy.diver.quirky
- **Grid Ref**: NL937424
- **Postcode**: PA77 6XQ

### Viewpoint 2 – Tràigh Bhi

- **Lat/Long**: 56.462704, -6.9495617
- **what3words**: ///plugged.snaps.equipment
- **Grid Ref**: NL952410
- **Postcode**: PA77 6UE

## Accessibility

Both beaches are easily accessed, but the tracks leading to the parking areas are quite bumpy. The beaches themselves are relatively flat and should pose no problems to walkers.

*Above: tracks in the sand at Tràigh nan Gilean (VP1), Fujifilm X–T2, 18–55mm f/2.8–f/4, ISO 200, 1/220s at f/8. Jun.*

## Best time of year/day

Tràigh nan Gilean is fantastic in the golden hour before sunset as the lower light picks out the cliffs on Ceann a'Mhara very well. It would suit most times of the year. Traigh Bhi would be great on a high tide with stormy conditions kicking up the waves against the rocks at the eastern end.

*Balephuil village (VP2), Fujifilm X–T2, 18–55mm f/2.8–f/4, ISO 200, 1/600s at f/5.6. Jun.*

## Viewpoint 2 – Tràigh Bhi

To the east of Ceann a'Mhara is Traigh Bhi, another fabulous beach. South facing, it attracts some pretty big waves and these can be used to create an interesting contrast with the pretty houses in the village of Balephuil perched above the shoreline. The view east takes in Ben Hynish, the highest point on Tiree, with the distinctive golfball shaped radar station on the summit. Looking south west you may be able to make out the remote lighthouse of Skerryvore on the horizon.

*__Opposite left__: summer swimming at Tràigh Bhi. Fujifilm X–T2, 55–200mm f/3.5–f/4.8, ISO 200, 1/750s at f/8. Jun. __Top__: surfing at Tràigh Bhi. Fujifilm X–T2, 55–200mm f/3.5–f/4.8, ISO 200, 1/640s at f/8. Jun. __Bottom__: cows on the beach at Tràigh nan Gilean. Fujifilm X–T2, 18–55mm f/2.8–f/4, ISO 200, 1/220s at f/8. Jun.*

*Buttercups at Tràigh Bhi. Fujifilm X–T2, 18–55mm f/2.8–f/4, ISO 200, 1/300s at f/4.5. Jun.*

*Above*: Tràigh Bhi and the radar station on Carnan Mòr. Fujifilm X–T2, 18–55mm f/2.8–f/4, ISO 200, 1/650s at f/8. Jun.

Gott Bay is the biggest beach on Tiree and if you have arrived by ferry it is the one you will have seen when approaching Scarinish. It's a favourite spot for windsurfing and on windy days many windsurfers can be seen racing at speed across the waves. Vaul is located to the north of Gott Bay. It feels a bit more sheltered, a lovely curve of white and grey sand with a rocky headland which encloses a blackhouse in an idyllic spot at the foot of a ruined broch.

In contrast to the other beaches on Tiree with their open aspect to the Atlantic, the beach at Caolas feels quite different. It looks out onto a narrow stretch of water called Gunna Sound (the word Caolas in Gaelic means Strait) to the isles of Gunna and Coll and provides a very interesting seascape, through which the Barra to Oban Calmac ferry passes once a week.

## What to shoot and viewpoints

### Viewpoint 1 – Gott Bay ♿

There a number of parking spots along the road which give access to the beach. If there is a big swell and high winds you are likely to see windsurfers so a long lens here will be useful if you want to capture the action. It may also be used for looking to the east to pull in the background hills of Mull as the beach itself can be quite featureless. However, under stormy skies or bright sun the colour of the water here can be very special. The beach looks at its best from the western end as the ferry terminal can dominate the view from the east. »

*Opposite top: post box on the dunes at Gott Bay, Fujifilm X–T2, 18–55mm f/2.8–f/4, ISO 200, 1/500s at f/8. Jun. **Middle left**: The An Turas shelter at the ferry terminal, Fujifilm X–T2, 18–55mm f/2.8–f/4, ISO 200, 1/900s at f/8. Jun. **Bottom left**: An old phone box at Gott Bay, Fujifilm X–T2, 18–55mm f/2.8–f/4, ISO 200, 1/125s at f/8. Jun. **Bottom right**: Kite surfing on Gott Bay (VP1), Fujifilm X–T2, 55–200mm f/3.5–f/4.8, ISO 200, 1/3800s at f/3.5. Jun.*

## How to get here

Head north from Scarinish on the B8068. At Gott Bay head east on the B8069. There are numerous places to stop on the right hand side of the road which give access onto the beach. To get to Vaul take the minor road on the left after you pass the hotel and follow until you reach a parking area for a couple of cars immediately above the eastern end of the beach. To reach Caolas head on east from Gott Bay, after you pass the phone box on the right, turn left and follow the minor road for 5 minutes. At the point where road splits in three directions there is space to pull off and park. From here it is an easy stroll across the machair to the beach.

### Viewpoint 1 – Gott Bay

- **Lat/Long**: 56.521518, -6.8085217
- **what3words**: ///budget.initiated.dwarf
- **Grid Ref**: NM043469
- **Postcode**: PPA77 6TW

### Viewpoint 2 – Vaul

- **Lat/Long**: 56.535171, -6.7997949
- **what3words**: ///interest.always.shook
- **Grid Ref**: NM050484
- **Postcode**: PA77 6TP

### Viewpoint 3 & 4 – Caolas Beach, The village and machair

- **Lat/Long**: 56.550129, -6.7530332
- **what3words**: ///commended.dynamic.windpipe
- **Grid Ref**: NM043469
- **Postcode**: PA77 6TS

### Accessibility

The beach at Gott Bay is very easily accessed, with the parking area pretty much on the sand! At Vaul the beach is also easily accessed and the path out to the broch is a fairly simple stroll over grazing land. The beach at Caolas is very easily accessed, just a short stroll across the machair. The village can be accessed from minor roads which are generally very quiet.

### Best time of year/day

To photograph the windsurfers at Gott Bay you will need a windy day with some waves. The beach itself looks great under bright summer conditions, however, it works equally well under stormy skies, providing a great contrast to the turquoise waters. Vaul is a good location for summer sunsets with the sun going down behind the uninhabited islands south of Vatersay. The fantastic rocks on the shoreline at Vaul look their best under overcast conditions. Caolas works well on a fair weather day, and if you want to maximise the views to Mull go on a day of clear visibility. It's a great spot for an autumn sunrise, with the sun coming up above the hills on Mull. If you are wanting to photograph the Calmac ferry as it winds its way through Gunna Sound, it is best to check the times at: *calmac.co.uk*

*Blackhouse on the beach near Vaul (VP2). Fujifilm X–T2, 55–200mm f/3.5–f/4.8, ISO 200, 1/480s at f/8. Jul.*

### Viewpoint 2 – Vaul

From the small parking area you have two choices; head east along the beach to explore it or head west through a stone gateway to explore the headland. The track to the west heads through grazing land above some rocky coves to a single blackhouse. From here the views open up to the north and on a clear day the the Small Isles of Eigg, Canna and Rum are visible on the horizon. Further on there are also the remains of an Iron Age Broch which can be explored. The rocky shoreline is fascinating with wave shaped rock offering plenty of opportunities for macro enthusiasts, especially good on those overcast days. >>

*Sheep on the route to the broch. Fujifilm X–T2, 55–200mm f/3.5–f/4.8, ISO 200, 1/200s at f/6.4. Jul.*

*The remains of Dún Mor broch. Fujifilm X–T2, 18–55mm f/2.8–f/4, ISO 200, 1/125s at f/8. Jul.*

*Sheep on the machair at Caolas (VP4). Fujifilm X–T2, 55–200mm f/3.5–f/4.8, ISO 200, 1/2000s at f/6.4. Jun.*

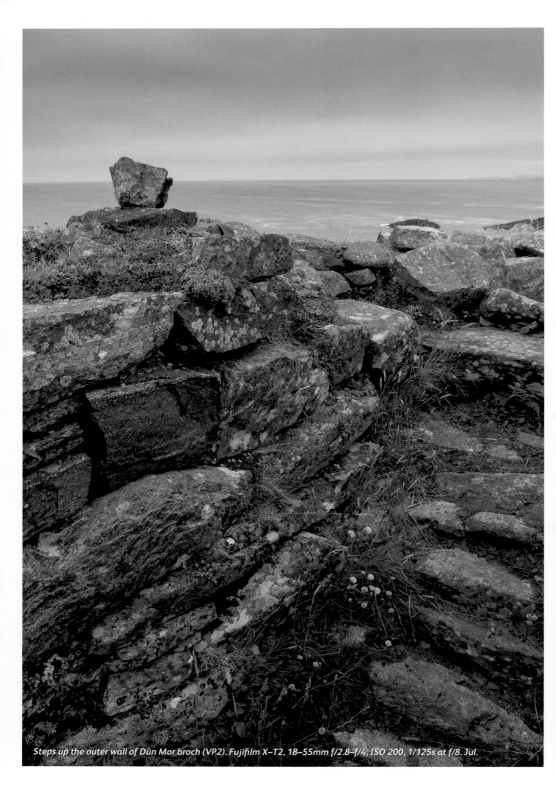

*Steps up the outer wall of Dùn Mor broch (VP2). Fujifilm X–T2, 18–55mm f/2.8–f/4, ISO 200, 1/125s at f/8. Jul.*

*Gott Bay under ominous skies. Fujifilm X–T2, 18–55mm f/2.8–f/4, ISO 200, 1/800s at f/8. Jul.*

*Caolas beach. Fujifilm X–T2, 18–55mm f/2.8–f/4, ISO 200, 1/840s at f/8. Jun.*

## Viewpoint 3 – Caolas Beach

The beach at Caolas is an intricate seascape and can be hard to make sense of immediately. If you spend some time here though will see many opportunities along the shoreline amongst the rocky outcrops and sandy areas. The view across to Mull and the mainland is fantastic on a sunny day. There are usually a number of small fishing boats anchored just off shore and these can make a fine subject in the wider landscape. The view south along beach to the house on the headland is particularly good with sinuous tidal areas forming some great lead-in lines.

*Looking south along Caolas beach (VP3). Fujifilm X–T2, 18–55mm f/2.8–f/4, ISO 200, 1/840s at f/8. Jun.*

*Boat in the shallows off Caolas beach, Fujifilm X–T2, 18–55mm f/2.8–f/4, ISO 200, 1/680s at f/8. Jun.*

*Gott Bay from the An Turas shelter at the ferry terminal. Fujifilm X–E3, 27mm f/2.8, ISO 200, 1/840s at f/8. Jun.*

## Viewpoint 4 – The village and machair

The village consists of a number of attractive blackhouses, some of which are particularity photogenic siting in the machair with the sea beyond. I'm always drawn to the rusting outhouses and there are a few of these which can make for interesting macro studies. The machair at the northern end of the beach is at its best in July and the profusion of buttercups is a sight to behold.

*On the machair above Caolas beach (VP4). Fujifilm X–T2, 18–55mm f/2.8–f/4, ISO 200, 1/850s at f/8. Jun.*

*Rusty shed and a cottage at Caolas (VP4). Fujifilm X–T2, 18–55mm f/2.8–f/4, ISO 200, 1/800s at f/8. Jun.*

# THE INNER ISLES

**The Inner Isles lie just off the coast of Argyll and are the closest Hebridean islands to the mainland. Each are fascinating in their own right and offer a variety of experiences. The Inner Isles make for great day trips if you are staying on the mainland.**

The largest island is Lismore. Known as the Great Garden, the underlying limestone rock gives rise to a rich fertile soil and it has settled, relaxed and plentiful feel to it. Situated at the seaward end of Loch Linnhe there are excellent views to the mountains of Lochaber and Argyll with the largest of them all, Ben Nevis looming on the horizon to the north. Lismore can be reached from Oban, via the Caledonian MacBrayne ferry or by the short passenger ferry from Port Appin.

Lying just offshore from Oban, and forming part of the the towns natural harbour, so crucial in its development as a large port town, is the island of Kerrera. Connected by a small passenger ferry, the island is a fantastic place to explore on foot or by bike with the route along the eastern coast to Gylen Castle in the south making an excellent day out.

The island of Seil is the closest Hebridean island to the mainland and is accessed by the famous Bridge over the Atlantic, a stone hump-backed bridge which crosses the narrow channel. Seil is one of the Slate Islands, known as the 'islands who roofed the world'. Famed for the quality of their slate the islands of Seil, Easdale, Luing and Belnhua supported a thriving industry in the 18th and 19th centuries. Today the slate quarries are abandoned, the result of flooding by a big storm in 1881 and then clay tiles replacing slate as the roofing material of choice. Many of the quarries have been reclaimed by nature, some you can swim in. They are fascinating post-industrial landscapes and make for some very unusual and distinctive photographs. The villages of Ellenabeich on Seil, Easdale island and Cullipool on Luing are also very photogenic with their narrow streets of whitewashed ex-miners cottage's particularly attractive and well preserved. There is much to explore on these islands with some diverse and distinctive landscapes located just off the mainland.

*Previous spread*: Cullipool beach at sunset. Fujifilm X–T2, 10–24mm f/4, ISO 200, 20s at f/9. Feb.

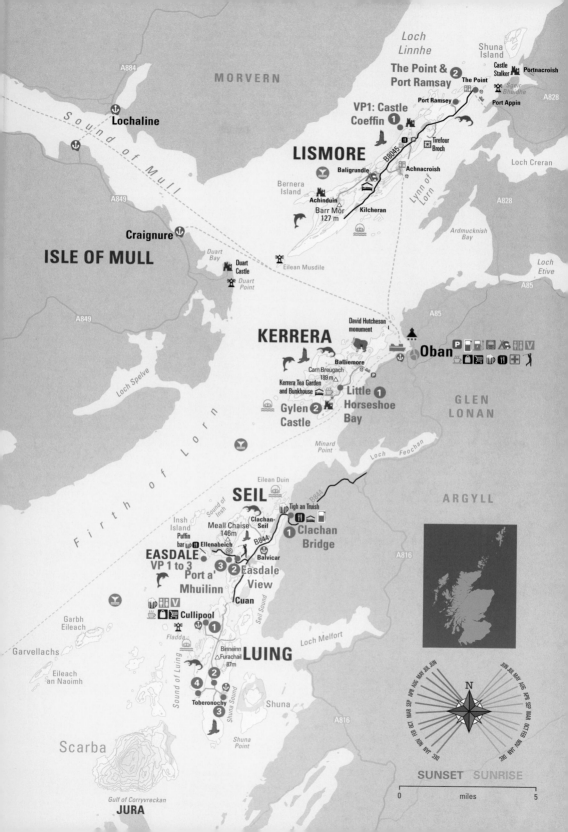

*Loch Linnhe*

Shuna Island

MORVERN

Castle Stalker · Portnacroish

The Point & Port Ramsay ❷ The Point

*Sound of Mull*

VP1: Castle Coeffin ❶ Port Ramsey · Port Appin

*Sgeir Bhuidhe*

A884

⚓ Lochaline Tirefour Broch

LISMORE A828

B8045 Achnacroish

Baligrundle *Loch Creran*

A849 Bernera Island

Achinduin *Lynn of Lorn* A828

⚓ Craignure Barr Mòr Kilcheran *Loch Etive*

127 m Ardmucknish Bay

ISLE OF MULL A85

A849 *Duart Bay* Duart Castle

*Duart Point* Eilean Musdile

David Hutcheson monument A85

KERRERA Oban 🅿 🚻 ✕ 🍴 🏥 V

Balliemore

*Loch Spelve* Carn Breugach 189 m

Kerrera Tea Garden and Bunkhouse GLEN LONAN

Gylen Castle ❷ Little Horseshoe Bay ❶

*Firth of Lorn*

*Minard Point*

*Loch Feochan*

⚓ Eilean Duin

SEIL B844 ARGYLL

Tigh an Truish

Insh Island *Sound of Insh* Clachan-Seil Clachan Bridge ❶ 🍴 🏠 ⛽

A816

Meall Chaise 146m

Puffin bar Ellenabeich Balvicar

EASDALE B844 ❷ Easdale View

VP 1 to 3 ❸ Port a' Mhuilinn

Cuan

🍺 V

☕ 🏠 Cullipool ❶

Garbh Eileach *Fladda*

*Sound of Luing*

Binnein Furachail 87m LUING *Loch Melfort*

Garvellachs ❷

Eileach an Naoimh ❹ *Shuna Sound*

Toberonochy ❸ Shuna A816

*Shuna Point*

Scarba

*Gulf of Corryvreckan*

JURA

N

SUNSET SUNRISE

0 miles 5

# LISMORE

The name Lismore derives from the Gaelic Lios Mòr, meaning either the great garden or the big enclosure. It's easy to see why; the island is incredibly lush and green with the underlying limestone giving rise to a very fertile land. Alternatively it is thought that the mountains which rise up on the mainland to each side of the low lying island could possibly be the big enclosure. Either translation works in its own way.

The island itself is 12 miles long and sits in Loch Linnhe just offshore from Port Appin. It has numerous historically important sites including an Iron Age broch, two ruined castles and was once a key site of early Celtic Christianity. Whilst it does not have the immediate or perhaps obvious appeal of other Hebridean islands, there are no lofty peaks or sandy beaches, it excludes a quiet calm with a sense of real settled history and is a delight to explore.

## How to get to Lismore

Lismore is accessed from the mainland in two ways: the car ferry from Oban which arrives in Achnacroish or the passenger ferry from Port Appin to The Point which is the northern tip of Lismore. There is parking at both of these locations and it is possible to explore the quiet roads of the island either of foot or by bike.

*Looking across to Morvern from the north of Lismore, Fujifilm X–T2, 18–55mm f/2.8–f/4, ISO 200, 3.7s at f/11. May.*

| LISMORE | |
|---|---|
| Scottish Gaelic | Lios Mòr (Great Garden). |
| Area | 9 sq. miles (23 sq. km). |
| Length/breadth | 10 × 1 miles. |
| Highest Elevation | Barr Mòr, 127m (417ft). |
| Owned by | Mixed including Argyll Estate. |
| Population | 170 |
| Largest settlement(s) | Achnacroish |
| Vehicles allowed | Yes, but only space for two camper vans to stay. Bringing camper vans to the island is discouraged. |
| Car/Bike rental | Land Rover tours at *explorelismore.co.uk*. Lismore Bike Hire: **07376 425 996**. Thistle Taxi and Tours: **07584 177 132**. |
| Public transport | No |
| Day trips from mainland? | Yes |
| Internet/mobile phone coverage | Yes |
| Power | Grid |
| Island website(s) | *isleoflismore.com* • *lismoregaelicheritagecentre.org* *southernhebrides.com* • *visitscotland.com* • *scotland.org.uk* |
| Festivals/Events | See the islands websites. |
| Accommodation | The Lismore Bunkhouse and Campsite, and there is a good selection of self-catering cottages. Visit: *isleoflismore.com* to book. |
| Provisions/Eating Out | Lismore Gaelic Hertitage Centre cafe, Lismore Stores. |
| Wildlife | The island is known for its peregrine falcons, sea eagles and seabirds including razorbills. The island's three lochs, as well as its islets and skerries, are designated as a Special Areas of Conservation. Porpoises, dolphins, seals, minke whales, basking sharks and otters may be seen on the coast. |
| Night Sky Bortle Scale | Class 2. |

## LOCATIONS

## Maps

• OS Landranger 49: Oban and East Mull (1:50 000)

*Previous spread: storm clouds gather on Mull. Fujifilm X–T2, 55–200mm f/3.5–f/4.8, ISO 200, 1/750s at f/8. May.*

## What to shoot and viewpoints

### Viewpoint 1 – Castle Coeffin

Castle Coeffin sits in an idyllic location on a promontory beside a small bay looking out across to Morvern and Mull. The ruined castle, its walls now covered with ivy rises out of the ground, almost appearing as a natural part of the landscape. The myths tell us that the castle was once home to a Viking princess who, distraught at her lovers' death in faraway Norway pined away and died in the castle. It is said that when the wind whispers through the castle walls it is the sound of her voice that you can hear. It's certainly an atmospheric place, and under a glowering sky it can be really dramatic. The walk down to the castle crosses some lovely undulating farmland with dry stone walls and the odd isolated tree providing a foreground of the views to Mull. Also appearing in the view is the Glensanda super quarry in Morvern, the largest of its kind in Europe, where a mountain is gradually being hollowed out to provide granite aggregate. It is quite a sight and fortunately it doesn't feature in the view of Castle Coeffin! The path switchbacks down to the bay, and at high tide in calm conditions the castle is reflected in the sea, where you can also see the curved wall of an old fish trap. The remains of the castle can be explored, however, the best views are gained from the shoreline or from the top of the switchback path. »

*Opposite: a distant view of Duart Castle on Mull from the coastline northeast of Castle Coeffin. Fujifilm X–T1, 55–200mm f/3.5–f/4.8, ISO 200, 1/350s at f/8. Feb.*

*Castle Coeffin from the track (VP1). Fujifilm X–T2, 18–55mm f/2.8–f/4, ISO 200, 1/600s at f/8. May.*

*Castle Coeffin with Mull on the far horizon. Fujifilm X–T2, 18–55mm f/2.8–f/4, ISO 200, 1/600s at f/8. May.*

*Tirefour Castle and the east coast of Lismore. Fujifilm X–T2, 55–200mm f/3.5–f/4.8, ISO 200, 1/750s at f/8. May.*

## Viewpoint 2 – The Point and Port Ramsay ♿

If you have arrived at The Point by the passenger ferry you will have departed the boat via the slipway. This itself makes a great subject at high tide with the handrails gradually disappearing into the water and the small sign popping up a the end. The pebble beaches and the spit of land which arcs off towards Appin also provide some lovely foregrounds to the wider landscape. The views here are superb, taking in the hills of Appin, the island of Shuna and on a clear day the great whaleback of Ben Nevis can be seen on the horizon to the north. Your eye will no doubt be drawn to the stunted hawthorn tree growing on the western side of the pebble beach which makes a fine foreground anchor for the view up Loch Linnhe. From here you may also notice Castle Stalker on the eastern shore – certainly not the usual angle that it is photographed from! It is possible to walk around the coast from here to Port Ramsay, however, if you are pushed for time it is just a short drive. Built to house workers from the lime industry, Port Ramsay is a charming collection of whitewashed houses which look out across a sheltered bay to the hills of Morvern. »

## How to get here

If you come by vehicle, head up from Achnacroish and take a right at the first junction. This road passes the shop and after a few minuted you will come to the Lismore Herritage Museum and Cafe. There is parking here. Continue on foot until on passing a farmhouse on the left, take the path which leads east through the gate and into the field. From here, a track leads you across the fields and down a steep track to the castle. The Point and Port Ramsay are at the northern end of the island and there are parking areas at each.

## Viewpoint 1 – Castle Coeffin

| | | |
|---|---|---|
| 📍 Lat/Long: | 56.528375, -5.4880528 |
| 📍 what3words: | :///fattest.legroom.self |
| 📍 Grid Ref: | NM855428 |
| 📍 Postcode: | PA34 5UL |

*Opposite left: a rainbow in Morvern seen from Castle Coeffin. Fujifilm X–T2, 55–200mm f/3.5–f/4.8, ISO 200, 1/2000s at f/4. May. Right: sunrise at The Point. Fujifilm X–T2, 18–55mm f/2.8–f/4, ISO 200, 120s at f/8. May.*

## Viewpoint 2 – The Point and Port Ramsay

| | | |
|---|---|---|
| **Lat/Long**: | 56.560106, -5.4276500 |
| **what3words**: | ///hush.keys.paddlers |
| **Grid Ref**: | NM894461 |
| **Postcode**: | PA38 4DF |

### Accessibility

Both sites are easily accessed from the main road, The Point in particular couldn't be any closer to the car park! Castle Coeffin is a half hours walk across largely unchallenging terrain.

### Best time of year/day

Castle Coeffin is a good sunset location, however, it's worth visiting at any time, particularly if visibility is good as the views across to Morvern and Mull are superb. The Point and Port Ramsay are both good sunset locations – The Point is also excellent at dawn. Lismore is great at any time of the year, but the island is particularly resplendent in the lush greenery of summer.

*Overleaf: scenes from the north of Lismore.*

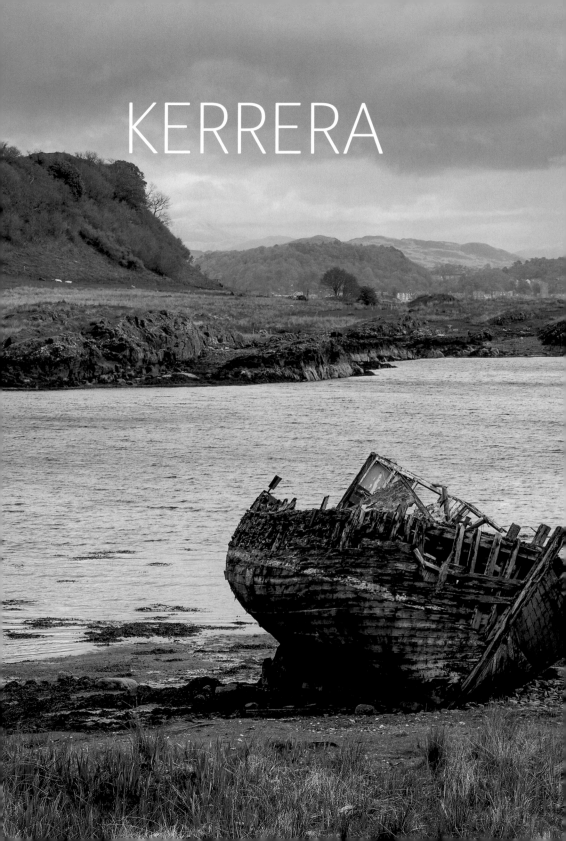

KERRERA

The small island of Kerrera is located to the west of Oban and the granite obelisk of the David Hutcheson monument at its northern end will be familiar to anyone who has taken a ferry to the islands of Mull, Lismore or Barra. The island itself is approximately six miles long and has no vehicle access for visitors, it's a calm, relaxed place and provides a welcome contrast to the hustle and bustle of Oban. Perhaps overlooked by many visitors who travel via Oban to other Hebridean islands, Kerrera has a lot to offer the photographer and is certainly worth a trip, especially if you have a free day either side of catching a ferry.

## How to get to Kerrera

Kerrera is accessed via the small ferry the MV Carvoria which makes the short crossing from Gallanach, just to the south of Oban. There is car parking at Gallanach or alternatively it can be reached by bus from Oban.

*Gylen Castle from the rocky shoreline to the south east. Fujifilm X–T2, 18–55mm f/2.8–f/4, ISO 200, 10s at f/11. May.*

| KERRERA | |
|---|---|
| Scottish Gaelic | Cearara (Copse island). |
| Area | 5 sq. miles (13 sq. km). |
| Length/breadth | 4 × 1 miles. |
| Highest Elevation | Carn Breugach 189m (620ft). |
| Owned by | Dunollie Estate and owner occupied. |
| Population | 68 |
| Largest settlement(s) | Balliemore |
| Vehicles allowed | No |
| Car/Bike rental | E-bikes at: *isleofkerrera.org/ebikes* |
| Public transport | No |
| Day trips from mainland? | Yes |
| Internet/mobile phone coverage | Yes |
| Power | Grid |
| Island website(s) | *isleofkerrera.org* • *kerreramarina.com* • *southernhebrides.com* *visitscotland.com* • *scotland.org.uk* |
| Festivals/Events | See the islands websites. |
| Accommodation | Kerrera Bunkhouse: *kerrerabunkhouse.co.uk*, Galley Cabin. |
| Provisions/Eating Out | Kerrera Tea Garden, Kerrera Marina and the Waypoint Bar & Grill, Ardentive Farm. |
| Wildlife | Wild goats, sika deer, otters, weasels, mink, white tip sea eagles, golden eagles, Greylag and canada geese, buzzards, hen harriers, kestrels, herons and oyster catchers. |
| Night Sky Bortle Scale | Class 3/4. |

## Maps

• OS Landranger 49: Oban and East Mull (1:50 000)

*Previous spread*: *a view up the east coast of Kerrera to Oban from Horseshoe Bay, Fujifilm X–T2, 55–200mm f/3.5–f/4.8, ISO 200, 1/350s at f/8. May.*

## What to shoot and viewpoints

### Viewpoint 1 – The Little Horseshoe Bay

On arrival, head up from the pier and take the first left. The minor road weaves around the eastern shoreline of Kerrera, passing below steep and wooded slopes. In springtime the slopes are carpeted with bluebells and the new born lambs in the fields to the east are always a joy to see. Continue straight on when the road branches right up to a farm and proceed through a gate. Roughly 30 minutes of walking will take you from the pier to Little Horseshoe Bay. As its name suggests this is small crescent shaped bay, and is backed by a row of pretty whitewashed cottages one of which used to house a parrot sanctuary. The wreck of a fishing boat sits at the eastern end of the

bay and makes a fascinating subject both as a focal point in the wider landscape or for detail studies of the decaying timbers. If you are wanting to get up close to the boat, time your trip with low tide. **»**

## How to get here

The walking descriptions for the viewpoints are in the viewpoint descriptions.

### Ferry

- **what3words**: ///improvise.news.enforced
- **Grid Ref**: NM835282
- **Postcode**: PA34 4QH

### Accessibility

Non-residents are not permitted to take a car to Kerrera, however, both viewpoints can be easily reached on foot or by bike. Allow approximately three hours for the trip to the castle, allowing for photography time along the way. There are some steep drops around the castle so care should be taken in high winds.

## Best time of year/day

Unless you are staying on the island your time on the island will be determined by the ferry, however, with careful planning you may be able to time your trip to coincide with the golden hours or sunrise/sunset. If not, the island still has plenty to offer. The textures of the shipwreck at Horseshoe Bay look especially good under overcast conditions. Gylen Castle has a distinctive silhouette and works well at both sunrise and sunset.

*Above left: the wreck of a fishing boat at Horseshoe Bay. Fujifilm X–T2, 55–200mm f/3.5–f/4.8, ISO 200, 1/420s at f/5. May.*

*Above: a young tree grows in the prow. Fujifilm X–T2, 55–200mm f/3.5–f/4.8, ISO 200, 1/420s at f/5. May.*

*Textures in the timber – studies of the decaying fishing boat at Horseshoe Bay.*

 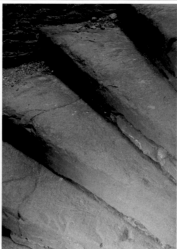 

*Gylen Castle (VP2). Fujifilm X–T2, 18–55mm f/2.8–f/4, ISO 200, 1/140s at f/10. May.*

*Well-worn steps within Gylen Castle. Fujifilm X–T2, 18–55mm f/2.8–f/4, ISO 200, 1/60s at f/5. May.*

*The castle from the beach to the north west. Fujifilm X–T2, 18–55mm f/2.8–f/4, ISO 200, 1/200s at f/9. May.*

### Viewpoint 2 – Gylen Castle

Gylen Castle is the main photographic opportunity on Kerrera. To reach it, continue along the track for another half hour past the farmhouse at Upper Gylen, passing numerous signs which point you in the direction of both the castle and the Tea Room and Bunkhouse at Lower Gylen. Once you have dragged yourself away from the cakes, the castle is accessed via a short stroll through the fields to the south (head past the composting toilet). The castle comes into view in a couple of minutes, situated high up on a rocky promontory and enjoying a fantastic location with far reaching views to Seil, Scarba and Mull. It is certainly a dramatic sight, the ruined castle towering above a rugged rocky shoreline, with ravens circling overhead; it definitely has a Game of Thrones feel to it. Constructed in 1582 by the MacDougalls the castle was primarily a defensive structure with a strategic location looking out over the busy shipping route of the Sound of Kerrera. However, it was only occupied for 70 years until it was burnt by the Covenanters and was in a ruined and perilous state until it was stabilised in 1995. There are many good spots for photographing the castle from the shore on both the northeast or southeast sides of the castle and there a compositions to be found either low down on the shoreline or up on the higher ground.

The position of the sun will more than likely determine the best side. In the morning it is best on the southeast and in the evening the northwest. Each side has its own plus points and it is worth taking the time to walk around the coastline in the vicinity of the castle. Gylen Castle can also be photographed from the promontory itself, however, the interpretation boards, whilst full of useful information, tend to get in the way of the composition. It's also possible to head further uphill inland if you wish to photograph the castle from above.

*The Kerrera ferry at sunset from the mainland. Fujifilm X–T2, 18–55mm f/2.8–f/4, ISO 200, 1/5s at f/8. May.*

SEIL

The island of Seil is the most populous of the Slate Islands and is the closest Hebridean island to the mainland, connected across the Atlantic by the elegant Clachan Bridge. As one of the 'islands that roofed the world' it's a place of real contrasts with many visible remnants of the slate industry sitting alongside farmland and pretty villages. It makes a fascinating destination for the photographer with a number of exciting locations within such a small island.

## How to get to Seil

Seil is located 12 miles south of Oban and it is a wonderful drive through some very scenic landscapes to get here. After 8 miles take the B844 on the right hand side and follow this winding single track road to Clachan Bridge where you can drive onto the island.

## Maps

- OS Landranger 55: Lochgilphead and Loch Awe (1:50 000)

*Previous spread*: the wild rocky shoreline at Port a' Mhuilinn (VP3). Fujifilm X–T2, 10–24mm f/4, ISO 200, 26s at f/8. Feb.

*Opposite*: looking across Port a' Mhuilinn to Easdale. Fujifilm X–T2, 10–24mm f/4, ISO 200, 16s at f/8. Feb.

*The Bridge over The Atlantic (VP1). Fujifilm X–T2, 18–55mm f/2.8–f/4, ISO 200, 1/100s at f/9. Oct.*

| SEIL | |
|---|---|
| Scottish Gaelic | Saoil (Hunting island). |
| Area | 5 sq. miles (13 sq. km). |
| Length/breadth | 3 × 2.5 miles. |
| Highest Elevation | Meall Chaise, 146m (479ft). |
| Owned by | Mixed |
| Population | 551 |
| Largest settlement(s) | Balvicar |
| Vehicles allowed | Yes |
| Car/Bike rental | Oban Cycles and Rusty Cycle Shed, Oban |
| Public transport | Yes, West Coast Motors. |
| Day trips from mainland? | Yes |
| Internet/mobile phone coverage | Yes |
| Power | Grid |
| Island website(s) | seil.oban.ws • slateislands.org.uk • southernhebrides.com visitscotland.com • scotland.org.uk |
| Festivals/Events | There are events at Seil Island Hall. |
| Accommodation | There is a wide range of self-catering accommodation on the island. Visit: seil.oban.ws to book. |
| Provisions/Eating Out | Shops at Ellenabeich and Balvicar. Oyster Bar and Restaurant, Ellenabeich; Puffer Bar and Restaurant, Easdale Island and Tigh an Truish at Clachan Bridge. |
| Wildlife | A hot spot for porpoises, dolphins, minke whales and basking sharks. Bird watching highlights include sea eagles, golden eagles and puffins, while otters, seals, and deer can be seen along the shore. |
| Night Sky Bortle Scale | Class 2. |

# What to shoot and viewpoints

### Viewpoint 1 – Clachan Bridge ♿

Clachan Bridge was originally constructed as a double arched bridge, it was rebuilt as a single arch to allow the passage of boats through Clachan Sound and is often known as The Bridge over the Atlantic. It's an interesting structure, which can be photographed from a variety of positions along the shoreline with a backdrop of trees on the eastern shoreline giving a lovely contrast in spring, summer and autumn. At high tide with still conditions the reflection of the bridge can make for some interesting studies. The views north and south from on top of the bridge are also very attractive, particularly to the north where the narrow channel is accentuated. On the Seil side of the bridge is the Tigh-an-Truish Inn, the House of Trousers, where islanders would change from the kilt (which was banned after the 1745 rebellion) into trousers. »

*Opposite: looking towards the bridge from Seil.*
*Fujifilm X–T2, 18–55mm f/2.8–f/4, ISO 200,*
*1/200s at f/8. Oct.*

*The narrow channel of the Atlantic below the bridge.*
*Fujifilm X–T2, 18–55mm f/2.8–f/4, ISO 200, 1/180s at f/9. Oct.*

*Clachan Bridge (The Bridge over The Atlantic) (VP1).*
*Fujifilm X–T2, 18–55mm f/2.8–f/4, ISO 200, 1/220s at f/8. Oct.*

## How to get here

There is roadside parking at all three locations. At Viewpoint 1, the large car park is for visitors to the pub, however, there is roadside parking to the south. At Viewpoint 2 there is a small lay-by before the road swings round to the left. Viewpoint 3 is accessed from a gravel parking area opposite the bus shelter.

### Viewpoint 1 – Clachan Bridge

🅿 **what3words**: ///suspect.inversion.unfocused
🅿 **Grid Ref:**    NM784196
🅿 **Postcode:**    PA34 4QZ

### Viewpoint 2 – Easdale view

🅿 **what3words**: ///dreams.hairspray.grand
🅿 **Grid Ref:**    NM755169
🅿 **Postcode:**    PA34 4RG

## Viewpoint 3 – Port a' Mhuilinn

🅿 **what3words**: ///halt.composts.bath
🅿 **Grid Ref:**    NM752168
🅿 **Postcode:**    PA34 4RG

### Accessibility

All three viewpoints are essentially roadside. The rocky beach at Port a' Mhuilinn is loose underfoot and you should be aware of big waves crashing over the rocks.

### Best time of year/day

Clachan Bridge is best at high tide, but works well at all times of the year. A low dawn sun suits it well. The view to Easdale is best on a clear day where you can pick out the cliffs on Mull. Port a Mhuilin is great on a high tide with some stormy conditions – it's a dramatic location and really suits a wild day.

### Viewpoint 2 – Easdale view

As you travel onwards to the village of Ellenabeich the road passes a tin church on the left, crests a hill and an incredible view opens up to the village, the island of Easdale and beyond that the rugged cliffs on the isle of Mull. It's a great spot albeit one which only really has one key view, however, its certainly worth stoping if the conditions are favourable.

### Viewpoint 3 – Port a' Mhuilinn

The small roadside beach at Port a' Mhuilinn offers a fantastically diverse rocky shoreline. The slate here is sculpted into some fascinating forms, with long spiky promontories rising from the sea like some sort of ancient leviathan emerging from the deep. The view out to see takes in the Garvellachs and the remote island of Scarba. It's an excellent location for long exposure images but also offers a wealth of opportunities for macro with the slate providing some interesting tonal contrasts and forms.

*Top: Tigh-an-Truish Inn, the House of Trousers (VP1). Fujifilm X–T2, 18–55mm f/2.8–f/4, ISO 200, 1/480s at f/8. Sep. Middle: cottages at Ellenabeich. Fujifilm X–T2, 18–55mm f/2.8–f/4, ISO 200, 1/850s at f/8. Sep. Bottom: a RIB approaches the harbour at Ellenabeich. Fujifilm X–T2, 18–55mm f/2.8–f/4, ISO 200, 1/420s at f/9. Sep.*

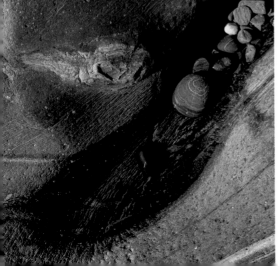

*Textures and patterns in the slate at Port a' Mhuilinn (VP3).*

EASDALE

Easdale is a fascinating island, a strange yet utterly compelling mixture of natural and man-made landscapes. It is the smallest permanently inhabited island in the Hebrides with a thriving community, museum, restaurant and is also home to the World Skimming Stone Championship. Easdale is a car-free island, accessed by a small passenger ferry from the village of Ellenabeich on Seil. In place of cars, a fleet of wheelbarrows are on hand to move goods from the dock to the old slate-miners whitewashed houses. Once occupied by 500 people at the height of the slate industry, its population declined to just four in the 1950s, but the island is now home to sixty people with most of the houses now restored and occupied.

*Previous spread: the west coast of Easdale looking to Mull. Fujifilm X–T2, 18–55mm f/2.8–f/4, ISO 200, 2s at f/11. Sep.*

## How to get to Easdale

Easdale is located a short 5 minute boat ride from Ellenabeich on Seil. From Clachan Bridge head south through Seil before branching off to the right at Balvicar. From here follow the road around the coast until you reach the village of Ellenabeich where there is on-street parking at the harbour side.

| LOCATIONS | | |
|---|---|---|
| 1 | The pools | 268 |
| 2 | Western Shore | 270 |
| 3 | The Village and Harbour | 272 |

## Maps

• OS Landranger 55: Lochgilphead and
  Loch Awe (1:50 000)

*Opposite: the football pitch in the centre of the village, Fujifilm X–T2, 18–55mm f/2.8–f/4, ISO 200, 1/240s at f/8. Sep.*

*A red boat against the distinctive slate quayside. Fujifilm X–E3, 55–200mm f/3.5–f/4.8, ISO 200, 1/90s at f/4.4. Sep.*

## EASDALE

| | |
|---|---|
| **Scottish Gaelic** | Eilean Èisdeal. |
| **Area** | 0.09 sq. miles (0.2 sq. km). |
| **Length/breadth** | 0.5 × 0.3 miles. |
| **Highest Elevation** | 125ft (38m). |
| **Owned by** | Easdale Island Company. |
| **Population** | 60 |
| **Largest settlement(s)** | Scattered homes. |
| **Vehicles allowed** | No |
| **Car/Bike rental** | Oban Cycles and Rusty Cycle Shed, Oban. |
| **Public transport** | No |
| **Day trips from mainland?** | Yes |
| **Internet/mobile phone coverage** | Yes |
| **Power** | Grid |
| **Island website(s)** | *easdale.org • easdaleisland.scot • slateislands.org.uk • easdalemuseum.org southernhebrides.com • visitscotland.com • scotland.org.uk* |
| **Festivals/Events** | The World Stone Skimming Cup, *stoneskimming.com* (September) and events at Easdale Island Community Hall. Seaweed foraging courses. |
| **Accommodation** | There are several self-catering cottages and a B&B on airbnb. |
| **Provisions/Eating Out** | Puffer Bar and Tearoom *pufferbarandrestaurant.co.uk* |
| **Wildlife** | Porpoises, dolphins, minke whales and basking sharks. |
| **Night Sky Bortle Scale** | Class 2. |

## What to shoot and viewpoints

There are numerous of photographic opportunities throughout the island so follow the path around the perimeter and spend time exploring the village.

### Viewpoint 1 – The pools

Easdale was famed for its slate and such was the quality of this material that it was shipped worldwide gracing the rooftops of buildings as far afield as Australia. However, the quarries, mainly located around the perimeter of the island were susceptible to flooding. In 1881, one of the worst storms the west coast has experienced sent waves crashing over the island and water inundated many of the quarries, bringing the industry to a standstill. Fortunately, the waves did not wash away the houses which hug the edges of the quarries, and they sit there to this day above beautiful

calm pools. A circular walk around the perimeter of the island visits all the former quarries and takes roughly an hour. The pools provide some lovely reflections of the houses clustered around them and can also form the foreground to wider views. The pools on the northern side are particularly attractive, looking across to Mull and up the Firth of Lorne. »

*The wheelbarrows. Fujifilm X–T2, 18–55mm f/2.8–f/4, ISO 200, 1/600s at f/8. Sep.*

*Textures of the slate pier. Fujifilm X–E3, 55–200mm f/3.5–f/4.8, ISO 200, 1/90s at f/4.4. Sep.*

### How to get here

A visit to the Easdale Island Folk Museum is definitely worth doing before visiting the island. From the village head down the slipway to the ferry shed and summon the boat with the push-button or klaxon inside. The timetable for the boat can be found at: *argyll-bute.gov. uk/ellenabeich-easdale-ferry-timetable*. The island itself is easily walkable with good grassy paths or slate tracks throughout.

### Viewpoint 1, 2 & 3

- **what3words**: ///presuming.earplugs.satellite
- **Grid Ref:**  NM742173
- **Postcode**:  PA34 4RE

### Accessibility

All three viewpoints are easily accessible, however, the slate can be loose under foot and care should be taken around the edges of the quarries.

### Best time of year/day

Easdale is one of those places which can work at any time of day and year. There is always something to photograph. Obviously the western shore is an ideal sunset location, however, the forms and textures of the slate can work equally well under cloud. Low tide is best on the western shore if you want to photograph the wave worn slate areas, but at high tide the waves crashing against the shoreline can still result in captivating images.

*Wave smoothed slate on the west coast of Easdale looking to Scarba.*
*Fujifilm X–T2, 18–55mm f/2.8–f/4, ISO 200, 1/10s at f/10. Sep.*

*Slate textures. Fujifilm X–T2, 18–55mm f/2.8–f/4, ISO 200, 1/35s at f/8. Sep.*

## Viewpoint 2 – Western shore

The western shore is an ideal spot for seascape photographers. The slate beaches are fantastic for macro studies, and are peppered with interesting rock formations. At low tide an area of undulating wave-smoothed slate is revealed which provides a great foreground to the view out to Scarba and the Garvellachs. Along the western shore are many piles loose slate and these can form very interesting foregrounds as well as being studies in their own right. »

*Piles of slate. Fujifilm X100S, 23mm f/2.8, ISO 200, 1/120s at f/8. Apr.*

*Opposite: looking across to Scarba from the slate mounds on the west coast. Fujifilm X–T2, 18–55mm f/2.8–f/4, ISO 200, 1/10s at f/11. Sep.*

Nature gradually reclaiming the slate mounds on the west coast. Fujifilm X–T2, 18–55mm f/2.8–f/4, ISO 200, 1/4s at f/11. Sep.

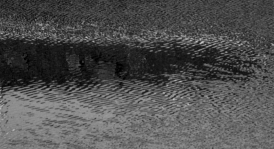

## Viewpoint 3 – The village and harbour

The village comprises old slate-miners cottages and these pretty whitewashed buildings and their setting around the old quarries are really interesting photographically. It's an idyllic village with the absence of cars making it a joy to walk around. The harbour has a number of boats to photograph and the walls made of stacked slate are particularly distinctive.

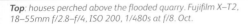

*Top*: houses perched above the flooded quarry. Fujifilm X–T2, 18–55mm f/2.8–f/4, ISO 200, 1/480s at f/8. Oct.

*Middle*: reflections in the quarry. Fujifilm X–E3, 55–200mm f/3.5–f/4.8, ISO 200, 1/240s at f/4.4. Sep.

*Bottom*: still pool on the eastern side of Easdale. Fujifilm X–T2, 18–55mm f/2.8–f/4, ISO 200, 240s at f/6.4. Sep.

*Opposite top left*: looking across the slate to Mull. Fujifilm X–T2, 18–55mm f/2.8–f/4, ISO 200, 1/4s at f/11. Sep. *Top right*: contrast between the rocks and bright blue water in the flooded quarry. Fujifilm X–T2, 18–55mm f/2.8–f/4, ISO 200, 1/420s at f/8. Sep. *Bottom*: the home of the World Skimming Stone Championship. Fujifilm X–T2, 18–55mm f/2.8–f/4, ISO 200, 1/420s at f/8. Sep.

The Crystal Waters at Tobermory. Fujifilm X-T2, 14mm f/2.8, ISO 200, 1/600s at f/8, Feb.

LUING

Luing is located to the south of Seil and is reached by a very short (200m) ferry journey across the fast flowing Cuan Sound. It is a lush and green island, especially in contrast to the black slate beaches on its coast. It is the home of Luing cattle, a breed developed on the island which are a hardy cross of highland cattle and beef shorthorn which are now farmed across Scotland and further afield. There are numerous and varied photographic opportunities on this small island, from the distinctive slate beaches, to ruined boats and churches and the island makes for a great short trip, together with Seil and Easdale.

## How to get to Luing

Luing is approached from Seil (page 258). Drive to Cuan at the south end of Seil (a 6-mile drive) where you can catch the ferry with your car (every half hour except 1pm). Bikes travel free.

## Maps

• OS Landranger 55: Lochgilphead and Loch Awe (1:50 000)

*Above the flooded quarry at Cullipool. Fujifilm X–T2, 18–55mm f/2.8–f/4, ISO 200, 1/210s at f/8. Feb.*

| LUING | |
|---|---|
| Scottish Gaelic | Luinn (Heather island). |
| Area | 5.5 sq. miles (14 sq. km). |
| Length/breadth | 6 × 1.5 miles. |
| Highest Elevation | Binneinn Furachail, 87m (285ft). |
| Owned by | Mixed ownership with some by Cadzow family. |
| Population | 195 |
| Largest settlement(s) | Cullipool |
| Vehicles allowed | Yes |
| Car/Bike rental | Bike hire from Sunnybrae Caravan Park • *oban-holiday.co.uk* |
| Public transport | No |
| Day trips from mainland? | Yes |
| Internet/mobile phone coverage | Yes |
| Power | Grid |
| Island website(s) | *isleofluing.org* • *southernhebrides.com* • *visitscotland.com* • *scotland.org.uk* |
| Festivals/Events | See: *isleofluing.org* |
| Accommodation | Sunnybrae Caravan Park has 8 self-catering holiday homes and two lodges (no camping or motorhomes). There are also several self-catering cottages. Book accommodation at: *oban-holiday.co.uk/accommodation*. |
| Provisions/Eating Out | Luing Stores and Post Office in Cullipool is the only shop on the island and is a licensed general store for all grocery and household needs, gifts, cards and local arts and crafts. The Atlantic Islands Centre (Cullipool) has a café – local baked goods and produce are served – a retail shop for local artists and an events programme and local history exhibitions. |
| Wildlife | Porpoises, dolphins, minke whales and basking sharks. |
| Night Sky Bortle Scale | Class 2. |

## What to shoot and viewpoints

### Viewpoint 1 – Cullipool ♿

The village of Cullipool is a pretty wee place. Whitewashed ex-miners cottages cluster around the narrow streets, hunkered down against the walls of the slate quarries and facing out towards the Garvellachs and Scarba. There are some great photographic opportunities within the village, particularly with a bit of elevation. By heading uphill from the community centre towards the old church, and bearing right at the fence it is possible to gain a great view across the flooded quarry, the village and north towards Mull and Easdale. The beach itself is the other draw and the combination of black slate sand and lighter boulders is really striking. The view south along the shoreline with the houses of Cullipool peaking over the beach and the wild island of Scarba on the horizon is particularly fine. It is worth exploring the coastline to the north of the village as well as there are many opportunities along here which vary with the tide. »

*Cullipool beach at sunset (VP1). Fujifilm X–T2, 10–24mm f/4, ISO 200, 17s at f/11. Feb.*

***Opposite left**: the Luing Ferry in Cuan Sound. Fujifilm X–T2, 35mm f/1.4, ISO 200, 1/340s at f/5.6. Feb. **Right**: Cullipool from the hill to the east. Fujifilm X–T2, 55–200mm f/3.5–f/4.8, ISO 200, 1/180s at f/8. Feb.*

### How to get here

There are only a few roads on the island so it's difficult to get lost. From the ferry head south across the island and you will reach a junction at the fire station. Turn right here for Cullipool, there is parking at the quarry at the northern end of the village. To reach the south end of the island, return to the fire station and turn right. Kilchattan Cemetery is on the left after 2 miles. From here you can turn right to Blackmill Bay or head on to Toberonochy.

### Viewpoint 1 – Cullipool

| | |
|---|---|
| **P Lat/Long**: | Lat/Long: 56.257866, -5.651677 |
| **P what3words**: | ///soaps.spaceship.fatter |
| **P Grid Ref**: | NM739132 |
| **P Postcode**: | PA34 4UB |

### Viewpoint 2 – Kilchattan Church

| | |
|---|---|
| **P Lat/Long**: | Lat/Long: 56.221008, -5.639828 |
| **P what3words**: | ///spectacle.press.ticking |
| **P Grid Ref**: | NM744091 |
| **P Postcode**: | PA34 4UG |

### Viewpoint 3 – Toberonochy

| | |
|---|---|
| **P Lat/Long**: | Lat/Long: 56.216852, -5.629976 |
| **P what3words**: | ///mows.victory.painting |
| **P Grid Ref**: | NM750086 |
| **P Postcode**: | PA34 4UE |

*Kiltchattan Church from the roadside (VP2). Fujifilm X–T2, 14mm f/2.8, ISO 200, 1/1250s at f/5.6. Feb.*

## Viewpoint 2 – Kilchattan Church

Heading south though the island you pass the new Kilchattan church, however, the more photogenic location is a bit further south at the old Kilchattan Church. The building itself is in a ruinous state, but it has an interesting form and could make a good silhouette for night photography. The graveyard also has some fascinating old and weathered gravestones. »

*Top right: the graveyard Kilchattan Church. Fujifilm X–T2, 14mm f/2.8, ISO 200, 1/1000s at f/5.6. Feb.*

*Right: Inscribed stones set in the wall surrounding Kilchattan Church. Fujifilm X–T2, 14mm f/2.8, ISO 200, 1/1000s at f/5.6. Feb.*

## Viewpoint 4 – Blackmill Bay

- **Lat/Long:** 56.213662, -5.658687
- **what3words:** ///passes.deflect.tightrope
- **Grid Ref:** NM732083
- **Postcode:** PA34 4TZ

### Accessibility

All viewpoints are close to the road. The beach at Cullipool is loose underfoot and the paths down can be slippery on the slate. Kilchattan Church is unsafe, with signs warning visitors not to go inside.

### Best time of year/day

The beach at Cullipool faces west so is an ideal sunset location. During the golden hour the village itself looks fantastic and the beach works well with low light on it, however, there is potential here even under overcast conditions, particularly for detail studies of the rock formations and patterns within the slate itself. Blackmill Bay is also west facing and is also a great sunset location, out of the two, Cullipool offers a little bit more interest though, so if you are selecting one over the other, Cullipool is probably your best bet.

*Opposite: Textures of the gravestones at Kilchattan Church*

*Detail on the side of the Crystal Waters. Fujifilm X–T2, 35mm f/1.4, ISO 200, 1/800s at f/5.6. Feb.*

*Ropes and knots on the Crystal Waters. Fujifilm X–T2, 35mm f/1.4, ISO 200, 1/160s at f/5.6. Feb.*

### Viewpoint 3 – Toberonochy ♿

The village of Toberonochy is at the southern end of Luing and faces east towards Shuna. It has a similar feel to Cullipool with whitewashed miners cottages, narrow streets and well tended gardens which cluster around a small harbour. The ruin of the Crystal Waters, a Banff-registered Trawler sits rusting and rotting away alongside the pier. It's a melancholy sight but makes for an interesting study in weathering and decay.

### Viewpoint 4 – Blackmill Bay ♿

On the south western side of Luing at Blackmill Bay is another black sand beach and is home to the old pier and ticket office. This was once a busy spot with boats arriving from Glasgow and Oban or leaving the island full with livestock or slate. Today it is much quieter but there is an excellent view to be had across to Scarba and the beach is worth visiting as well.

*The Crystal Waters at Toberonochy (VP3). Fujifilm X–T2, 35mm f/1.4, ISO 200, 1/500s at f/5.6. Feb.*

*Above*: the black sand beach at Toberonochy. Fujifilm X–T2, 35mm f/1.4, ISO 200, 1/480s at f/5.6. Feb.
*Below*: the remains of the pier at Blackmill Bay (VP4). Fujifilm X–T2, 14mm f/2.8, ISO 200, 1/750s at f/6.4. Feb.

*Below left*: lighthouse on Fladda from Cullipool (VP1). Fujifilm X–T2, 55–200mm f/3.5–f/4.8, ISO 200, 1/1700s at f/8. Feb.
*Below right*: Luing Cattle at Blackmill Bay. Fujifilm X–T2, 14mm f/2.8, ISO 200, 1/350s at f/8. Feb.

# THE SMALL ISLES

# THE SMALL ISLES – INTRODUCTION

**The Small Isles are a group of four islands (or five if you count the island of Sanday off the coast of Canna) which lie to the south of Skye. They are all served by the same Caledonian MacBrayne ferry which departs from Mallaig. In spring and summer the islands can also be visited on the MV Shearwater which sails from Arisaig.**

The largest is Rum. Wild and mountainous, it is truly an island for the adventurous. Roadless once you leave main settlement, you will have to be prepared to put in the effort to reach the locations on the other side of the island. To the north there is the beautiful Kilmory bay, home to a long running deer survey and one of the best locations to observe these creatures up close. It also provides a stunning outlook to Skye. To the west there is the remote abandoned settlement of Harris with its strange mausoleum. Rum rewards the adventurous and if you can brave the midges and the long walks you can create truly great images and fantastic memories on the island

Close by Rum is the community owned island of Eigg. A model of sustainability, powered by its own energy supplies from wind and solar, Eigg is a perfect example of how a small Hebridean island can thrive. Photographically it has become very popular, with the Bay of Laig and its incredible geology drawing photographers from far and wide. There are plenty of other opportunities across the island, from the dramatic pitchstone cliff of An Sgùrr to the cliffs above Cleadale and the small sandy bays on the east coast.

Muck is located to the south of Eigg and is the smallest of the Small Isles. It is a green and fertile island with agriculture as the main industry. It's a quiet and peaceful place with some wonderful beaches on the north coast providing a great foreground to the view north to Eigg and Rum.

The Isles of Canna and Sanday are the furthest west of the Small Isles and both offer an abundance of opportunities. Sanday is perfect for wildlife photographers where in summer months puffins nest on the sea stacks and bonxies patrol the skies, ready to divebomb the unwary. Canna is a relaxing island with a stunning black sand beach, overlooked by the dramatic ruins of Coroghon Castle castle at one end and a beautiful sandy bay with Staffa-esque basalt columns at the other.

*Opposite: the fantastic rocky shore at Laig Bay on Eigg. Fujifilm X–T2, 14mm f/2.8, ISO 200, 1/240s at f/8. Apr.*

*Previous spread: red deer at KIlmory Bay with the Cuillin on Skye in the distance. Fujifilm X–T2, 55–200mm f/3.5–f/4.8, ISO 200, 1/500s at f/4.2. Apr.*

SEA OF THE HEBRIDES

**CANNA**

Garrisdale Point

Tarbert ③
Above Campsite
② A' Chill
Canna Campsite
Coroghan Castle
① ⑤ Sanday
④ ⑥
Sanday Beach

Sound of Canna

bothy
Orval 571m

**Kilmory Bay** ③
Kilmory

Allt Slugan a' Choilich
**Kinloch Castle** ①
② Kinloch
Village Shop / Post Office
⑤ **Otter Hide**
Loch Scresort

**Harris** ④
Harris

**RÚM**

Scotland's National Nature Reserves

Askival 812m △
Ainshval 778m △
bothy

**Rum National Nature Reserve**

Oigh-sgeir
keir

Sound of Rúm

**EIGG**

**Singing Sands** ②
**Tràigh Chlithe / Bay of Laig** ①
Cleadale
③ **Above Cleadale**
Isle of Eigg Wildlife Reserve

An Sgurr 394m △
⑤ **Eastern Shores**
Galmisdale
Eilean Chathastail

Camas na Cairidh
④ **An Sgurr**

Gallanach ③
② ①
**Port Mor**

**MUCK**

Sound of Eigg

**SKYE**

Armadale
A851

Mallaig
⚓
🅿 ... 

Arisaig
A830

A861

N

JUN JUL MAY JUN
AUG APR
SEP MAR
OCT FEB
NOV JAN
DEC

SUNSET    SUNRISE

0    miles    5

EIGG

**Eigg is a truly inspirational island. Not only does it possess a natural landscape which is one of the most distinctive in the Hebrides but its transformation in the last 20 years has been remarkable. Previously owned by a succession of sometimes absentee landlords, Eigg is now thriving, an ecologically friendly island owned by its community and powered by its own sources of renewable energy. This has been a hugely significant move, and one which has been inspirational to other rural areas across Scotland. Since the buyout in 1997 the island has been owned by the Eigg Heritage Trust, which has managed the development of the island, sustainably growing the population whilst preserving its natural assets.**

The main attraction on Eigg for the landscape photographer is undoubtably the Bay of Laig. However, there are numerous other gems throughout the island from the dramatic pitchstone peak of An Sgùrr to the singing sand of Camas Sgiotaig.

## How to get to Eigg

To get to the Isle of Eigg, you catch a ferry from Mallaig. Glasgow is 150 miles (3.5 hours drive) from Mallaig, Edinburgh a 185 mile drive (4 hours) with public transport provided by Citylink (bus) and Scotrail, similarly for Arisaig. Caledonian Macbrayne operates the Small Isles ferry service to Eigg, Muck, Rum and Canna all year round. Additionally, during the summer months from late April to September you can also travel from Arisaig on MV Sheerwater: *arisaig.co.uk/islandferry*.

### Mallaig Car Park

| | |
|---|---|
| **Lat/Long**: | 57.005039, -5.8316083 |
| **what3words**: | ///apple.sideburns.ocean |
| **Grid Ref**: | NM674969 |
| **Postcode**: | PH41 4RA |

### Arisaig Car Park

| | |
|---|---|
| **Lat/Long**: | 56.910045, -5.8492488 |
| **what3words**: | ///gurgling.reheat.journals |
| **Grid Ref**: | NM657864 |
| **Postcode**: | PH39 4NL |

*The beaches on the east of Eigg looking towards the mainland (VP5). Fujifilm X–T1, 18–55mm f/2.8–f/4, ISO 200, 1/60s at f/8. May.*

| EIGG | |
|---|---|
| Scottish Gaelic | Eige (Notched island). |
| Area | 12 sq. miles (31 sq. km). |
| Length/breadth | 5.5 × 3 miles. |
| Highest Elevation | An Sgùrr, 393m (1,289ft). |
| Owned by | Eigg Heritage Trust. |
| Population | 107 |
| Largest settlement(s) | Cleadale and Galmisdale |
| Vehicles allowed | No |
| Car/Bike rental | Bike hire from Eigg Adventures: *eiggadventures.co.uk* or call Charlie on: **01687 482 404** for a taxi. |
| Public transport | No |
| Day trips from mainland? | Yes, you will have 4 hours on the island. |
| Internet/mobile phone coverage | Variable 3G/4G dependent on carrier. There is an internet cafe at the pier, and wifi at the learning centre in the primary school. |
| Power | Renewable: water, sun and wind. |
| Island website(s) | *isleofeigg.org* • *southernhebrides.com* • *visitscotland.com* • *scotland.org.uk* |
| Festivals/Events | There are regular guided nature walks and ceilidhs. Small Isles games each year, each island takes it in turns to host, so every isle gets a go once every four years (August). |
| Accommodation | A varied but small selection of accommodation options including camping, camping pods, bothies, a hostel, B&Bs, self-catering cottages and yurts. Book at *isleofeigg.org/accommodation*. |
| Provisions/Eating Out | Galmisdale Bay Cafe, Bar and Restaurant by Eigg pier, Lageorna Restaurant with Rooms on the north west of the island in Cleadale. The Isle of Eigg Shop stocks a wide range of local produce. Home-baking and refreshments at Rest and be Thankful in Cleadale |
| Wildlife | Otters, seals, dolphins and minke whales, 200 species of birds. |
| Night Sky Bortle Scale | Class 1. |

## LOCATIONS

## Maps

• OS Landranger 39: Rùm, Eigg, Muck & Canna (1:50 000)

*Previous spread*: Eigg from the Armadale to Mallaig Ferry. Fujifilm X–T2, 55–200mm f/3.5–f/4.8, ISO 200, 1/400 at f/8. Oct.

## What to shoot and viewpoints

### Viewpoint 1 – Tràigh Chlithe / Bay of Laig

Tràigh Chlithe at The Bay of Laig is a location which can provide days of inspiration for landscape photographers with each visit revealing more and more possibilities. The beach is comprised of two-tone grey and black sand which is sketched by the tide into fantastic patterns, presenting themselves particularly well under a skim of shallow water at low tide. These patterns draw the eye out to sea, to the saw-toothed mountains of Rum which dominate the view. The mysterious Rum Cuillin, often wreathed in swirling clouds, provide an excellent silhouette after sunset and the Bay of Laig is the perfect location to photograph this iconic Hebridean view. The bay is roughly 3 miles from the pier and comes into view as you descend towards Cleadale. As the road levels off take the second minor road on the left past the church and down onto the shore, from here you can explore the beach to the south and the coast all the way north to Camas Sgiotaig. »

*The Bay of Laig from the north (VP1). Fujifilm X–T2, 18–55mm f/2.8–f/4, ISO 200, 1/400s at f/8. Apr.*

## How to get here

From Cleadale where the ferry lands you have to walk or cycle to the viewpoints, use the text in the viewpoints and the map to navigate to the viewpoints.

## Accessibility

Eigg is a small island and as you are unlikely to have a car you will be relying on either walking to the viewpoints or bike hire which is available at the pier. Alternatively, there is a local taxi and minibus service and many of the locals will give you a lift if you stick a thumb out. The beaches are all accessible to able-bodied walkers, however, the rocks between Tràigh Chlithe and Camas Sgiotag can be very slippery and uneven. The routes up the hills are steep and moderately challenging for fit walkers. Whilst there are generally good paths, there are many steep drops and the routes are not advisable (or worth it!) in poor visibility.

## Best time of year/day

Eigg is a popular day trip from the mainland, but to experience it fully, and do it justice, you really need to spend some time on the island. It is possible to make it across the island to the beaches between the ferries, however, this will leave you with very little time to explore. At high tide many of the delightful rocky features which make it so special will be underwater as will much of the grey/black sand at Tràigh Chlithe so it is best to time your visit with low tide. Clear conditions are desirable if you are hoping to photograph the classic view of Rum from Eigg, however, the diversity of landscape features on the beach mean that even if the hills of Rum are shrouded in mist, there are still great opportunities to be had.

*Opposite: clouds rise from Rum at dawn on Tràigh Chlithe. Fujifilm X–T2, 14mm f/2.8, ISO 200, 480s at f/8. Apr.*

*Top*: looking down onto Cleadale and The Bay of Laig from An Sgùrr with Skye on the horizon. Fujifilm X–T1, 18–55mm f/2.8–f/4, ISO 200, 1/120s at f/8. May. **Left**: the rocky shore at Laig. Fujifilm X–T1, 18–55mm f/2.8–f/4, ISO 200, 1/250s at f/10. Jun. **Above**: looking east from the pier towards the mainland. Fujifilm X–T1, 18–55mm f/2.8–f/4, ISO 200, 1/900s at f/8. Jun.

**Opposite left top**: the heather clad hill and zigzag path at the northern end of Cleadale (VP3). Fujifilm X–T2, 55–200mm f/3.5–f/4.8, ISO 200, 1/250s at f/8. Apr. **Bottom**: sheep on the beach (VP5). Fujifilm X–T1, 18–55mm f/2.8–f/4, ISO 200, 1/1250s at f/5.6. Jun.

### Viewpoint 2 – Singing Sands

Heading north along the shore, the coastline changes and becomes what can only be described as the ultimate playground for the landscape photographer. Strange stone mushrooms rise from algae covered rocks, serrated ridges slide into the sea drawing the eye to Rum, circular pools filled with seawater like tiny worlds gaze up from wave smoothed sandstone, boulders scatter the surface like dice. It's an otherworldly place. As you progress north, there are caves, sea arches and and honeycomb rocks cut by waterfalls. The variety is incredible and there are innumerable images to be made along this stretch of coast. At the far end of the rocky shore are is Camas Sgiotaig, the Singing Sands, so called because the sand 'sings' if you scuff your boots along it. It actually squeaks, however, that is somewhat less poetic. To return to Tràigh Chlithe you can either retrace your steps along the shore or head up behind the beach and follow a track along the top of the cliffs.

### Viewpoint 3 – Above Cleadale

The ridge above Cleadale forms a natural amphitheatre to the Bay of Laig and this escarpment provides a fine walk to view both the beaches and the outlook to Rum. The highlight of the walk is the Finger of God, a soaring pinnacle which points skywards. The heather-clad slopes are a riot of colour and bees in the late summer. There is a very steep path which heads up through the bracken just before you reach the guest house Lageorna in Cleadale. The path winds up through the escarpment, rapidly gaining height and then can be followed along the ridge. It is possible to follow this path to the end of the escarpment and then descend to the northern end of Cleadale, returning through the village on the road. »

*Top: The Finger of God above Cleadale (VP3). Fujifilm X–T2, 18–55mm f/2.8–f/4, ISO 200, 1/480s at f/8. Apr.*

*Blooming heather and Rum (VP3). Fujifilm X–T2, 18–55mm f/2.8–f/4, ISO 200, 1/80s at f/8. Apr.*

*Above*: a natural arch on the way to the south of Singing Sands (VP2). Fujifilm X–T2, 18–55mm f/2.8–f/4, ISO 200, 1/240s at f/8. Apr.
*Below*: the rocky shoreline south of Singing Sands. Fujifilm X–T2, 18–55mm f/2.8–f/4, ISO 200, 1/210s at f/8. Apr.

*The dramatic pitchstone top of An Sgùrr. Fujifilm X–T1, 18–55mm f/2.8–f/4, ISO 200, 1/320s at f/8. Jun.*

### Viewpoint 4 – An Sgùrr

The giant pitchstone ridge of An Sgùrr is one of the most distinctive hills along the western seaboard visible from the mainland and many other Hebridean islands. The remnants of a volcanic eruption on Rum, this shear sided peak looks to be impregnable from below, but a path snakes up the northern side before doubling back to the summit. The view from the top is sensational, particularly to the north where the mountains of Skye appear on the horizon. The hill itself is best photographed from below where the vertiginous slopes can be best appreciated, and it pops up in the view across the island. From the shop follow the path west alongside the woodland towards Galmisdale House before picking up the path which branches off to the north. This gradually skirts the northern side of An Sgùrr, slowly gaining height before a short, steep climb following painted rocks to the airy summit plateau.

### Viewpoint 5 – The eastern shores

Whilst not as celebrated as the beaches on the west with their dramatic views to Rum, the beach on the east of Eigg has its own charms and provides a wonderful outlook back to the mainland. The grassland behind the beach is often grazed by sheep and cows which can animate the scene as they wander across the sand. It's close to the shop and cafe and is definitely worth a stroll if you have time to kill waiting for the the ferry.

*Opposite top: cows on the beach near Galmisdale. Fujifilm X–T1, 18–55mm f/2.8–f/4, ISO 200, 1/800s at f/5.6. Jun. **Left**: the small harbour near Galmisdale. Fujifilm X–T1, 18–55mm f/2.8–f/4, ISO 200, 1/680s at f/8. Jun. **Right**: An Sgùrr from the path west of Galmisdale. Fujifilm X–T1, 18–55mm f/2.8–f/4, ISO 200, 1/340s at f/8. Jun.*

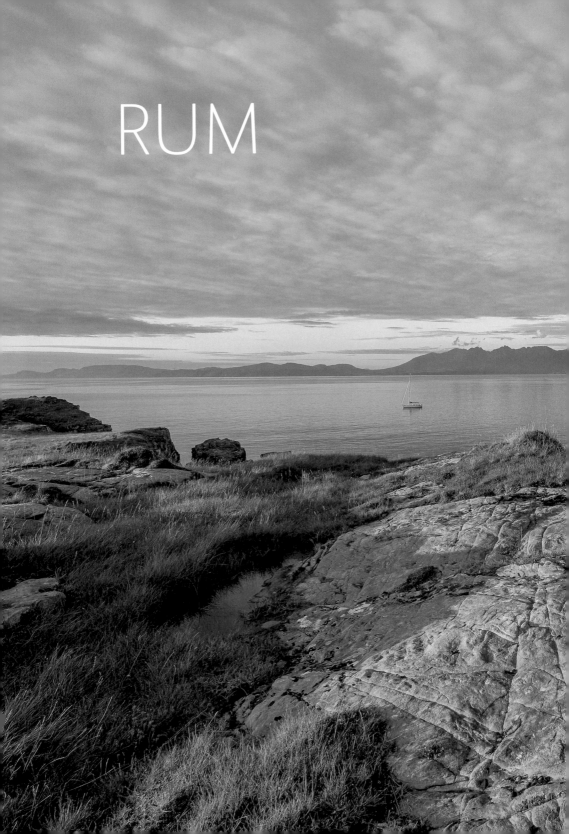

# RUM

# RUM – INTRODUCTION

**The Isle of Rum is the largest of the Small Isles and offers so much to the photographer who is willing to put a bit of effort in; there are no roadside opportunities here. It is owned by Nature Scot and the Isle of Rum Community Trust and is managed as a National Nature Reserve for its diverse range of habitats and wildlife which include deer, golden eagles, otters and 30% of the worlds' population of Manx Sheerwaters which nest high up on a mountainside.**

Dominated by its mountainous interior formed from extinct volcanoes, it has a wild, empty feel once you leave the the village of Kinloch. Beyond this, Rum is the domain of red deer and those in search of long walks, empty beaches and some locations which are a little less photographed.

## How to get to Rum

To get to the Isle of Rum, you catch a ferry from Mallaig. Glasgow is 150 miles (3.5 hours drive) from Mallaig, Edinburgh a 185 mile drive (4 hours) with public transport provided by Citylink (bus) and Scotrail, similarly for Arisaig. Caledonian Macbrayne operates the Small Isles ferry service to Eigg, Muck, Rum and Canna all year round. Additionally, during the summer months from late April to September you can also travel from Arisaig on MV Sheerwater: *arisaig.co.uk/islandferry*.

Visitors to Rum are not permitted to bring a vehicle, however, a mountain bike is perfect for getting around.

### Mallaig Car Park

- **Lat/Long**: 57.005039, -5.8316083
- **what3words**: ///apple.sideburns.ocean
- **Grid Ref**: NM674969
- **Postcode**: PH41 4RA

### Arisaig Car Park

- **Lat/Long**: 56.910045, -5.8492488
- **what3words**: ///gurgling.reheat.journals
- **Grid Ref**: NM657864
- **Postcode**: PH39 4NL

*The red sand beach at Kilmory Bay (VP3). Fujifilm X–T2, 10–24mm f/4, ISO 200, 1/400s at f/8. Aug.*

| RUM | |
|---|---|
| Scottish Gaelic | Rùm (Wide island). |
| Area | 40 sq. miles (103 sq. km). |
| Length/breadth | 7 × 7 miles. |
| Highest Elevation | Askival, 812m (2,664ft). |
| Owned by | NatureScot (Rum National Nature Reserve) and the Isle of Rum Community Trust. |
| Population | 40 |
| Largest settlement(s) | Kinloch |
| Vehicles allowed | No |
| Car/Bike rental | No |
| Public transport | No |
| Day trips from mainland? | Yes. Use the MV Sheerwater from Arisaig (summer only). You will have 3 hours on the island. |
| Internet/mobile phone coverage | Variable 3G/4G dependent on carrier. |
| Power | Hydroelectricity turbines and diesel backup generators. |
| Island website(s) | *isleofrum.com* • *southernhebrides.com* • *visitscotland.com* • *scotland.org.uk* |
| Festivals/Events | Small Isles games each year, each island takes it in turns to host, so every isle gets a go once every four year (August). See the island website. |
| Accommodation | Bunkhouse, cabins, guest house, mountain bothies at Guirdil and Dibidil, the Harbour BBQ Hut, campsite and wild camping. Book at: *isleofrum.com/accommodation* |
| Provisions/Eating Out | Kim's kitchen in the Village hall, isle of Rum general store. |
| Wildlife | Rum ponies, red deer, Manx shearwaters, red-throated divers, golden and white-tailed eagles, feral goats, otters, eider ducks, oystercatchers and curlews, Greylag geese, guillemots, kittiwakes and shags. |
| Night Sky Bortle Scale | Class 1. |

## LOCATIONS

## Maps

• OS Landranger 39: Rùm, Eigg, Muck & Canna (1:50 000)

*Previous spread: an ideal anchorage at Kilmory Bay (VP3). Fujifilm X–T2, 10–24mm f/4, ISO 200, 1/125s at f/8. Aug.*

## What to shoot and viewpoints

### Viewpoint 1 – Kinloch Castle

On approaching Rum from the sea, the imposing bulk of Kinloch Castle sits at the head of the Loch Scresort. Built by Sir George Bullough who was gifted the island of Rum by his wealthy father this sandstone mansion sits in crumbling splendour. A testament to the absurd landlordism that was prevalent throughout the Highlands and Islands where individuals used places as playthings for the wealthy. Although tours of the building were previously available, the castle is currently shut, and its long-term future us currently unknown. However, it is possible to peer through the windows at the fading late-Victorian opulence and photograph the building from the curtilage. »

### How to get here

See the viewpoint descriptions and the map to navigate to the viewpoints. All viewpoints are acted by a rough track.

### Accessibility

Rum isn't the most accessible of islands and all the viewpoints (save the Castle and Otter Hide) are accessed by long and sometimes rough tracks. A bike is the best way to get across the island. The cycle from Kinloch to Kilmory is 16km and from Kinloch to Harris is 25km, it is possible to combine them both into a long days cycling as they share the same route for some of the way.

### Best time of year/day

The sandstone of Kinloch Castle looks particularly attractive at dawn when the low sun turns it a fiery red, however, if you have a short time on the island, there are other more scenic places for sunrise. One of those is Kilmory, where you have a fine aspect to Skye on a clear day. It equally works as well at sunset, as the key view faces north to Skye and you benefit from the slanting side light across the foreground. If you visit in September you may experience the rut, where the stags battle each other for control of the breeding rights to the herd. The bellowing of the stags is an incredibly evocative sound! Due to the long distance you have to travel back from Harris it may be that you are visiting during daylight hours (unless you camp, or fancy a long walk back to Kinloch by torchlight), however, there is still plenty of interest at any time though. The route up Allt Slugan a' Choilich is worth a walk in the early morning when the low sun illuminates the pools. The otter hide is best visited at dusk or dawn when the otters are most likely to be out and about.

*Kinloch Castle (VP1). Fujifilm X–T2, 10–24mm f/4, ISO 200, 1/500s at f/5.6. Aug.*

**Opposite left**: *looking across to the mainland at dawn from Kinloch. Fujifilm X–T2, 55–200mm f/3.5–f/4.8, ISO 200, 1/80s at f/8. Aug.* **Right**: *Kinloch Castle picking up the dawn sunlight. Fujifilm X–T2, 10–24mm f/4, ISO 200, 1/125s at f/8. Aug.*

*One of the pools on the Allt Slugan a' Choilich (VP2). Fujifilm X–T2, 10–24mm f/4, ISO 200, 26s at f/8. Aug.*

## Viewpoint 2 – Allt Slugan a' Choilich

From the southwest corner of the castle, a path leads through a gate across a field into dense woodland. Cross the rushing burn and head southwest along the path. Gradually the trees this out into stands of small Scots pine and the hills come into view. There are lots of good opportunities here with the rushing burn cascading over rocks in to small pools. The path continues to ascend with the gradient steepening as you rise up the hill. A bench provides a welcome point for a rest and to take in the view across Kinloch and over to Skye and the mainland.

## Viewpoint 3 – Kilmory Bay

At the north end of Rum is Kilmory, a beautiful red sand beach with one of the finest views to the Skye Cuillin in the Hebrides. Not only does it have a stunning outlook and beach, it also has a huge population of red deer and is home to The Isle of Rum Red Deer Project, which has been conducted at Kilmory since 1953. It studies the population dynamics, natural selection, behaviour and the impact of climate change on the red deer population and is one of the longest running studies of its kind. There is a deer hide which is accessed to the right just off the main track as you approach the buildings and from here you can study and photograph the deer at close quarters. They seem totally unafraid of people and you will likely encounter them on the beach and amongst the dunes as well. There are plentiful spots along the beach for a fine sunset image, looking across to Skye, however, it is best with some elevation, either from the dunes or the raised ground at the western end of the beach. »

*Opposite: Kilmory Bay at dawn. Fujifilm X–T2, 10–24mm f/4, ISO 200, 1/170s at f/8. Aug.*

*The Bullough Mausoleum against a backdrop of the Rum Cuillin (VP4). Fujifilm X–T2, 10–24mm f/4, ISO 200, 1/500s at f/8. Aug.*

## Viewpoint 4 – Harris

On the far side of Rum is Harris, a wonderfully wild bay which was the islands main settlement in the 18th Century. Today there are just two houses. It has a strange, almost eerie atmosphere with the forbidding hills of the Rum Cuillin looming over the bay. It is also home to the Bullough Mausoleum, a ludicrous Doric sandstone temple which houses three sarcophagi. It does make a fine subject for images though and adds an interesting foreground element in the frame when placed either against the sea or the mountains. Just up the hill from it are the remains of the former mosaic-clad mausoleum, which peak out of the hillside. It was demolished when a visitor remarked that it looked like a public toilet!

*Looking southwest from the Bullough Mausoleum to Coll. Fujifilm X–T2, 10–24mm f/4, ISO 200, 1/640s at f/8. Aug.*

## Viewpoint 5 – Otter hide

On the southern shore of Loch Scresort is an otter hide. It is just a short walk from the ferry terminal through some lovely woodland and offers a chance to see otters up close. The views back to the mainland are superb on a clear day.

*Opposite: the fantastic deer of Kimory Bay (VP3)*

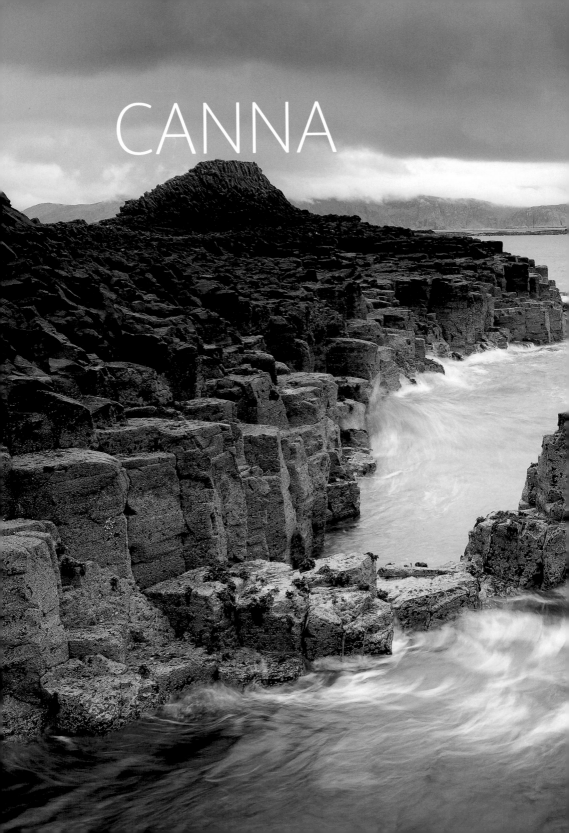

CANNA

**Hidden away behind the wild island of Rum and out of sight from the mainland is the lovely island of Canna. The island has been owned and managed by the National Trust for Scotland since 1981 when it was bequeathed by the former owners, John Lorne Campbell and Margaret Fay Shaw. The couple met in South Uist and lived together on Canna and were committed to the preservation of Hebridean culture, assembling a vast and historically important collection of Gaelic songs and stories. Shaw was also an influential photographer and her book *Eilean: The Island Photography of Margaret Fay Shaw* is a beautiful collection, documenting life in Canna, Barra, South Uist and the Aran islands in Ireland. Some of her images of Canna can be seen in the ferry waiting room.**

Canna supports a thriving community and with its cafe restaurant, campsite and well-stocked honesty shop it has all the facilities required for a really special stay. For a small island (Canna is only 4 miles long) it packs in a plethora of photographic opportunities from basalt rock columns to black sand beaches and a ruined clifftop prison. There are wide ranging views from the island which include Ben More on Mull and the Skye Cuillin, and a fantastic outlook to the coast of Rum. It's a great wee island and one which is off the beaten track of the usual photography hotspots. The low lying island of Sanday sits just offshore from Canna and forms the southern side of the sheltered harbour which has made Canna such a favoured anchorage for yachts. The island is accused by a bridge from Canna along the site of a former tidal causeway. Despite being even smaller than Canna, the island of Sanday manages to to rival its neighbour with a number of attractions including a beautiful sandy beach, a rugged coastline with distinctive stacks, a beautiful church and of course, the stars of the show, the puffins.

## How to get to Canna

To get to the Isle of Canna, you catch a ferry from Mallaig. Glasgow is 150 miles (3.5 hours drive) from Mallaig, Edinburgh a 185 mile drive (4 hours) with public transport provided by Citylink (bus) and Scotrail, similarly for Arisaig. Caledonian Macbrayne operates the Small Isles ferry service to Eigg, Muck, Rum and Canna all year round. Additionally, during the summer months from late April to September you can also travel from Arisaig on MV Sheerwater: *arisaig.co.uk/islandferry*.

Visitors to Canna are not permitted to bring a vehicle, however, most accommodation providers will pick up your luggage at the pier when you arrive by ferry. The ferry from Mallaig is a great journey taking in the little-seen coast of Rum including the wreck of the trawler Jack Abry II which ran aground 2011 and the beach at Kilmory famed for its deer study. There are plenty of car parking spaces in Mallaig either within the large car park on the left as you enter the town or on-street parking on East Bay around the harbour. If travelling from Arisaig on MV Sheerwater the skipper often stops when whales, dolphins or basking sharks are sighted, so keep a look out for these wonderful animals. As ever, you can great images shooting from the ferry of wildlife, the sea and the islands.

**Mallaig Car Park**

**P Lat/Long:** 57.005039, -5.8316083
**P what3words:** ///apple.sideburns.ocean
**P Grid Ref:** NM674969
**P Postcode:** PH41 4RA

**Arisaig Car Park**

**P Lat/Long:** 56.910045, -5.8492488
**P what3words:** ///gurgling.reheat.journals
**P Grid Ref:** NM657864
**P Postcode:** PH39 4NL

| CANNA | |
|---|---|
| **Scottish Gaelic** | Canaigh (Porpoise island). |
| **Area** | 4.4 sq. miles (11 sq. km). |
| **Length/breadth** | 4.3 × 1 miles. |
| **Highest Elevation** | Càrn a' Ghaill 210m (689ft). |
| **Owned by** | National Trust for Scotland. |
| **Population** | 67 |
| **Largest settlement(s)** | A' Chill. |
| **Vehicles allowed** | No |
| **Car/Bike rental** | No |
| **Public transport** | No |
| **Day trips from mainland?** | Yes. Use the MV Sheerwater from Arisaig (summer only). |
| **Internet/mobile phone coverage** | No phone coverage. There is broadband internet access. |
| **Power** | Diesel generator. |
| **Island website(s)** | *theisleofcanna.com* • *southernhebrides.com* • *visitscotland.com* *scotland.org.uk* |
| **Festivals/Events** | Canna 10K run (May). Small Isles games each year, each island takes it in turn to host, so every isle gets a go once every four year (August). |
| **Accommodation** | Canna self catering: *cannaselfcatering.co.uk* Canna Campsite: *cannacampsite.com* Tighard Guest House |
| **Provisions/Eating Out** | Café Canna, post office and phonebox, community shop, toilet and shower facilities at the pier. |
| **Wildlife** | Sea eagles, golden eagles, puffins, peregrine falcons, merlins, rare butterfly species, dolphins and smaller whales. |
| **Night Sky Bortle Scale** | Class 1. |

## Maps

• OS Landranger 39: Rùm, Eigg, Muck & Canna (1:50 000)

*Previous spread: the basalt columns at Tarbert Bay.*
*Fujifilm X–T2, 18–55mm f/2.8–f/4,*
*ISO 200, 0.6s at f/8. Jun.*

## What to shoot and viewpoints

### Viewpoint 1 – Coroghon Castle

The Coroghon Mor is a flat topped rock stack which rises above a swooping black and grey sand beach at the eastern end of Canna. A small ruin sits on the side of the stack and legend has it that it was used to confine the wife of a local laird. The laird was so worried that his wife would desert him that he locked her up in this lofty prison! There looks to be a sketchy path to the ruin, however, returning would be very tricky and climbing up is not recommended, it can be photographed well from below! There are two beaches either side of the stack, to the south is a graceful arc of black and grey sand, similar to that found at Talisker Bay on Skye and to the north is a pebble beach with a wonderful outlook to the Skye Cuillin. Both offer some great opportunities, with the patterns in the black sand being particularly appealing. The stack is also reflected in the shallow water of the receding waves. In spring, the carpet of bluebells on the rock stack of Alman adds a lovely pop of colour in the view to Rum. »

*The island phone box. Fujifilm X–T2, 18–55mm f/2.8–f/4, ISO 200, 1/1800s at f/5.6. Jun.*

### How to get here

On Canna there is only one road, Viewpoint 1 is accessed via a track which branches off to the right as the road curves around the waterside. Viewpoints two and three are accessed from the road. Viewpoints 4,5 and 6 are on Sanday. They can be accessed on foot from Canna and the route taking in the beach, church and cliffs takes about 3–4 hours.

### Accessibility

The whole island is all pretty accessible, however, some of the routes (particularly west to Tarbert) pass through fields with cows. They are generally easy to avoid, however, if you are worried about them it might be best to skip that viewpoint. The rocky basalt coastline is quite tricky to access at the eastern side, requiring a scramble down a steep slope. If you take your time it is fine, but a fall would be dangerous, and it is an isolated spot with no phone reception. If you aren't confident scrambling down it is easier to head straight to the beach at Tarbert on the good track and head back east along the shoreline.

### Best time of year/day

The majority of the viewpoints have an outlook south, and are backed by cliffs to the north. Therefore in summer, due to the sun rising and setting further north, you will find that during the golden hours your foreground may be in shadow. April is perhaps the ideal month to go to Canna, however, it is a beautiful island and images can be created at any time. All the viewpoints described are within an hour or so of each other, however, it's worth taking your time on the island and soaking up its relaxed pace. The puffins nest on Dun Mòr from late April to August and a clear day is desirable to make the most of the view to Rum. St Edward's Church works well at all times and will no doubt appear in many of your images as it tends to pop up in the view. The beach is lovely in spring at both sunrise and sunset and you are more than likely to have it all to yourself.

*Above middle: welcome to the Isle of Canna. Fujifilm X–T2, 18–55mm f/2.8–f/4, ISO 200, 1/800s at f/8. Jun. **Right**: St Columba's Church. Fujifilm X–T2, 18–55mm f/2.8–f/4, ISO 200, 1/340s at f/8. Jun.*

*The Coroghon Mor and the wonderful black sand beach (VP1). Fujifilm X–T2, 18–55mm f/2.8–f/4, ISO 200, 1/250s at f/8. Jun.*

*Looking to Rum at sunset from the slopes above the campsite (VP2). Fujifilm X–T2, 18–55mm f/2.8–f/4, ISO 200, 1/7s at f/8. Jun.*

## Viewpoint 2 – Above the campsite

Canna campsite is a fine place to stay whilst on the island and it also happens to provide a cracking view over Canna, Sanday and Rum. From the harbour follow the track round past the shop, cafe and and farm until a sign directs you through a gate and up to the campsite. The hillside behind the site is easily ascended with a number of sheep tracks to follow up through the outcrops of basalt rock. It's up to you how far you go up, however, the best views are obtained once you are high enough to create separation between the coast of Sanday and Rum. From this height, a 180 degree panorama taking in the mainland mountains, Canna and its harbour, Sanday, Rum and on a clear day Mull, Coll and Tiree! It's something of a one hit wonder photographically, but it is also just a delightful place to spend sometime taking in the view and tracing routes across the islands of Canna and Sanday.

*The view to Rum from Canna Campsite. Fujifilm X–T2, 18–55mm f/2.8–f/4, ISO 200, 1/500s at f/8. Jun.*

***Opposite middle**: a sheep on the path back from Tarbert Bay. Fujifilm X–T2, 18–55mm f/2.8–f/4, ISO 200, 1/12s at f/11. Jun.
**Bottom**: rock textures at Tarbert Bay (VP3). Fujifilm X–T2, 18–55mm f/2.8–f/4, ISO 200, 1/125s at f/4. Jun.*

*A cloud-topped Rum seen from Tarbert Bay (VP3). Fujifilm X–T2, 18–55mm f/2.8–f/4, ISO 200, 40s at f/8. Jun.*

### Viewpoint 3 – Tarbert

Heading west from the campsite the island becomes more rugged, with steep slopes looming over to the north and a fractured rocky shoreline to the south. Five miles out to sea the lonely lighthouse of Hyskeir sits on an isolated skerry. As the road begins to climb, the coastline to the south becomes more intriguing. Like a distant cousin of Staffa or the Giants Causeway, columnar basalt thrusts out into the ocean, sculpted into a series of pinnacles and deep channels. Thought to be the remnants of a lava flow from a volcanic eruption on Skye this basalt landscape forms an incredibly intricate coastline with plenty of photographic opportunities, extending all the way to the beach at Tarbert. The contrast between the hard basalt and the soft white sand at the beach is especially appealing and forms a wonderful foreground for the view out to Rum. This stretch of basalt coastline is a seascape photographers dream, and unlike on Staffa where you are surrounded by others and constrained by time, here you can wait for the light and spend a while fine tuning your compositions. »

*The beautiful Sanday beach. Fujifilm X–T2, 18–55mm f/2.8–f/4, ISO 200, 1/180s at f/11. Jun.*

*Chickens wandering the shoreline on Sanday. Fujifilm X–T2, 18–55mm f/2.8–f/4, ISO 200, 1/350s at f/8. Jun.*

### Viewpoint 4 – Sanday Beach

You will catch your first glimpse of the beach (strangely unnamed on the OS maps) as you cross the bridge from Canna to Sanday. At the roadside shrine with its stained glass window head right along the rocky shoreline and through a gate in the fence. From here, the beach is revealed. With its pretty arc of white shell sand it is a classic Hebridean beach and makes a fine spot for a swim after a long walk around Sanday. The black rocky outcrops at each end of the beach provide some nice contrast to the sand and in early summer the pink flowers of Sea Thrift add a lovely pop of colour. Up above the beach there are marram grass dunes which can form a nice foreground. The views out to the western end of Canna and back to a pretty white cottage are superb.

### Viewpoint 5 – St Edward's church

Completed in 1890, the Roman Catholic church of St Edward's was funded by the Marchioness of Bute in memory of her father and is a fine looking structure, appearing in many views throughout Canna and Sanday. The church is now deconsecrated and has had a chequered past with a struggle to find a viable use for the building. Heading east from the beach a rough track follows the shoreline, passing the tiny school and offering some nice views back across calm waters to Canna. The church appears to be a long way off, however, it does not take long to arrive. Once through a gate, a gravel track provides a sweeping lead-in line the building which looks fantastic against the backdrop of the rugged hills of Rum.

*Puffins in flight over Dun Mòr. Fujifilm X–T2, 55–200mm f/3.5–f/4.8, ISO 200, 1/2000s at f/4.8. Jun.*

## Viewpoint 6 – The stacks and the puffins

The southern coast of Sanday is a dramatic place to be. Rum appears tantalisingly close, its uninhabited coastline of steep cliffs and high hills providing a foreboding and mysterious presence on the horizon. The coastline of Sanday is equally as impressive with towering cliffs and two rock stacks (Dun Mòr and Dun Beag) offshore providing the drama. The main attraction is the puffin colony which nests on the larger of the two rock stacks Dun Mòr. The puffins make Sanday their home in the summer and it is possible to photograph them as they bob about in the water or dart back to their burrows laden with fish for their chicks (delightfully know as pufflings). If you are very lucky you might see huge numbers of puffins in flight together, which is a terrific sight to see. The cliffs

are also home to shags, cormorants, kittiwakes and fulmar and in summer it is a busy place! The other bird you need to keep your eyes out for (for very different reasons) are the Great Skuas or Bonxies. These aggressive piratical birds steal food from other seabirds, kill smaller birds like puffins and generally make a menace of themselves throughout the summer. They have been known to swoop down on people, so be aware, especially if you are close the cliff edge.

*Top left: St Edward's Church. Fujifilm X–T2, 18–55mm f/2.8–f/4, ISO 200, 1/340s at f/10. Jun. Right: Dun Beag rock stack on Sanday. Fujifilm X–T2, 18–55mm f/2.8–f/4, ISO 200, 1/350s at f/9. Jun.*

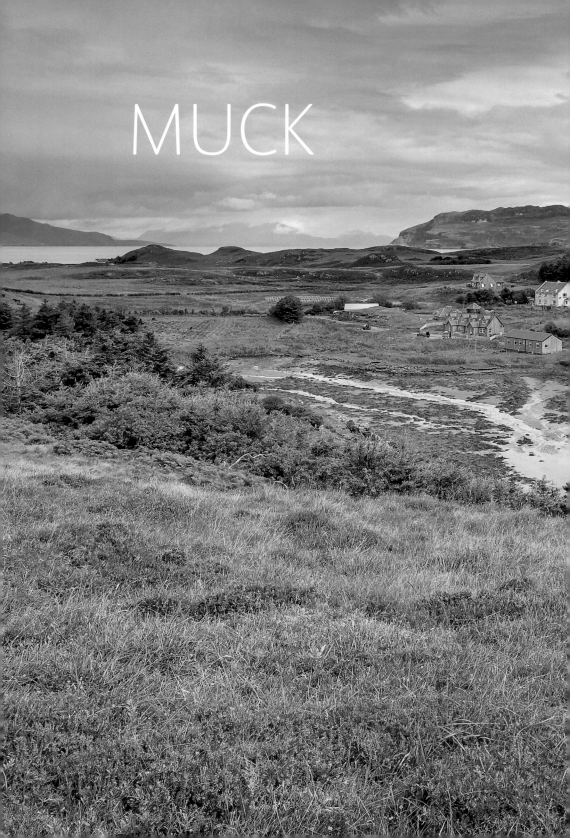

MUCK

The Isle of Muck is the smallest of the Small Isles, located to the south west of Eigg. The etymology of the name Muck is thought to derive from the Gaelic Muc, meaning pig, however, you are more likely to encounter cows these days which range across the island and can often be found on the beaches. The main settlement is Port Mòr, on the southern side of the island where you will find the bunkhouse, fantastic tearoom and the community centre. It's difficult to get lost on Muck with just one road on the island which stretches north from Port Mòr through farmland to the beaches of Gallanach.

## How to get to Muck

To get to Muck, you catch a ferry from Mallaig. Glasgow is 150 miles (3.5 hours drive) from Mallaig, Edinburgh a 185 mile drive (4 hours) with public transport provided by Citylink (bus) and Scotrail, similarly for Arisaig. Caledonian Macbrayne operates the Small Isles ferry service to Eigg, Muck, Rum and Canna all year round. Additionally, during the summer months from late April to September you can also travel from Arisaig on MV Sheerwater: *arisaig.co.uk/islandferry*.

Visitors to Muck are not permitted to bring a vehicle although Blue Badge holders can apply for a temporary permit.

*A boat pulled up onto the shore makes a great foreground in the view to Rum (VP2). Fujifilm X–T2, 10–24mm f/4, ISO 200, 1/550s at f/8. Jul.*

## MUCK

| MUCK | |
|---|---|
| **Scottish Gaelic** | Eilean nam Muc (Sea Pig or Whale island). |
| **Area** | 2 sq. miles (5 sq. km). |
| **Length/breadth** | 2 × 1 miles. |
| **Highest Elevation** | Beinn Airein (137m or 449ft). |
| **Owned by** | MacEwen family. |
| **Population** | 38 |
| **Largest settlement(s)** | Port Mòr. |
| **Vehicles allowed** | No |
| **Car/Bike rental** | No |
| **Public transport** | No |
| **Day trips from mainland?** | Yes. Use the MV Sheerwater from Arisaig (summer only). You will have 3 hours on the island. |
| **Internet/mobile phone coverage** | Mobile coverage is sporadic. There is broadband internet access. |
| **Power** | Wind/photovoltaic power scheme with a back-up diesel generator. |
| **Island website(s)** | *isleofmuck.com* • *islemuck.com* (hisytory) • *southernhebrides.com* *visitscotland.com* • *scotland.org.uk* |
| **Festivals/Events** | Craft courses. Small Isles games each year, each island takes it in turns to host, so every isle gets a go once every four year (August). |
| **Accommodation** | Gallanach Lodge, yurt, bunkhouse, 3 self-catering holiday cottages. Book at: *isleofmuck.com* |
| **Provisions/Eating Out** | Muck Craft Shop & Tea Room (does food and some provisions). Public toilets are also available at the Community Hall. |
| **Wildlife** | Otters, crabs, small purple sea urchins and the only British Coral; the 'Cup Coral'. Grey atlantic seals, Minke whales, common and bottlenose dolphins, porpoises, basking sharks and sometimes Orca (killer whales). Over 40 species of birds breed regularly on Muck including Manx shearwaters, guillemots, razor bills, cormorants, shags, fulmars, gannets, terns, puffins. |
| **Night Sky Bortle Scale** | Class 1. |

### LOCATIONS

### Maps

• OS Landranger 39: Rùm, Eigg, Muck & Canna (1:50 000)

*Previous spread*: the village of Port Mór from the headland to the west with a cloud-shrouded Eigg in the distance. Fujifilm X–T2, 10–24mm f/4, ISO 200, 1/340s at f/8. Jul.

## What to shoot and viewpoints

### Viewpoint 1 – Port Mór

As you enter the harbour your gaze may be drawn to a cylindrical hill which rises on the west side of the bay. This is the site of an Iron Age fortification, and the route to the hill provides the best view of Port Mòr and over to the Isle of Eigg. Head inland and take the track on the left at the ruins of the old village and head past the houses. The route rises up and a feint path branches off across the hillside.

After 15 minutes the hill comes into view. The view south is excellent, with Ardnamurchan and its lighthouse, and Mull and the Coll seen on the horizon. >>

*Opposite top*: Port Mór from the old village. Fujifilm X–T2, 10–24mm f/4, ISO 200, 1/220s at f/8. Jul. **Bottom**: The rocky shoreline of Camas na Cairidh (VP2). Fujifilm X–T2, 10–24mm f/4, ISO 200, 120s at f5.6. Jul.

*The village of Port Mór (VP1). Fujifilm X–T2, 10–24mm f/4, ISO 200, 1/450s at f/8. Jul.*

*Camas na Cairidh at sunset looking to Rum. Fujifilm X–T2, 10–24mm f/4, ISO 200, 120s at f/8. Jul.*

## Viewpoint 2 – Camas na Cairidh

As you head across the island, passing an agricultural shed on the right, the road turns a bend at a picnic table. From here a gate on the right gives access to a field which slopes down to a small sandy beach. The view of Rum here is fantastic, and one which is not often photographed. There is a basalt dyke which snakes out into the sea providing a great lead in line to the view across the sea to Rum and Skye on the distant horizon. The enclosing hill to the east of the bay also provides a good view to Eigg.

## Viewpoint 3 – Gallanach

The road continues on along the coast. The first opportunity is an old fishing boat pulled up out of the water in amongst the reeds. It makes a fine subject against the looming bulk of Rum with the wind blown foliage providing a great foreground. Further on there are a couple of sandy bays all enjoying a fine outlook to Rum. As you reach the end of the beaches, a path leads up the hillside past an idyllically located cottage, sitting in a lovely garden. From here, feint paths lead out to the end of the headland where there is a beautifully sited circle of gravestones and a small sandy bay with views of Eilean Àird Nan Uan and Eilean Nan Each (the island of the horses and the island of sheep). Depending on the level of the tide it is possible to cross to the islands. The views from here are sublime with the outer Hebrides glimpsed on the far horizon.

*Top: sandy shore at Gallanach (VP3). Fujifilm X–T2, 10–24mm f/4, ISO 200, 1/300s at f/8. Jul. **Bottom**: the fishing boat in the reeds at Gallanach (VP3). Fujifilm X–T2, 10–24mm f/4, ISO 200, 1/600s at f/8. Jul.*

## How to get here

Muck is a small island, 3×1 miles. It is about a mile to viewpoints 2 and 3 with directions in the viewpoint descriptions.

## Accessibility

There is one road on Muck and it is generally fine under foot and relatively flat. The path to the fort is rough and can be boggy, as is the path out to Àird Nan Eilean Uan. Otherwise it is simple walking. Please note that livestock roam free on the island so dogs should be kept on leads.

## Best time of year/day

Unless you are staying on the island your time of day may be constrained by the ferry, which doesn't give you a lot of time to explore. However, you should be able to complete the walk to all the viewpoints. If staying on the island, Gallanach and Camas an Cairidh make fine sunrise and sunset locations at any time of the year, particularly in summer though when the sun sets and rises at more northerly lattitude. Some of the best elements of Muck are the views to other islands, particularly Eigg and Rum, so good visibility is vital to make the most of your time on the island.

# SKYE & RAASAY

*Previous spread*: cloud-covered Cuillins from Elgol. Fujifilm X–T2, 18–55mm f/2.8–f/4, ISO 200, 17s at f/11. Sep.

*Below*: The Needle at The Quiraing. Fujifilm X–T2, 10–24mm f/4, ISO 200, 1/75s at f/8. Aug.

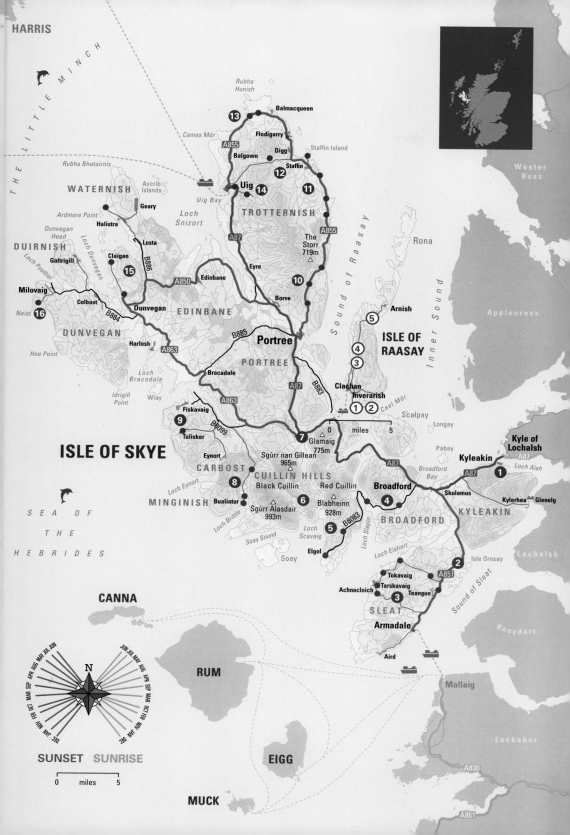

SKYE

**The Isle of Skye is arguably the most famous of all the Hebridean islands. It's certainly the most popular for visitors and is known across the world for its incredible landscapes, history and culture. If there is one island in the Hebrides which potentially gives a flavour of all the islands, it is Skye. There is a reason why Skye is popular. It is simply a fantastic place.**

From the jagged Cuillin hills to the crazy pinnacles and cliffs of the Quiraing, the upland landscape throughout Skye provides an abundance of opportunities for the photographer; there really is a lifetime of exploring to be had on the Isle of Skye. There are ruined castles to find, quiet beaches, distilleries, craggy mountain ridges, waterfalls, clifftop bothies, the bustling town of Portree with its pretty harbour; even the bridge which takes you 'over the sea to Skye' is an excellent spot for photography.

Skye is an easy island to visit compared to many others as it is connected to the mainland by a bridge, although for the romantics there is still the option of the ferry from Mallaig to Armadale on the Sleat peninsula. There are plenty of options for accommodation across the island, ranging from campsites and bothies to hotels and bed and breakfasts and there is something for every budget. Just be sure to book in advance as accommodation tends to fill up very quickly in the summer months and around school holiday times.

There is no doubt that Skye has suffered in recent years from the pressures of over-tourism. The infrastructure was simply not in place to cope with the huge numbers of visitors who flocked to the incredibly popular attractions such as the Fairy Pools in Glen Brittle, the Fairy Glen in Uig or The Quiraing and the Old Man Of Storr in Trotternish.

*Previous spread: Camasunary Bay from Elgol. Fujifilm X–T2, 55–200mm f/3.5–f/4.8, ISO 200, 1/320s at f/11. Sep*

However, in recent years some great work has been undertaken to address this, with dedicated parking areas and new path networks in place to mitigate some of the pressure of increased footfall on these delicate and precious landscapes. Even so, in terms of photography I wouldn't recommend visiting Skye in the summer period, its just too busy, especially if you are wanting to visit the most popular areas. Whenever you visit, treat the island with care. It is a special place.

## How to get to Skye

You can reach Skye by car over the Skye bridge, public transport and ferry.

### Car
Portree on Skye is 215 miles drive from Glasgow (5 hours), 235 miles from Edinburgh (5 hours drive) and 114 miles from Inverness (2.5 hours), and 300 miles drive from the Scottish-English border (6.5 hours).

### Public Transport
You can catch a train to Mallaig or Kyle of Lochalsh, then a bus or taxi to Portree (about an hour).

Scotrail Train from Glasgow (8 hours), Edinburgh (9 hours), Inverness (4.5 hours) to Skye.

Citylink Bus or Megabus from Glasgow (7 hours) Edinburgh (7 hours) Inverness (3 hours) to Skye

### Ferry
The Caledonian MacBrayne ferry between Mallaig and Skye runs daily from the port of Mallaig to Armadale in Sleat on the south of Skye. Glenelg ferry connects Glenelg on the mainland with Kylerhea on Skye. For more information visit: *skyeferry.co.uk*

## Maps

- OS Landranger 32: South Skye & Cuillin Hills (1:50 000)
- OS Landranger 23: North Skye – Dunvegan & Portree (1:50 000)

| SKYE | |
|---|---|
| Scottish Gaelic | An t-Eilean Sgitheanach (Island of the mist/cloud). |
| Area | 639 sq. miles (1655 sq. km). |
| Length/breadth | 50 × 25 miles. |
| Highest Elevation | Sgùrr Alasdair, 993m (3,258ft). |
| Owned by | Mixed including the John Muir Trust. |
| Population | 10,000 |
| Largest settlement(s) | The capital town of Skye is Portree. Larger villages include Dunvegan, Staffin, Uig, Carbost, Broadford, Kyleakin and Armadale. |
| Vehicles allowed | Yes |
| Car/Bike rental | Jans Bike Rental, Portree; Skye EBikes, Kilmuir; Skye MTB Adventures, Kyle of Lochalsh; Skye Bike Shack, Carbost. Skye Car Hire, Kyle of Lochalsh; DriveSkye, Armadale Garage; Morrison Car Hire, Portree; Isle of Skye Campervan rental, Armadale. |
| Public transport | Yes, Stagecoach: *stagecoachbus.com*. |
| Day trips from mainland? | Yes |
| Internet/mobile phone coverage | Yes, but variable 3G/4G coverage, dependent on your carrier. Broadband in hotels/residencies. |
| Power | Grid and renewables primarily wind. |
| Island website(s) | *isleofskye.com • isleofskye.net • southernhebrides.com • visitscotland.com scotland.org.uk* |
| Festivals/Events | Skye Live Festival (May). Skye Half Marathon (June). Isle of Skye Highland Games (August). |
| Accommodation | There is a wide selection of accommodation on Skye including 8 camping/caravan/motorhome sites (marked on the maps), a selection of yurts, several hostels and huts, and many self-catering cottages and B&Bs. There are great listings at: *isleofskye.com* and *isleofskye.net*. |
| Provisions/Eating Out | There are supermarkets and smaller food shops in most of the larger villages with Co-op's in Portree and Broadford. Skye has over 20 pubs with restaurants and cafes in most of the larger villages (some marked on our maps) with a good listing on *isleofskye.com*. |
| Wildlife | Red deer, otters, sea eagles, seals, dolphins, porpoises and whales. |
| Night Sky Bortle Scale | Class 2 and 3. |

## LOCATIONS

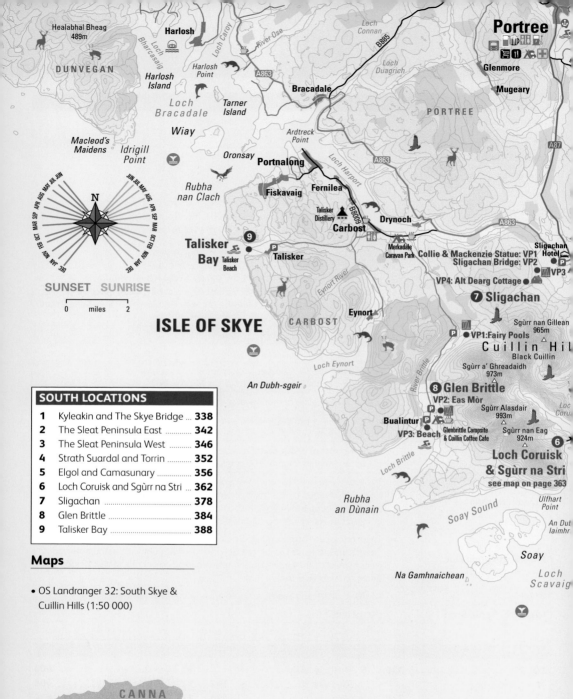

**Portree**

Healabhal Bheag
489m

Harlosh

D U N V E G A N

Loch
Bharcasaig

Harlosh
Island

Harlosh
Point

Harlosh
Point

River Ose

Loch Caroy

A863

B885

Loch
Connan

Loch
Duagrich

Loch
Bracadale

Tarner
Island

Wiay

Bracadale

P O R T R E E

Glenmore

Mugeary

A87

Macleod's
Maidens

Idrigill
Point

Oronsay

Ardtreck
Point

Loch Harport

A863

A863

Rubha
nan Clach

Portnalong

Fiskavaig

Fernilea

Talisker
Distillery

B8009

Drynoch

Carbost

N

SUNSET   SUNRISE

0    miles    2

Talisker
Bay

Talisker
Beach

9

Talisker

Merkadale
Caravan Park

Collie & Mackenzie Statue: VP1
Sligachan Bridge: VP2

Sligachan
Hotel

VP3

VP4: Alt Dearg Cottage

**7** Sligachan

**ISLE OF SKYE**

C A R B O S T

Eynort

Eynort River

An Dubh-sgeir

Loch Eynort

VP1: Fairy Pools

Sgùrr nan Gillean
965m

C u i l l i n   H i l l

Black Cuillin

Sgùrr a' Ghreadaidh
973m

River Brittle

**8** Glen Brittle

VP2: Eas Mòr

Sgùrr Alasdair
993m

Loch
Coru

Bualintur

VP3: Beach

Glenbrittle Campsite
& Cuillin Coffee Cafe

Sgùrr nan Eag
924m

**6**

**Loch Coruisk
& Sgùrr na Stri**

see map on page 363

Loch Brittle

Rubha
an Dùnain

Soay Sound

Ulfhart
Point

An Dut
Iaimhr

Na Gamhnaichean

Soay

Loch
Scavaig

## Maps

- OS Landranger 32: South Skye &
  Cuillin Hills (1:50 000)

C A N N A

M U L L

# ISLE OF RAASAY

④ Inver Beach
③ Balmeanach
Dun Caan 444m
astianavaig
Holoman Bay
avaig Bay
Oskaig
Raasay Walled Garden
Dun Caan
Rubha na' Leac
Ollach
Clachan
Isle of Raasay Distillery
Inverarish
Narrows of Raasay
① East Suishnish
② Eyre Point

inchorran

Sconser
Loch Ainort

Scalpay

Longay

APPLECROSS

Kyle of Lochalsh

Kyle Akin

Kyleakin
VP1: Skye Bridge
① VP2: Caisteal Maol

Luib
Dunan
Caolas Scalpay

A87

Guillamon Island
Pabay

Sgùrr na Coinnich 739m △

Kylerhea

Glenelg

sco
6m
d Cuillin
Beinn na Caillich 732m
Broadford
Broadford Bay  Ashaig Beach
Corry
Skulamus

Blà Bheinn 928m
Strath Suardal & Torrin
④ Torrin
VP1: Cill Chriosd
VP2: Loch Cill Chriosd
BROADFORD
Allt Mòr
KYLEAKIN

Loch na Crèitheach
na Stri 495m
VP3: Loch Slapin
B8083

Kinloch

3.2km/2 miles walk
Kirkibost
VP4: Camasunary
Kilmarie
clearance villages of Suishish & Boreraig
Heaste
Eilean Heast
Drumfearn
VP1
Loch na Dal

VP1: Beach
⑤ Elgol
Elgol & Camusunary
Pier 3: Cliffs
VP2:
Glasnakille
Rubha Suisnish
Loch Eishort
VP4: Ord  Ord
Isleornsay
② Sleat Peninsula (East)
Isle of Ornsay
Eilean Sionnach
Camuscross
VP1

Rubha na h-Easgainne
an na Airde
Tokavaig
VP3: Tokavaig
VP5: Loch Meadal
VP2: Torabhaig Distillery
Camas Barabhaig

Tarskavaig
Tarskavaig Point
Bàgh Tharsgabhaig
Achnacloich
VP2: Tarskavaig
VP1: Achnacloich
Teangue
Knock Bay

Sleat Peninsula (West) ③
Kilmore

Inver Dalavil
SLEAT
Kilbeg
A851

RubhaCharn nan Cearc
Armadale Castle, Gardens & Museum
Armadale
Armadale Bay

Sound of Sleat

KNOYDART

Aird
Point of Sleat
Camus Daraich

Before the opening of the Skye Bridge in 1995, Kyleakin was the gateway to the island, connected to the mainland by a ferry which plied the waters between the village and Kyle of Lochalsh. It was a village with all the hustle and bustle of a busy port. However, today Kyleakin, bypassed by the bridge, is a much more peaceful and tranquil village. With an attractive harbour and a ruined 14th century castle it offers some great photographic opportunities and is great spot to break up your journey to or from Skye.

## What to shoot and viewpoints

### Viewpoint 1 – The Skye Bridge ♿

By 1971 the romance of getting a ferry across to Skye was waning. An increase in visitors meant that the small ferries were unable to cope with the demand and queues were often a frustration to locals and visitors alike. A bridge connecting Kyle of Lochalsh via Eilean Bàn to Skye was proposed to alleviate this and was eventually opened in 1995. Initially a toll bridge but with sustained pressure and protests from local people the toll was thankfully dropped. The bridge touches briefly on Eilean Bàn (White Island) which was once the home of the naturalist and author Gavin Maxwell who wrote the classic Ring of Bright Water about his time with the otters at Sandaig and the island also houses a Stevenson lighthouse which now appears to sit under the bridge. The bridge itself is best photographed from the bouldery shore as you enter the village of Kyleakin, where its graceful span arcs across the water, framing the lighthouse superbly. »

*Sunlight hits the bridge (VP1). Fujifilm X–T2, 55–200mm f/3.5–f/4.8, ISO 200, 1/300s at f/4.5. Dec.*

*The Skye Bridge and Eilean Bàn. Fujifilm X–T2, 10–24mm f/4, ISO 200, 30s at f/8. Dec.*

## Viewpoint 2 – Caisteal Maol

The ruins of Caisteal Maol (Bare Castle) are to be found at the eastern side of Kyleakin and guard the narrowest part of the loch (Kyle Akin). Legend has it that a Norwegian princess named 'Saucy Mary' once lived in the castle and would charge any boats who wished to sail through the strait a toll. On payment of the toll she would remove the chain which stretched from castle to mainland and then thank them by flashing her breasts. Not a method employed by the folk who manned the tolls on the Skye Bridge. The castle itself sits above a pretty little bay with old ruined boats beached on the pebbly shore. The boats, particularly the larger of the two, provide some great opportunities to photograph the beautiful patterns of decay and also make an excellent foreground to the castle. There is also a great view from the castle itself which takes in the view over Kyleakin, the Skye Bridge and Raasay.

### How to get here

Kyleakin is easily accessed from the A87. On descending from the bridge, take the first left at the roundabout and follow the road into the village. There is ample parking at the waterside. To photograph the bridge, head west along the shoreline. For Caisteal Maol head across the village green and take the road south across the bridge before turning left. Follow the road for 10 minutes until a small pier is reached. From here follow the path above the shoreline for a minute or two before the bay is reached. The castle itself is not easily accessed at high tide however, most of the best photographic opportunities are looking towards the castle rather than from it.

### Parking for both viewpoints

**P Lat/Long**:  57.272842, -5.7302417
**P what3words**: ///expansion.goats.rungs
**P Grid Ref**:  NG752264
**P Postcode**:  IV41 8PL

*Above*: old boats, the castle, and the view back over Kyleakin from Caisteal Maol.

## Accessibility

The bouldery shore along Loch Alsh can be slippery underfoot. Be wary of boats sailing under the bridge – the wake from the larger vessels can catch you unaware if you are at the waters edge. The narrow path to Caisteal Maol is suitable for most able-bodied walkers but, be aware of the tide times if you are crossing over to the castle.

*Above*: *the wreck of an old boat lies in the bay in front of Caisteal Maol (VP2), Fujifilm X–T2, 10–24mm f/4, ISO 200, 1/210s at f/8. Sep.*

## Best time of year/day

The Skye bridge can be photographed well under most conditions, even grey overcast days can work as its bold shape can be used to form strong, graphic compositions. It works well for long exposures, with the racing clouds and tides contrasting well with its sturdy architecture. Caisteal Maol is best at high tide, as the bay provides scope for reflections, however, at low tide the boats themselves (and the castle) can be more readily explored. It is equally as good at sunrise where the bold shapes of the castle can form an interesting silhouette against the brightening sky or also at sunset when the sun hits the west face of castle.

Whilst lacking the drama provided by views to the Cuillin found on the west, the east coast of the Sleat Peninsula is still a lovely part of the island. Green and lush and relatively low-lying, it is easy to see how it has earned its name as the 'The Garden of Skye'. There is still plenty to interest the photographer including ruined castles, island lighthouses and a distillery all backed by a fantastic outlook east to the mountains of Knoydart.

## What to shoot and viewpoints

### Viewpoint 1 – Isle Ornsay &

On the east coast of the Sleat Peninsula is the pretty village of Isle Ornsay. The harbour was once thronged with herring fishing boats and it was also a destination for the paddle steamers which sailed the waters off the west coast from as far afield as Glasgow. Today the whitewashed buildings are home to a hotel, bar and gallery which provide an interesting subject. However, the main photographic opportunities are from the road which heads south east along the coast. The view east from the sheltered bay to the lighthouse (Eileen Sionnach) on the island (Isle Ornsay) is superb, with the mountain of Beinn Sgritheal towering over the loch. There is good scope here for using a telephoto lens to pull the mountains of Knoydart into the image as well as wider shots showing the lighthouse in context within the bay. There also a great view across The Sound of Sleat to be had from the lay-by on the A851 at NG700151 (*57.168908, -5.8060658* and *what3words:///rock.noun.formed*) where a lonely white cottage across Loch na Dal provides a pop of intrigue in the mid-ground. >>

*Sun hits the lighthouse of Eileen Sionnach (VP1). Fujifilm X–T2, 55–200mm f/3.5–f/4.8, ISO 200, 1/210s at f/8. Nov.*

*Eileen Sionnach and the towering Knoydart hills on the mainland. Fujifilm X–E3, 55–200mm f/3.5–f/4.8, ISO 200, 1/80s at f/11. Sep.*

## Viewpoint 2 – Torabhaig Distillery ♿

The newest distillery on Skye is Torabhaig and it sits in an idyllic position on the coast overlooking the ruins of Caisteal Camus. The distillery buildings are attractive in their own right, but it is certainly worth walking down to the shore. There is a fantastic outlook to the mainland with the mountains of Knoydart prominent on the horizon with Mallaig visible to the south east and numerous rocky skerries providing mid-ground interest. The ruined castle, sitting out on a rocky promontory provides a good focal point for the view north east.

*Top: the wee house across Loch na Dal with Beinn Sgritheal beyond. Fujifilm X–T2, 55–200mm f/3.5–f/4.8, ISO 200, 1/125s at f/8. Nov. **Left**: Hotel Eilean Iarmain. Fujifilm X–T2, 10–24mm f/4, ISO 200, 1/35s at f/8. Nov.*

## How to get here

Isle Ornsay is accessed by the small road which branches off the A851 signposted to Camus Croise and Eilean Iarmain. Follow the road down and once over the bridge turn left. There is parking at the hotel. Torabhaig Distillery is also accused from the A851 at Teangue and is signposted from the road, there is parking at the distillery.

### Viewpoint 1 – Isle Ornsay

| | |
|---|---|
| Lat/Long: | 57.145484, -5.7992144 |
| what3words: | ///gone.crunching.lights |
| Grid Ref: | NG702124 |
| Postcode: | IV43 8QR |

### Viewpoint 2 – Torabhaig Distillery

| | |
|---|---|
| Lat/Long: | 57.113176, -5.8489648 |
| what3words: | ///topples.indicates.flask |
| Grid Ref: | NG670090 |
| Postcode: | IV44 8RE |

## Accessibility

Both viewpoints are essentially roadside. The pebble beaches and rocky foreshores can be uneven, but it is not essential to cross these to visit. Be careful crossing the large areas of seaweed at low tide, these can be incredibly slippery as well as hiding rock-pools.

## Best time of year/day

Both viewpoints are east facing and make obvious sunrise destinations. However, they also work well at sunset particularly when the low sun hits the lighthouse. There are images to be made here at all times of the year, but good visibility is required to make the most of these viewpoints.

*Above: Torabhaig Distillery (VP2). Fujifilm X–T2, 18–55mm f/2.8–f/4, ISO 200, 1/400s at f/8. Apr.*

*Opposite: Caisteal Camus from the shoreline below Torabhaig Distillery. Fujifilm X–T2, 18–55mm f/2.8–f/4, ISO 200, 1/480s at f/8. Apr.*

The western side of the Sleat Peninsula has a very different character to the east with dramatic views across to the jagged saw-toothed ridge of the Cuillin and glimpsed views southwest to Canna and Rum. It's simply a wonderful part of Skye. A tortuous single-track road snakes its way along the coast through stands of woodland with each hill and corner revealing another glorious outlook over Loch Eishort. There are a number of small settlements along the road and each offer something different for the landscape photographer to savour.

## What to shoot and viewpoints

### Viewpoint 1 – Achnacloich

Approaching from the south east, the first settlement reached is Achnacloich. At low tide a huge expense of grey/black sand is revealed, over which the Gillean Burn flows in braided channels. The sinuous form of the burn can provide some great lead-in lines to the view of the wider landscape. It is here that the Cuillin are first seen across the water, their steep grey flanks contrasting well with the scattered white cottages of Glasnakille. To the south west the islands of Rum and Canna appear on the horizon.

*Tarskavaig church from Achnacloich beach (VP1). Fujifilm X–E3, 55–200mm f/3.5–f/4.8, ISO 200, 1/200s at f/11. Oct.*

### Viewpoint 2 – Tarskavaig

Heading north, the road climbs steeply and reveals the settlement of Tarskavaig with its pretty houses sheltered in a shallow valley. Again, the Cuillin dominate the view north, with the full range arrayed on the horizon. There are also great views of Rum from the high point of the road where it branches off to the village. »

## How to get here

The western coast of the Sleat Peninsula is best travelled in an anti-clockwise direction, starting at Kilbeg on the A851. It is a very narrow road with some tight corners, and is unsuitable for caravans. The route described above finishes back on the A851 to the north of Torabhaig. Allow 45 minutes at least to drive the route, however, you are likely to spend a lot of time at the various viewpoints. Each viewpoint is essentially roadside. There are obvious areas to park at each location, but take special care not to park in passing places, if there is no space available come back at another time.

### Viewpoint 1 – Achnacloich
Small parking area at road bend

- 🅿 **Lat/Long:**     57.106205, -5.9856087
- 🅿 **what3words:** ///annual.empires.earpiece
- 🅿 **Grid Ref:**     NG587087
- 🅿 **Postcode:**    IV46 8SB

### Viewpoint 2 – Tarskavaig
Small area to park at cattle grid

- 🅿 **Lat/Long:**     57.113585, -5.9859387
- 🅿 **what3words:** ///huddling.pelting.swinging
- 🅿 **Grid Ref:**     NG587095
- 🅿 **Postcode:**    IV41 8PL

*Above*: the Cuillin from Achnacloich beach (VP1). Fujifilm X–T2, 18–55mm f/2.8–f/4, ISO 200, 1/150s at f/8. Oct.
*Below*: looking across to Rum from the road south of Tarskavaig (VP2). Fujifilm X–T2, 10–24mm f/4, ISO 200, 1/120s at f/8. Dec.

### Viewpoint 3 – Tokavaig

The road heads inland and after 10 minutes the settlement of Tokavaig is reached. Flanked by twisted birch trees, the rocky beach here offers an incredible view across Loch Eishort to the Cuillin. There is plenty of foreground interest, with some fascinating wave smoothed rocks providing an excellent foil for the serrated ridge of the distant mountains. There are a number of great opportunities at this beach, and it is really worth spending time here exploring the coastline; the foreshore of straggly birch trees and wandering sheep and the outlook to the Cuillin is a classic Hebridean scene. At the northern end of the beach, perched on a promontory is the ruined Dunscaith Castle which can offer a bit of mid-ground intrigue. >>

*Gnarled trees alongside the road at Tokavaig (VP3). Fujifilm X–T2, 18–55mm f/2.8–f/4, ISO 200, 1/75s at f/8. Oct.*

*The pebble beach at Tokavaig (VP3). Fujifilm X–T2, 18–55mm f/2.8–f/4, ISO 200, 1/250s at f/8. Oct.*

### Viewpoint 3 – Tokavaig
**Small parking area alongside road**

- **Lat/Long:** 57.132125, -5.9715194
- **what3words:** ///held.lasts.icebergs
- **Grid Ref:** NG597115
- **Postcode:** IV44 8QL

### Viewpoint 4 – Ord
**Parking area on the shoreside of road at bend**

- **Lat/Long:** 57.147164, -5.9414694
- **what3words:** ///shrugging.helpfully.wording
- **Grid Ref:** NG616131
- **Postcode:** IV44 8RN

### Viewpoint 5 – Loch Meadal
**Small area to park at cattle grid**

- **Lat/Long:** 57.130692, -5.8707889
- **what3words:** ///applauded.plotting.siesta
- **Grid Ref:** NG658110
- **Postcode:** IV44 8RR

### Accessibility

All these locations are easily accessible from the roadside, but some require walking on bouldery beaches.

### Best time of year/day

With the views to the Cuillin forming such a key part of these views, the best time to go is a clear day with good visibility. Being generally west facing they are all good locations for sunset. However, sunrise and winter mornings when the low sun hits the Cuillin can be equally as good. If you are lucky enough to have snow on the Cuillin then even better. In summer time, this area can be quite busy and the road is not so enjoyable to drive.

***Opposite top**: looking across to a snow-capped Cuillin from Tokavaig (VP3), Fujifilm X–T2, 10–24mm f/4, ISO 200, 50s at f/11. Dec. **Bottom**: the ruins of Dunscaith Castle from Tokavaig beach (VP3) Fujifilm X–T2, 10–24mm f/4, ISO 200, 55s at f/11. Dec.*

*Looking across to Suisnish from Ord (VP4). Fujifilm X–E3, 55–200mm f/3.5–f/4.8, ISO 200, 1/200s at f/11. Oct.*

## Viewpoint 4 – Ord

Next up is the small bay at the village of Ord. A rocky shore with interesting skerries, it has its charms but is possibly not as varied as the beach at Tokavaig. However, it is still worth a visit and with a telephoto lens it is possible to pick out the clearance village at Suisnish, across Loch Eishort with the forlorn sight of a rusting red roof under the glowering bulk of Blà Bheinn all that remains.

*Right above: the Cuillin viewed from Ord. Fujifilm X–T2, 18–55mm f/2.8–f/4, ISO 200, 1/640s at f/8. Oct. Below: rocky beach at Ord. Fujifilm X–T2, 18–55mm f/2.8–f/4, ISO 200, 1/300s at f/8. Oct.*

*Across Loch Meadal to Blà Bheinn (VP5). Fujifilm X–E3, 55–200mm f/3.5–f/4.8, ISO 200, 1/140s at f/11. Oct.*

## Viewpoint 5 – Loch Meadal

After the drama of the coast it feels a shame to head back into the interior of Sleat, however, there is still one more viewpoint to take in on this fantastic scenic route. Loch Meadal is a beautiful reed-fringed lochan which offers both the opportunity for abstract studies of the reeds and also a great foreground for the view back to Blà Bheinn.

*Detail of Reeds on Loch Meadal. Fujifilm X–E3, 55–200mm f/3.5–f/4.8, ISO 200, 1/240s at f/11. Oct.*

It is tempting when heading south from Broadford to keep on going to the photographers Shangri-La of Elgol at the end of the road. However, that would mean missing out on some of the most delightful landscapes in Skye. From isolated stands of gnarled old birch trees and reed fringed lochans to views of the towering Blà Bheinn, this location has plenty to occupy the landscape photographer and deserves to be a destination in its own right.

## What to shoot and viewpoints

### Viewpoint 1 – Cill Chriosd

The peaceful Strath Suardal used to support a thriving population and Cill Chriosd (Christ's Church) was the focal point for a large community which included the villages of Boreraig and Suisnish to the south. It was also the heart of Skye Marble industry with evidence of quarrying found from as early as 1707. The industry peaked in the early 20th Century with a railway line built to transport the quarried marble to Broadford, the route of which can be walked today. Very little of the original industry is evident these days although there is a large marble quarry which can be glimpsed to the left on the approach to Torrin. The church itself sits on small rise adjacent to the road and it is easy to see why it was chosen, sitting as it does against a backdrop of majestic mountains with sweeping views along the Strath. The ruined church makes a fine subject to be silhouetted against a sunrise sky. >>

### How to get here

From Broadford take the B8083 which is signposted to Elgol. After 5 minutes Cill Chriosd is reached; there is parking on the left hand side of the road adjacent to the church. From here you can explore the church and the loch itself which is just a short stroll along the road. Continue on the B8083 through Torrin to reach the shore of Loch Slapin, where there is a parking area on the loch side.

### Viewpoint 1 – Cill Chriosd & Viewpoint 2 – Loch Cill Chriosd

| | |
|---|---|
| **P Lat/Long**: | 57.214582, -5.9479675 |
| **P what3words**: | ///arriving.ranted.scrolled |
| **P Grid Ref**: | NG617206 |
| **P Postcode**: | IV49 9AS |

*Above: stunted birch trees on a small hill alongside the road in Strath Suardal. Fujifilm X–T2, 10–24mm f/4, ISO 200, 1/9s at f/8. Dec.*

## Viewpoint 3 – Loch Slapin

- **P Lat/Long**: 57.217836 , -6.0236056
- **P what3words**: ///culling.prefect.hops
- **P Grid Ref**: NG571212
- **P Postcode**: IV49 9BA

### Accessibility

All these locations are easily accessible from the roadside. You may want to wear wellies if you are getting in amongst the reeds at Loch Cill Chriosd.

### Best time of year/day

A dusting of snow always heightens the drama of the hills but these locations offer something at all times of the year. Loch Cill Chriosd is best at dawn in late autumn / early winter when the reeds have yellowed. The shore at Loch Slapin is also best photographed at dawn and a higher tide also suits the scene better than low tide when a large area of stony shore can be a bit featureless. On a still day, the reflections on Loch Slapin can also be very appealing.

*Looking over Loch Cill Chriosd to a snowy Blà Bheinn (VP2).*
*Fujifilm X–T2, 10–24mm f/4, ISO 200, 1/40s at f/8. Dec.*

## Viewpoint 2 – Loch Cill Chriosd

Loch Cill Chriosd is an absolute gem. Known locally as
'The Hairy Loch' for its reedy appearance it provides an
excellent reflecting pool for the mountain Beinn Na Caillich
which rises on the opposite shore. There is plenty to occupy
the photographer here, and as the road runs along the side
of the loch it is no hardship to stroll along and find your
ideal composition. Towards the western end of the loch,
the mighty Blà Bheinn comes into view, its rocky face
providing a fantastic contrast to the lush vegetation and
smooth sided hills surrounding the loch. The loch also
provides scope for compelling detail studies of the reeds
themselves. At the far western end, beyond the loch are
some fascinating stands of straggly birch trees perched
on a small rise. These survivors make a great subject,
either individually or as a group.

*The shoreline of Loch Slapin northwest of Torrin (VP3). Fujifilm X–T2, 10–24mm f/4, ISO 200, 1/170s at f/8. Dec.*

*A house nestles below the snow-covered face of Blà Bheinn. Fujifilm X–T2, 55–200mm f/3.5–f/4.8, ISO 200, 1/250s at f/8. Dec.*

## Viewpoint 3 – Loch Slapin

As you pass through Torrin the road drops down to the shore of Loch Slapin and an incredible vista opens up. The full length of Blà Bheinn forms the backdrop to one of the finest views on Skye. The rocky shore offers some interesting foreground options where it meets the grass, and a single whitewashed cottage on the far shore lends a sense of scale, nestled in below the bulk of the mountain. The steep face of Blà Bheinn is fantastic with a dusting of snow upon it, which highlights the cracks and gullies offering good scope for some studies with a telephoto lens.

*Opposite middle left*: *abstract of reeds in Loch Cill Chriosd (VP2). Fujifilm X–T2, 55–200mm f/3.5–f/4.8, ISO 200, 1/125s at f/4.2. Dec.* **Right**: *Loch Cill Chriosd reflections. Fujifilm X–T2, 55–200mm f/3.5–f/4.8, ISO 200, 1/280s at f/3.5. Dec.* **Bottom**: *Beinn Na Caillich and Loch Cill Chriosd. Fujifilm X–T2, 18–55mm f/2.8–f/4, ISO 200, 1/180s at f/11. Mar.*

On an island where the Cuillin loom large on the skyline from many locations, it is perhaps at Elgol that you are granted their finest aspect. Across the loch from the small fishing village at the end of the winding road the Cuillin can be appreciated in all their dark, foreboding glory. Rising straight from the sea, the jagged crenelated ridge forms one of the most dramatic landscape in the UK and the coast around Elgol provides the perfect foreground for this epic view.

In recent years the popularity of Elgol as a photographic destination has reached fever-pitch with lines of tripods found along the shoreline at popular times. Don't let that put you off though, there are still great opportunities to find original compositions without the need to slavishly replicate those of photographic masters.

## What to shoot and viewpoints

### Viewpoint 1 – The beach

For most photographers the beach at Elgol is the main focus. The bouldery beach itself can be a good spot at high tide, but most photographers make a bee-line for the rocky shore at the headland to the north. Here there are numerous compositions to be found, regardless of the level of the tide with wave sculpted rocks, platforms and boulders all providing bounteous foreground options for the view. A large honeycombed wall makes a fascinating subject in its own right and you could spend a long time here photographing the weathered textures of its pebble-studded face. The classic image at Elgol usually takes in the whole Cuillin range, however, there are powerful compositions to picked up with a telephoto lens, with the compression effect really pulling the viewer into the Mordor-esque landscape of shattered peaks and steep sided chaos. »

## How to get here

From Broadford take the B8083 which is signposted to Elgol. Whilst only 14 miles from Broadford, the single track will likely take 40 minutes to drive. There is plentiful car parking in the village of Elgol. For the 3.2km/2 miles walk to Camasunary, park in the car park beyond Kilmarie and take the signposted track on the opposite side of the road. This route gradually climbs up to the pass of Am Màm before descending to Camasunary.

## Viewpoint 1 – The beach, Viewpoint 2 – The pier & Viewpoint 4 – Camasunary

| | |
|---|---|
| **Lat/Long**: | 57.145539, -6.1072306 |
| **what3words**: | ///regular.speeded.executive |
| **Grid Ref**: | NG516135 |
| **Postcode**: | IV49 9BJ |

## Accessibility

The bouldery shore can be slippery at high tide and the rock platforms to the north will require a bit of boulder-hopping. As always at coast, beware of freak waves, particularly at high tide. The cliff top route is generally fine, but some routes down to the shore are trickier than other so use your judgement as to which looks the safest.

## Best time of year/day

Elgol is a classic sunset location, but also works well at sunrise. As the outlook to the Cuillin is the main element it is best to visit on a day where there is decent visibility although changeable conditions work well with swirling clouds, passing showers or fleeting light lending even more drama to the scene. There are countless foreground options regardless of the level of the tide. In the summer months it will be very busy with photographers.

*Opposite: a flash of light amongst the gloom of the Cuillin (VP1). Fujifilm X–T2, 55–200mm f/3.5–f/4.8, ISO 200, 1/480s at f/3.5. Sep.*

*Top: the Cuillin from the beach at Elgol (VP1). Fujifilm X–T2, 18–55mm f/2.8–f/4, ISO 200, 12s at f/11. Sep. Middle: the famous Joe Cornish boulder at the far end of the beach. Fujifilm X–T2, 10–24mm f/4, ISO 200, 480s at f/11. Dec. Bottom left: textures in the cliff beside the beach. Fujifilm X–T2, 18–55mm f/2.8–f/4, ISO 200, 1/120s at f/11. Oct. Bottom right: well balanced stones. Fujifilm X–T2, 18–55mm f/2.8–f/4, ISO 200, 1/160s at f/11. Oct.*

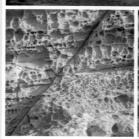

*Stormy sunlight illuminating the flanks of Gars-bheinn from the pier at Elgol (VP2).*
*Fujifilm X–T2, 55–200mm f/3.5–f/4.8, ISO 200, 1/210s at f/5.6. Apr.*

*An idyllic house on the road down to the pier in Elgol. Fujifilm X–T2, 55–200mm f/3.5–f/4.8, ISO 200, 1/90s at f/5.6. Apr.*

***Above***: *the Cuillin at dawn from Elgol Pier (VP2). Fujifilm X–T2, 55–200mm f/3.5–f/4.8, ISO 200, 1/60s at f/5.6. Apr.* ***Below left***: *the bouldery beach beside the school. Fujifilm X–T2, 10–24mm f/4, ISO 200, 480s at f/11. Apr.* ***Below right***: *a textured foreground gives a good lead-in line, Fujifilm X–T2, 10–24mm f/4, ISO 200, 10s at f/9. Apr.*

*A stormy sunset at Elgol Pier (VP2), Fujifilm X–T2, 10–24mm f/4, ISO 200, 20s at f/8. Apr.*

### Viewpoint 2 – The pier ♿

For all the natural elements which provide foreground interest, it is also worth considering the pier itself. The hard, geometric form reaches out into the loch, and provides a nice contrast to the chaotic jumble of peaks across the water. This works particularly well as a long exposure, with the blurred water and clouds providing a softness to the image offset against the hard concrete of the pier, and the even harder gabbro of the Cuillin.

### Viewpoint 3 – The cliffs to the south

If you are seeking a bit of solitude, want something a bit more unique from this location or are just tired of tripping over tripod legs, head south from the upper tier of the car park where a rough path gives access to less visited area. It is possible to descend to the beach after a hundred or so metres via a break in the cliffs where the bouldery shore provides some interesting foreground options. Alternatively stay up on the cliffs and eventually the Isle of Rum appears on the horizon to the southwest with the edge.

### Viewpoint 4 – Camasunary

A 3.2km/2 miles walk. Glimpsed from the beach at Elgol, the house at Camasunary looks a lonely old spot against the dark peaks. Together with the new bothy which tends to blend into backdrop in the view from Elgol, these two buildings sit in a lovely location with a sandy beach backed by pasture. There are some great options from the beach, but the most powerful composition is from the the west of Am Màm where a good view of Sgùrr na Stri and the Cuillin can be found.

*__Opposite top left__: a rainbow between Elgol and Blà Bheinn, Fujifilm X–T2, 55–200mm f/3.5–f/4.8, ISO 200, 1/200s at f/11. Apr. __Middle left__: sea pinks in the rocks, Fujifilm X–E1, 18–55mm f/2.8–f/4, ISO 200. 1/420s at f/5.6. Jun. __Top right__: the view south to Rum (VP3). Fujifilm X–E1, 18–55mm f/2.8–f/4, ISO 200, 1/60s at f/11. Jun. __Bottom__: a glimpse into Camasunary Bay from Elgol (VP4). Fujifilm X–T2, 55–200mm f/3.5–f/4.8, ISO 200, 1/320s at f/11. Sep.*

From ancient mythological warriors to the painter J.M.W Turner, to modern day mountain bikers and photographers, Loch Coruisk and the peak of Sgùrr na Stri hold a magnetic appeal. The loch is hidden away in the centre of the Cuillin Hills, encircled by the serrated peaks of that ancient volcano, an epic place of myth and legend. Sgùrr na Stri is the wee brother of the Cuillin, with all the precipitous drops and jagged rock of its bigger siblings just scaled down into a slightly more manageable 494m. It rises to the east of the loch and provides what is undoubtedly the finest mountain viewpoint in the UK.

## Getting to Loch Coruisk

There are a number of routes up Sgùrr na Stri, with the most popular being the long walk in from Sligachan or the walk round over the 'Bad Step' from Camasunary. The bad step is a short sea-level scramble over rocks with a drop off (3/4m) into the sea. An alternative, and in my opinion more attractive route, is to go via the boat from Elgol to Loch Coruisk. This allows you to experience the loch and reach the summit of Sgùrr na Stri, with a bit less effort ensuring you still have enough energy to make images.

The boat trip from Elgol is a great experience and really whets your appetite for the day ahead, with the guides providing some excellent tales of ancient mythology as well as pointing out all the main sights. As you sail across the water and into Loch na Cuilce the hills gain prominence in the view with what appears to be an impassable wall of rock straight ahead. The steep slopes of Gars Bheinn on the left and Sgùrr na Stri enclose you in a cirque of rocky peaks which will have you craning your neck to see the tops. Seals lie basking on the rocks and on a rocky outcrop a small set of steps leads you from the boats and onto land.

You are now deep in the heart of The Cuillin.

## What to shoot and viewpoints

### Route up Sgùrr na Stri
8km/5miles round trip with 495m/1600ft of elevation gain. 4/5 hours round trip.

The path up to the loch roughly follows the line of the Scavaig River, said to be the shortest river in Britain, as it winds its way from Loch Coruisk and rushes into the sea. Loch Coruisk is soon revealed, a finger of water stretching into the Cuillin, wild and untamed, loomed over by towering hills. The walk around its shores gets you closer to these fine mountains and the views from the southern end of the loch where it flows into the Scavaig River are fantastic, albeit slightly tricky to give a sense of scale. If you are lucky to visit on a calm day the peaks will be reflected in the loch. However, be on your guard as according to legend, a Kelpie (a mythical Scottish water spirit) lives in Loch Coruisk. Once in the water, the Kelpie drags its victims down to their deaths and even a great photo isn't worth that risk.

From the loch itself, cross the Scavaig River via the stepping stones and pick up the faint and very boggy path which heads north along the eastern shore of the loch. As you reach the waterfalls turn away from the loch and head northeast along the southern side of the Allt a' Choire Riabhach. Follow this until Loch a' Choire Riabhach is visible ahead then turn southeast, ascending the broad ridge of Sgùrr na Stri. The path is vague and intermittent, but the route up is fairly obvious and it's best to pick your way up across the rocky slabs as the black gabbro rock provides great friction. There are numerous interesting spots to stop at on the way up as the views open up, including a large flat platform of rock with small boulders strewn across it like the aftermath of a particularly fractious game of bowls between two giants.

You may also come across some of the scattered wreckage of the USAF F111 plane which crashed on the hill in the winter of 1982. On a training exercise from RAF Lakenheath, despite having terrain-following radar the F111 flew straight into a rock face on Sgùrr na Stri. The pilot Major Burnley L Rudiger (37) from Norfolk, Virginia and the Weapons systems operator 1st Lt Steven J Pitt (28), from East Aurora, New York both perished in the crash. »

**Plan and navigate using OS Explorer 411: Map of Skye – Cuillin Hills 1:25 000**
**BE PREPARED FOR BAD WEATHER, AND IN WINTER, SNOW AND ICE.**

Loch a' Choire
Riabhach

Loch na
Crèitheach

*Sgùrr Hain*
*420m*

Allt a' Choire
Riabhach

Loch
Coruisk

**Captain
Maryon's
▲ Cairn**

The path is vague and intermittent,
but the route up is fairly obvious
and it's best to pick your way up
across the rocky slabs as the
black gabbro rock provides great friction.

**Dubh Ridge
Slabs**
A moderately graded rock climb
that Danny MacAskill rode
down on his mountain bike.

route down to
Camasunary

*Meall
na Cuilce
183m* △

Junior Mountaineering
Club of Scotland
**Coruisk
Memorial Hut**

**The UK's finest
mountain view**
*Sgùrr na Stri*
△ *495m*

Ilt a' Chaoich

can be impassable
after heavy rain

**Stepping
Stones**

Viewpoints of the Cuillin
Ridge down to Loch
Coruisk and out to sea

**Landing
Stage** ▪

*Scavaig
River*

**The
Bad Step**
scramble over
sea level
rocks with drop off

▲ **F111
crash site**

3.2km from the landing stage
with 495m of ascent.
Allow 2hrs plus for your ascent
depending on fitness.

**Camasunar
Bothy**

*Eilean Glas*

*Loch
na Cuilce*

*Loch
nan Leachd*

*Camas
Fhionnairigh*

*Elgol*

*LOCH
SCAVAIG*

from Elgol

**N**

0        miles        0.5

*Walkers crossing the stepping stones at the outflow of Loch Coruisk.*
*Fujifilm X–T2, 10–24mm f/4, ISO 200, 1/180s at f/8. Apr.*

*The Scavaig River plunging into the sea. Fujifilm X–T2, 10–24mm*
*f/4, ISO 200, 1/600s at f/8. Apr.*

*Aboard the Misty Isle en-route to Loch Coruisk, Fujifilm X–T2, 10–24mm f/4, ISO 200, 1/210s at f/8. Apr.*

**Top left**: *seals bask on the rocks of Eilean Glas. Fujifilm X–T2, 55–200mm f/3.5–f/4.8, ISO 200, 1/280s at f/6.4. Apr.*
**Left**: *Coruisk Memorial Hut, Fujifilm X–T2, 10–24mm f/4, ISO 200, 1/600s at f/8. Apr.*

**Opposite**: *Allt a' Chaoich (The Mad Burn) flowing down to Loch Scavaig. Fujifilm X–T2, 10–24mm f/4, ISO 200, 1/250 at f/8. Apr.*

## How to get here

From Broadford take the B8083 which is signposted to Elgol. Whilst only 14 miles from Broadford, the single track will likely take 40 minutes to drive. There is plentiful car parking in the village of Elgol. The route described here is via the boat from Elgol. There are two tour companies; The Misty Isle and Bella Jane, both offering a variety of tours at different times of the day. If you are intending to climb Sgùrr na Stri you will need to leave on the first boat in the morning and return on the last boat in the afternoon to give you enough time. From the landing stage allow 2 hours to reach the summit and 1 to 2 hours for the descent, as well as time for photography.

**The Misty Isle**: *mistyisleboattrips.co.uk* • 01471 866 288
**Bella Jane**: *bellajane.co.uk* • 01471 866 244

### Elgol

| | | |
|---|---|---|
| Ⓟ **Lat/Long**: | 57.145539, -6.1072306 |
| Ⓟ **what3words**: | ///regular.speeded.executive |
| Ⓟ **Grid Ref**: | NG516135 |
| Ⓟ **Postcode**: | IV49 9BJ |

### Map

OS Landranger Map 32 (1:50 000) South Skye & Cuillin Hills

## Accessibility

There are steep steps at the landing stage when disembarking the boat and the ground and paths around the loch can be boggy. Whilst relatively small compared to the surrounding hills Sgùrr na Stri is no simple undertaking. It is steep, rocky, boggy, pathless in parts and requires a good level of hill fitness. This route also necessitates crossing the Scavaig River either via stepping stones or wading across, it is worth checking with the boat operators prior to your trip as they can advise on the current level of the water. A map and compass, and the ability to use them is a must. Do not take this walk lightly, it is a steep hill with large drops on all sides and route finding can be tricky, particularly in poor visibility.

You will be isolated, in a remote location and with sporadic phone signal at best. In winter, only experienced mountaineers should attempt it.

## Best time of year/day

To see the full majesty of the Cuillin ridge from Sgùrr na Stri you will require a clear day, however visitors to Skye will know that a clear sky will not always coincide with your trip. However, even on a grey day there will still be opportunities, particularly around Loch Coruisk, which can look very mysterious with a bit of low cloud and mist. The boat trips generally run from April to October, but booking is advisable before you set off.

The glorious Loch Coruisk. Fujifilm X-T2, 10–24mm f/4, ISO 200, 1/400s at f/8, Apr

*Panorama looking south from the summit of Sgùrr na Stri. Fujifilm X–T2, 10–24mm f/4, ISO 200, 1/5000s at f/8. Apr.*

## The views

As height is gained and the ridge narrows you will get a clear view of Blà Bheinn in the east and on the western side gain what feels like an aerial view of Loch na Cuilce and Loch nan Leachd. The boats from Elgol look like children's bath-time toys on the bright blue water. However, it is the view north-west towards Loch Coruisk and the Cuillin that really grabs the attention. It is difficult to take in the sheer awesome splendour of the view and you find your eye bouncing along the ridge, taking in the serrated peaks and vertiginous slopes. It really is a sublime viewpoint. There are numerous spots to compose images all along the western side of the ridge so it's just a case of taking your time to explore. Wherever you choose, you will definitely need to use an ultra wide angle lens or shoot a panorama to take in the vastness of the full view. Alternatively there are great opportunities with a telephoto lens to pick out the individual peaks of the Cuillin and you may even spot a climber edging their way up the

Inaccessible Pinnacle (the only Munro which requires actual rock climbing to reach the top). From the summit the view from east to south to west takes in the mainland mountains, the Ardnamurchan peninsula, Mull, distant Iona, Eigg, Muck, Rum and Canna; it is quite the panorama.

*Top left: waterspout on the way up Sgùrr na Stri, Fujifilm X–T2, 10–24mm f/4, ISO 200, 1/40s at f/8. Apr. Middle: remains of the USAF F111 plane, Fujifilm X–T2, 10–24mm f/4, ISO 200, 1/75s at f/8. Apr. Right: an ideal shelter on a wet day on the main ridge of Sgùrr na Stri, Fujifilm X–T2, 10–24mm f/4, ISO 200, 1/300s at f/8. Apr.*

*Opposite: looking across to Gars-Bheinn from the summit of Sgùrr na Stri, Fujifilm X–T2, 10–24mm f/4, ISO 200, 1/400s at f/8. Apr.*

*Next spread: looking straight down from the top to the crystal blue waters of Loch na Leachd, Fujifilm X–T2, 55–200mm f/3.5–f/4.8, ISO 200, 1/320s at f/5.6. Apr.*

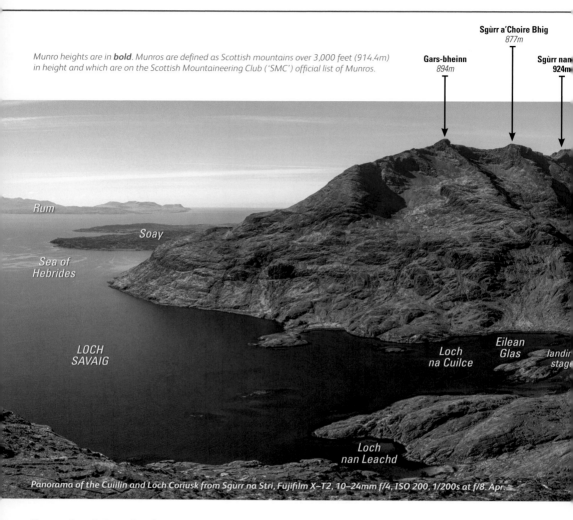

*Munro heights are in **bold**. Munros are defined as Scottish mountains over 3,000 feet (914.4m) in height and which are on the Scottish Mountaineering Club ('SMC') official list of Munros.*

Sgùrr a'Choire Bhig
877m

**Gars-bheinn**
*894m*

**Sgùrr nan**
**924m**

Rum

Soay

Sea of
Hebrides

LOCH
SAVAIG

Loch
na Cuilce

Eilean
Glas

landir
stage

Loch
nan Leachd

*Panorama of the Cuillin and Loch Coriusk from Sgùrr na Stri, Fujifilm X–T2, 10–24mm f/4, ISO 200, 1/200s at f/8. Apr.*

The view from Sgùrr na Stri of the Cuillin Ridge is considered by many to be one of Scotland's finest mountain views. The Cuillin Ridge, also known as the Skye Ridge, is formed by the peaks of the Black Cuillin, 11km/7.5 miles of jagged black gabbro and it is one of the finest mountaineering challenges in Europe. The ridge consists of 17 separate peaks, 11 of them Munros with Sgùrr Alasdair being the tallest at 992m/3254ft. It is a true ridge with exciting exposure for most of the way with steep drops, cliffs and scree slopes. Most of the peaks require scrambling to summit using hands and feet with an ascent of the Inaccessible Pinnacle usually requiring a rope, it is graded

'moderate' in rock climbing difficulty. It is usual to start early from Glen Brittle with a steep ascent then you follow the ridge all the way then down to the bar of the Sligachan Hotel. Mere mortals usually take close to 20 hours to complete the traverse, and some do it over two days. The current record stands at an incredible 2hrs 59mins 22 secs set by Finlay Wild in 2013. In winter, if covered in snow and ice, it is a serious alpine mountaineering challenge.

The ridge was formed from the remains of magma chambers which fed volcanic eruptions which were then eroded by glaciers, water, wind and freeze-thaw action,

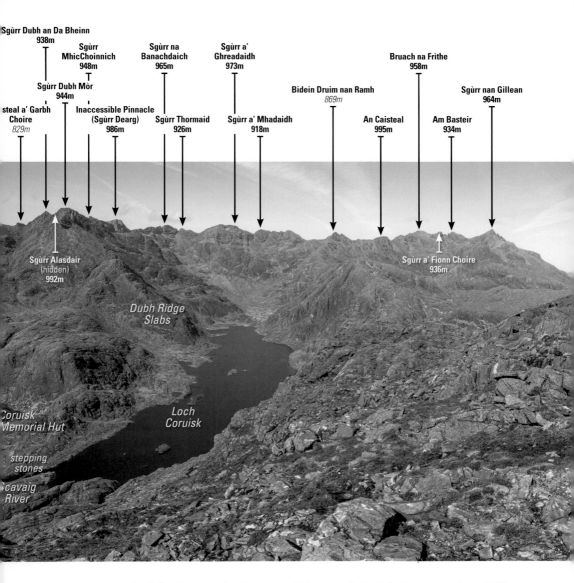

Sgùrr Dubh an Da Bheinn
938m

Sgùrr
MhicChoinnich
948m

Sgùrr Dubh Mòr
944m

Sgùrr na
Banachdaich
965m

Sgùrr a'
Ghreadaidh
973m

Bruach na Frithe
958m

steal a' Garbh
Choire
829m

Inaccessible Pinnacle
(Sgùrr Dearg)
986m

Sgùrr Thormaid
926m

Sgùrr a' Mhadaidh
918m

Bidein Druim nan Ramh
869m

An Caisteal
995m

Am Basteir
934m

Sgùrr nan Gillean
964m

Sgùrr Alasdair
(hidden)
992m

Sgùrr a' Fionn Choire
936m

Dubh Ridge
Slabs

Loch
Coruisk

Coruisk
Memorial Hut

stepping
stones

Scavaig
River

the area is a classic example of glacial topography. There is very little vegetation on the ridge itself, small pockets of alpine flowers such as alpine rock-cress are found, below the ridge the lower slopes are composed of bog, rough grassland and heather moorland The ridge is home to both both golden and white-tailed eagles, and is considered one of the best places to spot them, the area is known as Tir Nan Iolaire (Land of Eagles). The whole area is designated as the Cuillin Hills National Scenic Area.

There are a couple of theories about the etymology of Cuillin, it may be derived from the Old Norse word *kjölen*,

which means the keel of a boat or an upturned Viking longship or from Gaelic *cuilionn*, meaning 'holly', because of the mountains' jagged shape.

The walk up from Loch Coruisk to the summit of Sgùrr na Stri, whilst arduous, is relatively straightforward in the summer or in good weather. If the weather is bad, or you attempt the ascent in winter, make sure you are well-prepared and have some basic mountaineering and navigation skills.

*Looking into the heart of the Cuillin from Sgurr na Stri. Fujifilm X–T2, 10–24mm f/4, ISO 200, 1/280s at f/11. Apr.*

*Above left*: *looking towards Loch Coruisk from the ridge. Fujifilm X–T2, 10–24mm f/4, ISO 200, 1/400s at f/8. Apr.* **Right**: *the Inaccessible Pinnacle on Sgurr Dearg. Fujifilm X–T2, 55–200mm f/3.5–f/4.8, ISO 200, 1/950s at f/5.6. Apr.*

*A distant glimpse of The Old Man of Storr. Fujifilm X–T2, 55–200mm f/3.5–f/4.8, ISO 200, 1/1000s at f/5.6. Apr.*

*Above*: a view along Loch Coruisk from the start of the walk up Sgùrr na Stri. Fujifilm X–T2, 10–24mm f/4, ISO 200, 1/400s at f/8. Apr.
*Below*: a rock-strewn platform on the ridge. Fujifilm X–T2, 10–24mm f/4, ISO 200, 1/250s at f/10. Apr.

For many walkers and climbers Sligachan is the epicentre of Skye. Long walks and hair-raising climbs into the foreboding Cuillin hills start from this small village with its excellent hotel, pub and campsite. It is a location which will inspire all who visit whether you venture into the Cuillin or simply want to view the peaks from the roadside. On approaching Sligachan, it will be your first chance to see the magnificent mountains of Sgùrr nam Gillean and Am Basteir up close. With their jagged peaks often shrouded with clouds, it is a dramatic location and can be appreciated from both the roadside and from the rugged landscape along the rivers which flow from the hills. It is also home to an unfathomable number of midges, so it may be a place to avoid in summer if you are especially midge-phobic.

## What to shoot and viewpoints

### Viewpoint 1 – Collie and Mackenzie Statue ♿

Professor Norman Collie from Alderley Edge in Cheshire and John Mackenzie of Skye were the two pioneers of climbing in in the Cuillin, venturing up routes which nobody had previously attempted. Clad in tweed and hobnail boots, they headed into unknown territory in what is the most difficult terrain in Britain. Despite coming from very different backgrounds (Collie a chemist and MacKenzie a crofter) they formed a great friendship, climbing together throughout their lives. In 2020 a bronze statue in their honour was unveiled at Sligachan. It is an excellent sculpture and can be worked into numerous compositions, with the two men silhouetted against the surrounding peaks. »

## How to get here

Sligachan is located on the A87 road, midway between Broadford and Portree. There is a parking area on the left when approaching from the south.

### Parking for all three viewpoints

| | | |
|---|---|---|
| 📍 Lat/Long: | 57.290442, -6.1709750 |
| 📍 what3words: | ///cherished.park.sailing |
| 📍 Grid Ref: | NG487299 |
| 📍 Postcode: | IV47 8SW |

### Accessibility

Access is relatively simple, with well trodden paths leading towards the Cuillin which can be occasionally muddy. There is a gravel path up to the statue. The view of the old bridge is road side, however, be aware of photographing from the new bridge as the pavement is narrow and the road can be very busy. Venturing further into the Cuillin can be a little bit more difficult …

## Best time of year/day

With the peaks of Sgùrr nam Gillean and Am Basteir facing north they often hold onto a bit of snow which always heightens the drama but on days of low cloud the area loses the spectacle of the mountain views. Sunrise and sunset can work equally well here with sidelight illuminating the cracks and gullies on the face of the hills. Midges are a problem here in summer, but the trade off with the blooming of the heather (flowers in August) may be enough for you to risk a few bites. The river and the waterfalls look at their best after rainfall, which shouldn't be a problem in Skye.

*Above: cloud swathes the peaks above the Collie and Mackenzie Statue (VP1), Fujifilm X–T2, 55–200mm f/3.5–f/4.8, ISO 200, 1/1000s at f/5.6. Mar.*

*Collie and Mackenzie silhouetted against Marsco.*
*Fujifilm X–T2, 55–200mm f/3.5–f/4.8, ISO 200,*
*1/1700s at f/7.1. Mar.*

*The statue of Collie and Mackenzie. Fujifilm X–T2,*
*55–200mm f/3.5–f/4.8, ISO 200,*
*1/1000s at f/5.6. Mar.*

### Viewpoint 2 – Sligachan Bridge ♿

From the small car park to the east of the new bridge it is just a few metres walk to the old Sligachan bridge. With three graceful arches spanning the River Sligachan it is a popular spot for visitors and in summer you are very unlikely to have it all to yourself. It can be photographed from the new bridge or form either bank, with Sgùrr nam Gillean and Am Basteir prominent in the view from the western side or Marsco and the Red Cuillin from the east.

### Viewpoint 3 – Sligachan Waterfalls

From the western side of the old bridge a path follows the right side of the river uphill in the general direction of the Black Cuillin. Views open up along the river Sligachan with the distinctive profile of Marsco making a fine subject. After a short walk a footbridge is reached. From here you can either cross the bridge and into a boggy area of pools, some of which can form excellent reflective foregrounds for the mountain views. Alternatively you can stay on the path towards Allt Dearg Cottage. On this route there are numerous small waterfalls to explore, which can form the perfect foreground to the peaks of Sgùrr nam Gillean and Am Basteir. »

*Stewart and Jenna on the bridge at sunset (VP2). Fujifilm X–T1, 18–55mm f/2.8–f/4, ISO 200, 2s at f/11. Dec.*

***Opposite top***: *the old Sligachan Bridge. Fujifilm X–T2, 10–24mm f/4, ISO 200, 1/250s at f/8. Mar.*
***Bottom***: *Marsco from the riverside. Fujifilm X–E1, 18–55mm f/2.8–f/4, ISO 200, 1/420s at f/5.6. Jun.*

*The Allt Dearg Cottage and Sgùrr nan Gillean (VP4). Fujifilm X–T2, 10–24mm f/4, ISO 200, 20s at f/8. Dec.*

## Viewpoint 4 – Alt Dearg Cottage

As you progress up the path, the Allt Dearg Cottage, with its whitewashed walls providing a lovely pop of contrast to the black hills beyond appears in the mid-ground. It makes a fine subject and can be combined in a nice composition together with the upper waterfalls. It is holiday house, so please give the residents privacy; it is best photographed from a distance anyway.

*Lochan reflecting Sgùrr nan Gillean (VP4). Fujifilm X–T2, 10–24mm f/4, ISO 200, 1/350s at f/8. Apr.*

***Opposite top**: Sgùrr nan Gillean from the waterfalls (VP3). Fujifilm X–T1, 18–55mm f/2.8–f/4, ISO 200, 2s at f/11. Dec.*

Glen Brittle plays host to three very different viewpoints, all of which have plenty for the landscape photographer to appreciate. Most only venture as far as the Fairy Pools, which are without doubt the star of the show, but the dramatic waterfall Eas Mòr and the beach at Glenbrittle are also great destinations in their own right. Unlike many locations around the Cuillin, these viewpoints can also be enjoyed when the peaks are shrouded with cloud with the intricacy of the waterscape making up for the lack of mountain top views. In summer the clear blue pools at are particularly tempting, and you may wish to cool off with a quick dip after a hard days landscape photography.

## What to shoot and viewpoints

### Viewpoint 1 – The Fairy Pools

The Fairy Pools is the name given to the numerous waterfalls which are formed by the Allt Coir' a Mhadaidh and the Allt Coir' a' Tairneilèar which flows down through Coire na Creiche from the Cuillin. They are an incredibly popular destination and over the last decade the path which follows the bank on the left hand side has become an ugly wide scar and parking at the roadside has become very problematic, with inconsiderate visitors parking on the verges and blocking the road. Although it is still very busy, the new car park (pay and display) has made a huge difference. Now the negatives are out the way; the Fairy Pools are a stunning. A series of of fantastic crystal clear plunge pools, water cut channels, tight gorges and spouts all backdropped by the Cuillin. Long exposures and a polarising filter can be used here to great effect. From the car park the path descends down and after a short walk uphill the first falls come into view. If the water level is low you can generally find spots to hop over to the other bank, however, most of the opportunities are on the left hand side (looking upstream). Although after heavy rain (a common occurrence) the falls become a raging torrent and crossing is not recommended. After heading uphill the dramatic gorges and pools diminish in size and attractiveness and the path veers away from the falls, it is worth continuing on as the path does return to the waterside and it is from this upper level that a great

## How to get here

From Sligachan take the A683 for 5.2 miles and turn left onto the B8009. Continue to the turnoff for Carbost and take the minor road on the left. Follow this road for 4 miles until there is a good parking area on the right. It is pay and display and in summer it fills up quickly. Don't be tempted to park on the verge or in any passing places, as this has become a huge problem at this popular location. Eas Mòr is a kilometre to the south and there is a parking area for a couple of cars on the left hand side of the road opposite the Glen Brittle Hut. The beach is located another kilometre further on, there is a parking area on the right just before the campsite.

### Viewpoint 1 – The Fairy Pools

| | | |
|---|---|---|
| P Lat/Long: | 57.249503, -6.2736879 |
| P what3words: | ///thus.playroom.symphonic |
| P Grid Ref: | NG423257 |
| P Postcode: | IV47 8SG |

### Viewpoint 2 – Eas Mòr

| | | |
|---|---|---|
| P Lat/Long: | 57.211856, -6.2882537 |
| P what3words: | ///revealing.vibe.youth |
| P Grid Ref: | NG411216 |
| P Postcode: | IV47 8TA |

### Viewpoint 3 – Glenbrittle Beach

| | | |
|---|---|---|
| P Lat/Long: | 57.203409 , -6.2920139 |
| P what3words: | ///equipping.backers.guides |
| P Grid Ref: | NG408206 |
| P Postcode: | – |

## Accessibility

The path alongside the Fairy Pools is badly eroded and can be very muddy after heavy rainfall. There are steep drops and slippery rocks beside the stream and care should be taken particularly when you are preoccupied with finding a great shot. Some of the pools are best photographed from the water itself so a pair of wellies might be a good bet. Eas Mòr is reached via a steep but generally good grass path and should present no real difficulties, the route into the gorge is not recommended. Glen Brittle beach is road side.

## Best time of year/day

The Fairy Pools can be photographed well at any time and you can easily lose hours at this varied location. Under overcast conditions the fantastic colours of the bedrock comes to the fore and whilst you lose the views of the peaks, sometimes the mist can heighten the atmosphere. The Coire faces roughy west so does pick up the sun later in the day. Your main issue will be finding a way to photograph the falls without visitors in shot, as this location is incredibly popular in summer. The best bet is to visit late in the day or save the falls for the winter when they can look especially good against the snowy peaks. Eas Mòr is great in the autumn and winter as in summer the foliage can obscure the waterfall from the lower viewpoint. The beach at Glen Brittle is worth a visit at anytime.

*Coire na Creiche from the upper level of the falls (VP1). Fujifilm X–T1, 18–55mm f/2.8–f/4, ISO 200, 45s at f/11. Sep.*

view of the great bowl of Coire na Creiche. This is an especially popular spot for photographers, so you may find yourself sharing the pool with others. A low waterfall perfectly frames the great prow of Sgurr an Fheadain with its distinctive Waterpipe Gully cut across its face. Throughout the Fairy Pools there are options for both intimate studies of the water smoothed rocks, and wider landscapes with the waterfalls as the perfect foreground and it is a pleasure to really explore this fascinating landscape. »

*The water cascades through numerous canyons (VP1). Fujifilm X–E1, 18–55mm f/2.8–f/4, ISO 200, 1.6s at f/11. Aug.*

*A Rowan overhangs one of the pools (VP1). Fujifilm X–T1, 18–55mm f/2.8–f/4, ISO 200, 2s at f/11. Sep.*

## Viewpoint 2 – Eas Mòr

Little visited in comparison to the Fairy Pools, the waterfall Eas Mòr is definitely worth some of your time. From the Glenbrittle Hut a faint path ascends the hillside to the east. On passing some gorse bushes a footbridge comes into view, cross the bridge and make your way uphill and the waterfall is revealed. A single graceful waterfall flows into a dark pool surrounded by a tree clad gorge all backdropped by the flanks of Sgùrr na Banachdaich. Anywhere else on Skye it would be busy with visitors, but most stay at the Fairy Pools. There are a few obvious spots for the composition, and a narrow slippery path also descends into the gorge but this is not recommended.

## Viewpoint 3 – Glenbrittle Beach

At the end of Glenbrittle the beach itself is worth a visit. A wide expanse of two-tone sand provides opportunities for abstract studies particularly alongside the River Brittle as it makes its way to the sea. The Cuillin are a strong presence to the east, but it is difficult to work the hillsides into a satisfying composition. The best long views are out to sea where Rum and Canna lie tantalisingly on the horizon.

*A pale tree provides a nice counterpoint to Eas Mòr (VP2). Fujifilm X–T2, 10–24mm f/4, ISO 200, 1s at f/8. Dec.*

***Top**: a glimpse of light on the hillside from the road. Fujifilm X–E1, 18–55mm f/2.8–f/4, ISO 200, 1.6s at f/11. Aug.*

*Above*: Eas Mòr and Sgùrr na Banachdaich. Fujifilm X–T2, 10–24mm f/4, ISO 200, 1s at f/8. Dec. **Below**: the grey sandy beach at Glenbrittle looking south to Rum and Canna. Fujifilm X–T2, 10–24mm f/4, ISO 350, 1/350s at f/10. Dec.

**If you have driven the narrow road to get to Talisker Bay, in the hope of a dram from the famous distillery of the same name you may be disappointed to find no sign of it. Luckily, the charms of the two-tone sandy beach with its distinctive sea stack more than make up for the shortage of whisky. The distillery is just around the corner at Carbost anyway, so you can always sample later once you have drunk your fill of the views. The bay itself is a dramatic spot, with its sea stack, steep cliffs and black sand offering a number of opportunities in all conditions. Like many of the best photographic locations on Skye, it is very popular in the summer months, and space for parking is at a premium.**

## What to shoot and viewpoints

From the parking area head towards Talisker House on the signposted footpath and continue by the buildings to the shore. This is grazing land so be sure to close all gates and keep dogs on a lead. After a mile, the path terminates at the southern end of the beach. A short walk over the close cropped grass leads to a bouldery foreshore.

At low tide a huge expanse of black and grey sand is revealed, shifted by each tide, and the patterns formed between different colours can form some fascinating abstract studies. As you head across the beach, the distinctive sea stack (made even more famous by the Talisker Whisky branding) reveals itself.

The beach itself is enclosed to the north by very steep cliffs, over which a waterfall cascades. After periods of heavy rain, this feature can be very dramatic and it can form the basis for an image itself. The beach is also bisected by a river which offers a great opportunity for long exposure photography. Get down low amongst the black boulders and the combination of outflowing river and inflowing waves can form some compelling images. The view back upstream towards the distinctive hill of Preshal Mor also provides a different take than the usual view to the sea stack.

*Opposite top: high tide on the beach. Fujifilm X–T1, 18–55mm f/2.8–f/4, ISO 200, 7s at f/11. Sep.*

## How to get here

From the B8009 heading towards Carbost, take the signposted road for Talisker. The narrow road winds its way down to Talisker Bay for 4 miles before ending at a small turning area.

**⚲ Lat/Long**: 57.287606, -6.4383361
**⚲ what3words**: ///airbag.sounding.threading
**⚲ Grid Ref**: NG326306
**⚲ Postcode**: IV47 8SF

## Accessibility

The beach is easily accessed along a good track from Talisker House. The rocky areas of the beach are slippery and beware of the incoming tide if you are exploring the northern end. The main issue with this location is parking; the small turning area provides space for a few cars at the roadside, however, it also forms the access to Talisker House and Talisker Farm. Please be considerate when parking here, do not park on verges or block driveways, gates or any other access points. This is particularly important at popular locations such as this one, where the pressure of increasing numbers of visitors can cause needless conflict with residents. If there are no spaces, come back at another time.

## Best time of year/day

The beach is best visited at low tide, where the black sand is revealed. The location can work at sunset at all times of the year, however, the northern cliffs fall into shadow during summer sunsets. It is an ideal location on days when low cloud shrouds the mountains as there are opportunities to be found here at all times.

*Opposite left: the cliffs and waterfall on the northern side of the bay. Fujifilm X–E3, 55–200mm f/3.5–f/4.8, ISO 200, 1/680s at f/7.1. Mar.*
*Right: looking back inland towards the hill Preshal More. Fujifilm X–E1, 18–55mm f/2.8–f/4, ISO 200, 1/400s at f/11. Jun.*

*A calm day above the beach. Fujifilm X–E1, 18–55mm f/2.8–f/4, ISO 200, 1/170s at f/9. Jun.*

**Opposite top left**: *patterns in the sand, Fujifilm X–E1, 18–55mm f/2.8–f/4, ISO 200, 1/340s at f/8. Jun.*
**Right**: *foxglove by a barn door at Talisker House, Fujifilm X–E1, 18–55mm f/2.8–f/4, ISO 200, 1/100s at f/8. Jun.*
**Middle**: *silhouette of the stack at Talisker Point, Fujifilm X–E3, 55–200mm f/3.5–f/4.8, ISO 200, 1/1000s at f/7.1. Oct.*
**Bottom left**: *agricultural sheds on the way to Talisker with The Cuillin behind, Fujifilm X–E1, 18–55mm f/2.8–f/4, ISO 200, 1/100s at f/11. Jun.* **Right**: *a stormy evening on the beach, Fujifilm X–T2, 0–24mm f/4, ISO 200, 20s at f/11. Oct.*

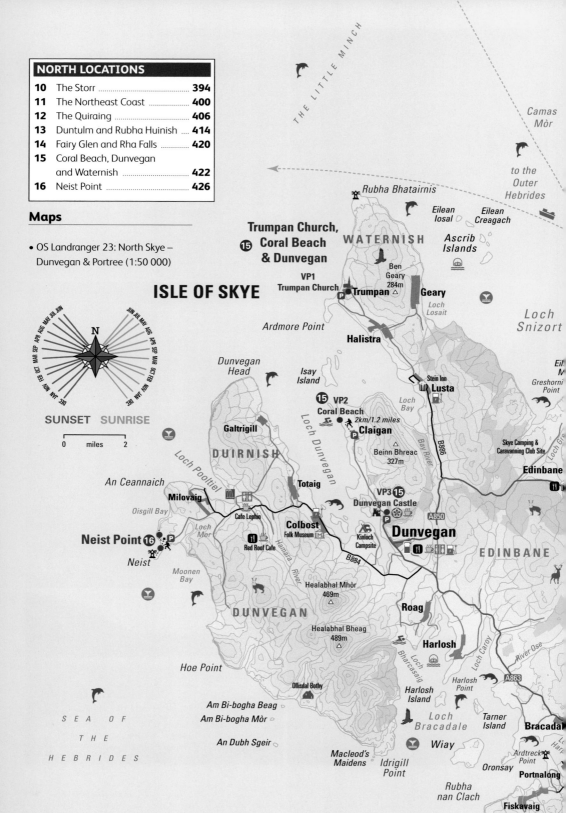

**Maps**

• OS Landranger 23: North Skye – Dunvegan & Portree (1:50 000)

**ISLE OF SKYE**

N

SUNSET   SUNRISE

0    miles    2

**THE LITTLE MINCH**

Camas Mòr

to the Outer Hebrides

Rubha Bhatairnis

Eilean Iosal

Eilean Creagach

Trumpan Church,
**15** Coral Beach
& Dunvegan

**WATERNISH**

Ascrib Islands

VP1
Trumpan Church

Ben Geary 284m

Trumpan

Geary

Loch Losait

Loch Snizort

Ardmore Point

Halistra

Eil M

Dunvegan Head

Isay Island

**15** VP2
Coral Beach

2km/1.2 miles

Stein Inn
Lusta

Greshorni Point

Loch Bay

Galtrigill

Claigan

B886

Bay River

Beinn Bhreac 327m

Skye Camping & Caravanning Club Site

**DUIRNISH**

Loch Dunvegan

Edinbane

An Ceannaich

Milovaig

Totaig

VP3 **15**
Dunvegan Castle

Oisgill Bay

Cafe Lephin

Loch Pooltiel

Loch Mor

Colbost
Folk Museum

A850

Kinloch Campsite

**Dunvegan**

**EDINBANE**

**Neist Point 16**

Neist

Red Roof Cafe

Glamaig River

B884

Healabhal Mhòr 469m

Moonen Bay

Healabhal Bheag 489m

Roag

Harlosh

**DUNVEGAN**

Hoe Point

Ollisdal Bothy

Loch Bharcasaig

Loch Caroy

River Ose

A863

Harlosh Island

Harlosh Point

Tarner Island

**Bracada**

Ardtreck Point

**S E A   O F**

**T H E**

**H E B R I D E S**

Am Bi-bogha Beag

Am Bi-bogha Mòr

An Dubh Sgeir

Macleod's Maidens

Idrigill Point

Loch Bracadale

Wiay

Oronsay

**Portnalong**

Rubha nan Clach

**Fiskavaig**

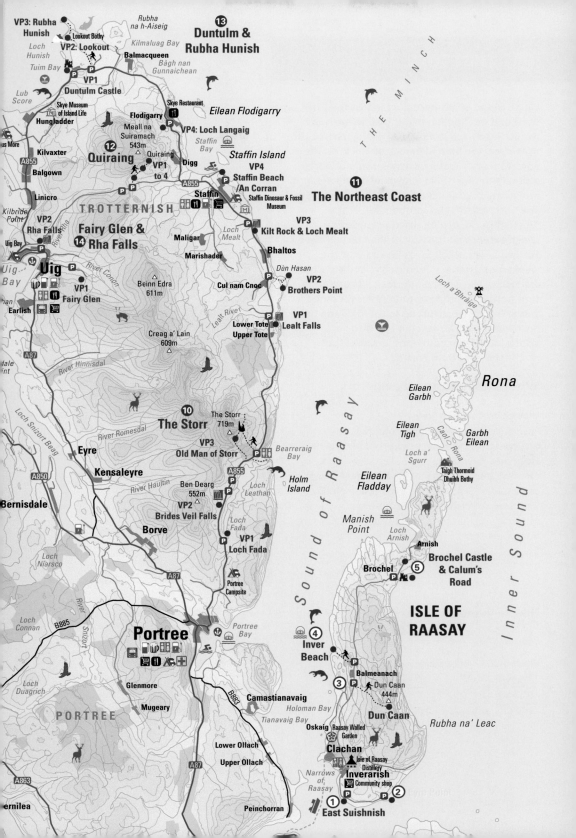

On an island of extraordinary landscapes, the Storr and its Old Man might just be the most iconic. Seen from as far away as the road south of Portree, the 50m high rock pinnacle on the eastern side of Trotternish peninsula attracts visitors from far afield, drawn by its unique form and numerous appearances on the silver screen. The Storr itself is the southern hill of the Trotternish ridge, a fascinating landscape which extends all the way to the north of Skye. Formed when basalt lavas flowed over the weaker sandstone, this caused a landslip which resulted in the cliffs, pinnacles and landforms that have delighted photographers for many years. It is a steep walk up to the Old Man of Storr viewpoint, however, it can also be appreciated from numerous low-level spots on the the road from Portree.

## What to shoot and viewpoints

### Viewpoint 1 – Loch Fada

Approaching from the south, the road crests alongside a sheepfold and there is an excellent view north to the Storr across the waters of Loch Fada. At dawn, in still conditions the loch can form a mirror for the Storr and together with the small fishing boats moored offshore, the scene couldn't be more idyllic. It is possible to park at the sheepfold, there is a good elevated view from here, or alternatively make your way down to the waterside. »

## How to get here

From Portree head north on the A855. The viewpoints are all accessed from this road.

### Viewpoint 1 – Loch Fada

- **Lat/Long**: 57.457592, -6.1826639
- **what3words**: ///alley.prawn.critic
- **Grid Ref**: NG492485
- **Postcode**: IV51 9HT

### Viewpoint 2 – Brides Veil Falls

- **Lat/Long**: 57.479583, -6.1803056
- **what3words**: ///regretted.improve.score
- **Grid Ref**: NG495509
- **Postcode**: IV51 9HX

### Viewpoint 3 – The Old Man

- **Lat/Long**: 57.499419, -6.1579270
- **what3words**: ///thrashing.rubble.bike
- **Grid Ref**: NG509530
- **Postcode**: IV51 9HX

## Accessibility

Loch Fada and Brides Veil Falls are easily accessed from the roadside, providing there is space to park. Both only require short walks, however, the route to the falls can be muddy. The Old Man of Storr is roughly a 5km round trip and is relatively steep in places but generally the paths are good and anyone with a good level of fitness should manage it. It is a very popular spot, and there are now a network paths around most of the features, some of these paths are better than others, a few skirt some steep ground on which care will be required. Pay attention to the possibility of rock fall along the base of the cliffs.

## Best time of year/day

Loch Fada is excellent on a still morning where the reflections add a lot to the scene. Brides Veil Falls can work at any time and even when the top of the Storr is under cloud, the waterfall itself provides interest. The Old Man is a classic sunrise location at all times of the year, but be aware in summer you are unlikely to avoid other photographers at the traditional viewpoint. If you are venturing up pre-dawn, make sure you are experienced and equipped with a head torch as the path can be tricky in the dark.

*Above*: *The Old Man of Storr and Loch Fada (VP1). Fujifilm X–T2, 18–55mm f/2.8–f/4, ISO 200, 1/125s at f/11. Mar.*

*Top: the path weaving behind The Old Man. Fujifilm X–T2, 18–55mm f/2.8–f/4, ISO 200, 1/420s at f/9. Mar. **Above**: The Old Man. Fujifilm X–T2, 18–55mm f/2.8–f/4, ISO 200, 1/420s at f/8. Mar.*

*The Old Man and The Cathedral. Fujifilm X–T2, 55–200mm f/3.5–f/4.8, ISO 200, 1/1000s at f/5.6. Mar.*

### Viewpoint 2 – Brides Veil Falls

Just a short drive further on are Brides Veil Falls suited on the opposite side of the road to Loch Leathan. A popular spot for tourist buses, the falls are located up a short and sometimes muddy path. When the river is in spate, it can be tricky to cross but there is usually a shoogly (shaky or unsteady) plank of wood across the water. The falls create a great foreground to the view north with the water cascading down the slopes providing a wonderful counterweight to the jagged pinnacle of the Old Man.

### Viewpoint 3 – The Old Man

The Old Man of Storr is a much-loved location and the new car park is testament to its popularity. From the car park the cliffs of the east face of the Storr form a dramatic backdrop, but the Old Man and the rock feature known as the Cathedral are difficult to pick out unless aided by the separation provided by swirling mist. To explore this incredible landscape head through the gate and follow the steep path up the hill through the remains of the cleared commercial forestry. At the gates continue up the path and as height is gained the Old Man becomes more prominent. The views east over to Rona and the mainland open up; if you are making your way up in the pre-dawn light this may give you your first indication to the possibility of a good sunrise. At an obvious break in the path, take the fork on the left, bearing towards the left hand side of the Old Man. The path emerges at the area known as the Sanctuary; an area of flat ground below the escarpment of the Storr with some fascinating gothic-looking rock architecture. The Cathedral and the Old Man are just a few of the excellent features and it is possible to spend a long time immersed in this area. The base of the cliffs are prone to rockfall, so be aware of this risk especially if you are absorbed in the scene. Continuing north, the path gradually rises to a small elevated hillock. From this lofty perch you gain the classic view of the Old Man of Storr. It is a magnificent location with Rona, Raasay and the mainland visible to the east, the shattered chaos of the Cuillin way beyond Loch Fada to the south and in the centre, the Old Man standing proud of the the Storr, the focal point of this epic vista. It is the Hebrides, and perhaps Scotland at its very best. Don't let the popularity of the traditional image put you off, it is a classic for a reason and it is a vista that every landscape photographer should savour.

*Top*: *Brides Veil Falls and the Old Man of Storr (VP2). Fujifilm X–T2, 18–55mm f/2.8–f/4, ISO 200, 1/6s at f/9. Mar.* **Above**: *looking up to the Old Man and The Cathedral at dawn. Fujifilm X–T2, 55–200mm f/3.5–f/4.8, ISO 200, 1/1000s at f/6.4. Mar.*

*The iconic view of The Old Man of Storr (VP3). Fujifilm X–T2, 18–55mm f/2.8–f/4, ISO 200, 1/400s at f/9. Mar.*

Sandwiched between the landslip of the Trotternish hills and cliffs that tumble into the sea are a number of small villages which culminate in the larger crofting settlement of Staffin. This is a strong Gaelic-speaking area with over 60% of residents speaking the language and it retains a distinct atmosphere. The landscape here is sublime, with the Trotternish hills providing an ever intriguing backdrop and far reaching views back to the mainland mountains; driving the road will provide many "stop the car!" moments. Luckily, there are a number of good places to stop and appreciate this unique landscape and there are numerous great photographic opportunities afforded by the waterfalls, beaches and cliffs. There are even dinosaur footprints to find on Staffin beach!

## What to shoot and viewpoints

### Viewpoint 1 – Lealt Falls

Approaching from the south the road crosses the Lealt falls as they slice through a steep sided gorge and wind their way down to the sea. A recently built viewing platform cantilevered out above the gorge provides an easy viewpoint, however, the wider composition which takes in the Trotternish ridge is slightly marred by the road, a tight crop of the waterfall itself may be more powerful. A path also leads up onto the cliffs to the north where another good view of the falls can be had from another viewpoint. It is also possible to descend with care down to the shore via a slippery switchback path where the remains of the old diatomite factory can be explored. From the shore it is also possible to follow the river Lealt back into the gorge.

### Viewpoint 2 – Brothers Point

Next up on the northwest coast is Brothers Point, a finger of land which extends into the sea, forming the easternmost point of the Trotternish Peninsula and once thought to be home to a monastic community. A short but steep walk from the road leads down to the shore, passing the remains of an old salmon netting station on the left. The black sandy shore offers some scope for images as does the view north along the cliffs where Kilt Rock can be seen and with its waterfall cascading down to the sea. »

*Lealt Falls and the Trotternish ridge from the viewing platform (VP1). Fujifilm X–T2, 10–24mm f/4, ISO 200, 1/1000s at f/8. Mar.*

*Looking east along the Lealt Falls gorge to the sea. Fujifilm X–T2, 10–24mm f/4, ISO 200, 1/250s at f/8. Mar.*

***Opposite top:*** *Alfie showing me the way to Brothers Point (VP2). Fujifilm X–T2, 18–55mm f/2.8–f/4, ISO 200, 1/300s at f/9. Mar. **Middle**: warning sign en-route to Brothers Point. Fujifilm X–T2, 18–55mm f/2.8–f/4, ISO 200, 1/350s at f/8. Mar. **Bottom**: looking back up from the beach beside Brothers Point to Culnacnoc. Fujifilm X–T2, 18–55mm f/2.8–f/4, ISO 200, 1/180s at f/9. Mar.*

# How to get here

These viewpoints are all accessed from the A855 which runs in a loop from Portree up and around the north of Skye. There is a roadside car park for Lealt Falls 20 minutes north of Portree and the route to the viewpoint is signposted. For Brothers Point, park in the small lay-by on the A855 at Culnacnoc. Walk back down the road verge and take the first track on the left, this passes some holiday houses. Head through the gate and down the steep grassy path to the shore. Kilt Rock and Mealt Loch are a little further north with the car park signposted from the road. Staffin Beach is accessed from a minor road which branches off the A855 to the right after passing the shop. There is parking area at An Corran where a ramp gives access to the beach.

## Viewpoint 1 – Lealt Falls

- **Lat/Long:** 57.565942, -6.1542306
- **what3words:** ///comply.owner.humid
- **Grid Ref:** NG516604
- **Postcode:** IV51 9JW

## Viewpoint 2 – Brothers Point

- **Lat/Long:** 57.584922, -6.1577472
- **what3words:** ///blurs.smokers.browsers
- **Grid Ref:** NG515626
- **Postcode:** IV51 9JH

## Viewpoint 3 – Kilt Rock and Loch Mealt

- **Lat/Long:** 57.610404, -6.1729305
- **what3words:** ///generated.minus.alien
- **Grid Ref:** NG508654
- **Postcode:** IV51 9JE

## Viewpoint 4 – Staffin Beach (An Corran)

- **Lat/Long:** 57.636314, -6.2043444
- **what3words:** ///airtime.pave.beak
- **Grid Ref:** NG491684
- **Postcode:** IV51 9JT

## Accessibility

Apart from Brothers Point all the locations are easily accessible, Kilt Rock and Mealt Falls are particularly easy to access. The route to Brothers Point requires some care as the grass can be slippery above some large drops and the path up Dùn Hasan is eroded and can be dangerous.

## Best time of year/day

All of these viewpoints are ideal at dawn or early morning located as they are on the east coast of the island. Brothers Point and Kilt Rock are particularly appealing on a winter morning as the low sun picks out the colour and textures of cliffs to great effect. An Corran is best visited at low tide, for both the chance to find the dinosaur footprints and to reveal a large expanse of sand. These are all quite popular locations on the Isle of Skye visitor route so can be very busy in the summer. Like many locations on Skye, it may be best to visit out of the summer if you like a bit of solitude.

*The flat-topped cliffs of Brothers Point (VP2). Fujifilm X–T2, 18–55mm f/2.8–f/4, ISO 200, 1/480s at f/8. Mar.*

It's a quiet, peaceful spot and you may be lucky enough to spot otters along this stretch of coast. From the beach, Dùn Hasan on the point is visible and is reached by picking your way along the shoreline which passes alongside a sign warning of the steep drops from the cliffs. The best views are to be found shooting towards Dùn Hasan although it is possible to ascend this on a tricky, eroded path before descending to the grassy area beyond.

### Viewpoint 3 – Kilt Rock and Loch Mealt ♿

The famous sea cliff of Kilt Rock is a popular visitor destination, and is easily accessed from a large parking area just off the A855. With its basalt columns said to resemble the pleated folds of a kilt and Mealt Falls falling in an unbroken line to the sea below it is a spectacular scene and worth visiting despite its popularity. Photographically it is a bit of one-shot wonder with the typical image shot from the viewing platform. However, there are also some interesting compositions to be found nearby, of the cliffs to the south where Brothers Point can be seen or on a clear day the mountains of Torridon to the east. Heading back to the road will bring you to Loch Mealt, which offers a great view of the Trotternish Hills and even the backside of the Old Man of Storr. On a calm day, the reflections can be superb here and there also the possibility to pick out some detail shots with a telephoto lens of the vertiginous cliffs of the Trotternish Ridge. »

*Opposite left: a fishing boat below the cliffs to the south of Kilt Rock. Fujifilm X–T2, 14mm f/2.8, ISO 200, 1/10s at f/11. Sep.*

*Kilt Rock at dawn (VP3). Fujifilm X–T2, 18–55mm f/2.8–f/4, ISO 200, 1/25s at f/8. Mar.*

**Top**: *the island of Rona and the Torridon mountains from Kilt Rock (VP3).* **Middle**: *Loch Mealt at dawn. Fujifilm X–T2, 55–200mm f/3.5–f/4.8, ISO 800, 1/90s at f/7.1. Mar.* **Above**: *moonset over the Trotternish Hills. Fujifilm X–T2, 55–200mm f/3.5–f/4.8, ISO 200, 1/100s at f/6.4. Mar.*

**Top**: *looking to the cliffs of Sgeir Bhàn from the slipway at Ob nan Ron. Fujifilm X–T1, 14mm f/2.8, ISO 200, 1/100s at f/9. Sep.*
**Above**: *Staffin Bay from An Corran. Fujifilm X–T2, 10–24mm f/4, ISO 200, 1/550s at f/8. Mar.*

### Viewpoint 4 – Staffin Beach (An Corran)

In 2001 two dog walkers made a remarkable discovery at An Corran, the sandy bay to the south west of Staffin. A dinosaur footprint thought to be that of a Megalasaurous which walked through the shallow mud here, about 166 million years ago. Seventeen more footprints have since been discovered along this rocky shore and the best chance of seeing them is at low tide after a storm when the sand and seaweed has been washed away. The beach itself offers a great view back up across Staffin to the Quiraing and the grey and white sand can make a compelling foreground, particularly at low tide.

*Looking across Staffin Bay from An Corran to the Quiraing. Fujifilm X–T2, 10–24mm f/4, ISO 200, 1/800s at f/8. Mar.*

The Trotternish ridge runs up the spine of the peninsula that bears its name. On its western side, the ridge is characterised by whale-backed hills which give no hint to the chaotic spectacle of their eastern faces. There is drama throughout the ridge but it reaches a crescendo at its northern area where the hillside of Meall na Suiramach tumbles into a series of cliffs and valleys, peaks and crags known as the Quiraing. Formed by a series of landslips, the land here is still moving and the road needs to be repaired on a yearly basis as the ground continues to shift below.

It is an other-worldly landscape, and an absolute delight for the landscape photographer to explore. Whether you are shooting from the roadside or in amongst it, the Quiraing is an epic location and one which invites repeat visits.

## What to shoot and viewpoints

### Viewpoint 1 – Roadside view ♿

From the car park, the obvious path leads north and after 100m you're met with the most popular viewpoint. A small prow of rock rises up and offers a fantastic view south to Cleat and the Trotternish ridge. To the north of this, in a steep gully, a small tree clings to the slope which may be the most photographed tree in Scotland since the one on Rannoch Moor blew down. It is a popular spot and at dawn it is not uncommon to see a group of photographers taking it in turns to record this scene. There are plenty of other compositions to be found within this area, so explore! »

*The popular tree near the roadside (VP1). Fujifilm X–T2, 18–55mm f/2.8–f/4, ISO 200, 1/25s at f/8. Mar.*

### How to get here

From Portree take the A855 to Staffin. On reaching Brogaig take the minor road on the left signposted to the Quiraing. The road climbs up via switchbacks to a large new car park (pay and display) at the bealach. Be aware that the road is very steep and in winter can pose difficulties. The route starts to the north of the road beside an information board. Do not park in passing places or on the switchbacks as it blocks the route for busses. The Loch Langaig viewpoint is accessed from the A855. Instead of turning left at Brogaig, continue on for 2km/1.2 mi until a parking area on the left of the road is reached.

### Viewpoint 1 – Roadside view, Viewpoint 2 – Cnoc a' Mheirlich & Viewpoint 3 – The Prison, The Needle, and the Table

| | | |
|---|---|---|
| 📍 **Lat/Long**: | 57.628207, -6.2913019 |
| 📍 **what3words**: | ///mulls.column.tricks |
| 📍 **Grid Ref**: | NG439679 |
| 📍 **Postcode**: | IV51 9LB |

*Above: sheep graze amongst the chaotic terraces near The Prison. Fujifilm X–T1, 18–55mm f/2.8–f/4, ISO 200, 1/25s at f/9. Sep.*

## Viewpoint 4 – Flodigarry / Loch Langaig

- **Lat/Long**: 57.657619, -6.2540365
- **what3words**: ///snacking.reported.healthier
- **Grid Ref**: NG463710
- **Postcode**: IV51 9HZ

### Accessibility

There is a good path from the car park and should be manageable by all walkers. The only tricky spot is roughly 0.5km/0.3 mi along where a burn crosses the path, but even that can be negotiated reasonably easily by most walkers. The route up beside the Needle and on to The Table is rough and bouldery and is tricky to descend.

### Best time of year/day

Facing east, the Quiraing is an ideal sunrise location. It can work at anytime of the year with a plethora of features to catch the early morning light. Viewpoint 1, despite being usually photographed at dawn also works well in the slanted light of a late winter afternoon, as the wee tree picks up the rays. In winter a dusting of snow helps to pick out the forms of the land. There are great images to be made here at any time of year, and under most conditions.

*Top: the classic view south from The Quiraing (VP1). Fujifilm X–T1, 18–55mm f/2.8–f/4, ISO 200, 125s at f/8. Sep. **Above**: a wider view taking in the road which snakes up to the bealach, Fujifilm X–T1, 18–55mm f/2.8–f/4, ISO 200, 2s at f/11. Sep.*

*Cnoc a' Mheirlich in the late afternoon sun (VP2). Fujifilm X–T2, 18–55mm f/2.8–f/4, ISO 200, 1/300s at f/8. Mar.*

### Viewpoint 2 – Cnoc a' Mheirlich

Continuing on along the path into the Quiraing the scenery gets more dramatic, with steep cliffs rising above to the west and excellent views opening up to the south. On crossing a small stream, which involves a slightly tricky scramble continue on for a few minutes until the sharks fin of Cnoc a' Mherlich becomes prominent in the mid-ground. It is a classic view and there are great foreground options afforded by the scattered boulders which adorn the slopes, you may even find there are sheep grazing, adding another bit of interest to this quintessential Skye scene.

### Viewpoint 3 – The Prison, The Needle, and the Table

The Prison is visible from the start of the route, but as you get closer to it and scramble up the bouldery path between it and the face to the east it is here that you gain the most appreciation of it. A fantastic rocky spire, it provides a great view for those bold enough to scramble up it via the narrow tracks which cling to its flanks. To the west the

*Looking north into the Quiraing from near the road (VP1), Fujifilm X–T2, 18–55mm f/2.8–f/4, ISO 200, 1/480s at f/8. Mar.*

*__Opposite top__: the Needle from below. Fujifilm X–T2, 18–55mm f/2.8–f/4, ISO 200, 1/250s at f/8. Mar. __Bottom left__: The Prison. Fujifilm X–T2, 18–55mm f/2.8–f/4, ISO 200, 1/70s at f/8. Mar. __Middle right__: two walkers below the dramatic cliffs at The Needle. Fujifilm X–T1, 18–55mm f/2.8–f/4, ISO 200, 125s at f/8. Dec. __Bottom right__: Loch Langaig. Fujifilm X–T2, 10–24mm f/4, ISO 200, 1/400s at f/8. Mar.*

*Loch Langaig reflections (VP4). Fujifilm X–T2, 10–24mm f/4, ISO 200, 1/250s at f/8. Mar.*

slender rock tower of the Needle juts out of the cliffs. Impressive from below, the best view is perhaps from above where it can be appreciated from the top of a very steep and bouldery route. From here it is possible to continue on, picking your way uphill on a network of paths which eventually leads to the Table. A large section of flat grassy ground has detached itself from the hillside and has began its slow descent to the valley below. It is a surreal spot and provides excellent views along the ridge. Arguably the best view of the Table is from the ridge above, where the grassy sward can be best appreciated among the jumble of cliffs. This involves following the path from the car park which leads directly up the hill in a series of relentless switchbacks, some of which are rough and eroded then following the edge of the escarpment.

## Viewpoint 4 – Flodigarry / Loch Langaig
The northern end of the Quiraing area is also worth a visit and is a short walk from the parking area at Flodigarry on the A855. Follow the path south for a couple of minutes until Loch Langaig is reached where you will gain an excellent views of the cliffs. On still days the shallow, rock studded loch provides the ideal reflecting pool for the dramatic eastern face.

*Looking down towards Staffin from the path north of the Quiraing. Fujifilm X–T2, 18–55mm f/2.8–f/4, ISO 200, 1/250s at f/8. Mar.*

The far northern tip of Skye is a great spot for those long sunny days in summer where the lingering light plays upon the basalt cliff faces. The views west from here are superb with the Outer Hebrides etched along the horizon almost beckoning you to check when the next ferry leaves Uig. There are many beautiful spots along this coastline, however, two of the finest are at the northern end: Duntulm Castle with its haunted atmosphere and ruined walls looking like a set from Game of Thrones and Rubha Hunish where the Isle of Skye stretches out into the Minch beneath foreboding sheer cliffs.

## What to shoot and viewpoints

### Viewpoint 1 – Duntulm Castle

With its dramatic location, surrounded on three sides by steep basalt cliffs, it is easy to see why this site has been used as a fort since the Iron Age. Raided and taken by the Vikings, then squabbled over by the MacDonalds and the Macleods it has a grisly old history. Tales such as feeding

an imprisoned MacDonald nothing but salt fish and salt beef until the unfortunate captive ate his own hand; or the nursemaid who killed an infant by dropping it out of a window who was then punished by being set adrift in a boat. It's perhaps understandable why people think it could be haunted. The castle itself is best photographed from the low promontory to the west where its situation on top of the cliffs can be best appreciated. It is also worth exploring the beach to the south, the castle itself is only just visible, but the beach itself offers some great foregrounds to the view back towards the cliffs. >>

## How to get here

Take the A855 north from Uig, passing through the townships along the western coast of the Trotternish peninsula. After passing the rocky beach on the left, the road climbs to the north and there is a parking area for Duntulm Castle on the left. It can be busy here and parking is limited. The castle is reached by walking back down the road and following the path through the gate. The walk to the lookout bothy starts at a small car park a few minutes to east at a red phonebox. Take the signposted track to Rubha Hunish which takes roughly 45 minutes (2km/1.2 mi) to reach the Bothy on Meall Tuath. Rubha Hunish itself is located down a very steep path which descends from the bealach between Meal Deas and Meal Tuath.

### Viewpoint 1 – Duntulm Castle

| | | |
|---|---|---|
| 🅿 Lat/Long: | 57.682078, -6.3445611 |
| 🅿 what3words: | ///spouting.slot.mainframe |
| 🅿 Grid Ref: | NG411741 |
| 🅿 Postcode: | IV51 9UF |

### Viewpoint 2 – The Lookout & Viewpoint 3 – Rubha Hunish

| | | |
|---|---|---|
| 🅿 Lat/Long: | 57.684029, -6.3256764 |
| 🅿 what3words: | ///file.waged.flap |
| 🅿 Grid Ref: | NG422742 |
| 🅿 Postcode: | IV51 9UG |

## Accessibility

Duntulm Castle is accessed via a path from the roadside and there are some slippery grass terraces to descend in order to reach the best viewpoint. The Lookout Bothy is a 45 minute walk from the car park along a good but occasionally muddy path. Descent to Rubha Hunish below the cliffs is a tricky scramble and not recommended unless you are comfortable on steep ground and big drops.

## Best time of year/day

Both of these viewpoints are west facing with a fine outlook across the Minch to the Outer Hebrides and therefore are ideal sunset locations. The cliffs below the Lookout Bothy are great at sunset during the summer, when the sun sets further to the northwest, illuminating the rocks with a beautiful orange glow. The Lookout is a fine spot on a clear day, but is equally good in squally conditions where the clouds racing over the Minch can be very dramatic. On a clear winter night it would also be the ideal location to view the northern lights as it offers an uninterrupted view to the north without any light pollution (and you could stay in the warm bothy as well).

*Above: Duntulm Castle from the route to Rubha Hunish (VP1). Fujifilm X–T2, 55–200mm f/3.5–f/4.8, ISO 200, 1/250s at f/9. Mar.*

*Duntulm Castle (VP1). Fujifilm X–T2, 10–24mm f/4, ISO 200, 1/350s at f/8. Mar.*

*The view across to Harris from The Lookout (VP2). Fujifilm X–T2, 55–200mm f/3.5–f/4.8, ISO 200, 1/350s at f/9. Mar.*

## Viewpoint 2 – The Lookout

The Lookout is a former Coast Guard watch station which was built in the early 20th century. Today it has been repurposed as a bothy which can sleep up to seven people. Perched on the edge of the cliffs at Hunish, it commands an incredible view across The Minch with the islands of Lewis, The Shiants, Harris, North Uist and even South Uist seen on a good day. The bothy provides a great space to sit out a storm, and also makes a fine spot for sunset with the tantalising outline of the Outer Hebrides hills forming a beautiful horizon. It is also a great spot for whale watching, so keep your eyes peeled. On the return route back to the car park you get a distant view of Duntulm Castle which can be picked out with a long lens. It takes roughly 45 minutes (2km/1.2 mi) to get to the Lookout. >>

*Above right: storm clouds racing in towards The Shiants. Fujifilm X–T2, 55–200mm f/3.5–f/4.8, ISO 200, 1/250s at f/9. Mar.*

*Bottom row: scenes from the Lookout, the bothy on top of the cliffs.*

*The Lookout and the cliffs (VP3). Fujifilm X–T2, 10–24mm f/4, ISO 200, 1/1000s at f/8. Mar.*

## Viewpoint 3 – Rubha Hunish

If you have peered over the edge of the cliffs you will have noticed an area of land stretching out into the sea. This low-lying headland is reached via a difficult scrambly path but if you have a head for heights it is worth making the trip down to it. On the east side there are sea stacks to explore and in the centre, a number of lochans offer a great place for catching the reflections of the cliffs. The Lookout Bothy can be seen from below at some areas, with its whitewashed wall lending a sense of scale to the dramatic sheer cliffs. A haven for wildlife, you may see otters, seals and even whales in the seas surrounding the peninsula.

*Sheep pose in front of the dramatic cliffs of Hunish (VP3). Fujifilm X–T2, 10–24mm f/4, ISO 200, 1/1000s at f/8. Mar.*

*__Right__: the path at the base of the cliffs on the way to Rubha Hunish (VP3). Fujifilm X–T2, 10–24mm f/4, ISO 200, 1/800s at f/7.1. Mar.*

*__Opposite left__: sea stack on the eastern side of Rubha Hunish. Fujifilm X–T2, 10–24mm f/4, ISO 200, 1/220s at f/8. Mar.*
*__Right__: looking down on Rubha Hunish from the cliffs. Fujifilm X–T2, 10–24mm f/4, ISO 200, 1/850s at f/8. Mar.*

In recent years the Fairy Glen has become a bit of a visitor hotspot. Nestled in the hillside above Uig, this dramatic mountain-scape in miniature has become a victim of its own beauty with its increased popularity resulting in erosion, misguided attempts at land art and bad parking. Fortunately a new car park has alleviated some of the problems of the latter and recently the stone circles have also been removed. However, don't let the problems put you off, visit off-season and enjoy the fascinating landscape, a place which really requires a bit of time to explore and understand. The Rha falls are a bit quieter and provide a nice alternative to the hustle and bustle of the Fairy Glen.

## What to shoot and viewpoints

### Viewpoint 1 – The Fairy Glen ♿

The new parking area located at the western side of the Fairy Glen is the obvious place to start and you can either walk east along the minor road or head up the obvious path to the left. This route weaves its way through steep sided conical hills, with glimpsed views through to the cottages to the north or Castle Ewen itself. Although steep,

the hillsides can be carefully scrambled up to provide views along the glen. As the path emerges back onto the road, a small lochan creates a great foreground to Castle Ewen providing good reflections on a calm day. Castle Ewen itself isn't actually a castle, but a flat topped basalt pinnacle which has weathered over the years into its fortified appearance. It is possible to scramble up to the top of it, however, the views from the top obviously lose the castle as the focal point. Around the back of the castle is a nice area of close cropped grass, unfortunately this lawn-like surface has been marred by a series of rings formed by visitors placing rocks over the years. The spirals may be of interest as a foreground element, however, there are more compelling views of the castle from some of the other hills. It is worth exploring the other hills on the southern side of the road, their steep sides and tiny summits provide some intriguing views.

### Viewpoint 2 – Rha Falls

Located just a short walk from the village, the signposted path along the river to the falls provides a good spot to stretch the legs when waiting for a ferry. The falls themselves cascade down through a wooded gorge and are particularly dramatic after heavy rain.

## How to get here

To the south of Uig a minor road branches off the A855 adjacent to the Uig Hotel. Signposted to Siadair and Baile nan cnoc the Fairy Glen parking area is reached after roughly mile. The car park is pay and display and takes both cards and cash. Alternatively it is 30 minute walk from Uig itself. To reach Rha falls, park in the village opposite the police station and head along the minor road signposted to Staffin. At a gap in the wall on the right a set of steps provides access to the riverside.

### Viewpoint 1 – The Fairy Glen

| | |
|---|---|
| **P** Lat/Long: | 57.584769, -6.3332056 |
| **P** what3words: | ///silly.rank.scratches |
| **P** Grid Ref: | NG411632 |
| **P** Postcode: | IV51 9YF |

### Viewpoint 2 – Rha Falls

| | |
|---|---|
| **P** Lat/Long: | 57.592036, -6.3586111 |
| **P** what3words: | ///flame.shook.imitate |
| **P** Grid Ref: | NG396641 |
| **P** Postcode: | IV51 9XP |

## Accessibility

Some of the hillsides in the Fairy Glen are quite steep, so use your judgement when ascending and descending. Castle Ewen can viewed from the roadside at the lochan. The Fairy Glen can be very busy, although the new car park should help to alleviate some of the problems, however, if there are no spaces, return at another time or alternatively walk from Uig. There are steep steps and a narrow path to the Rha falls.

## Best time of year/day

The Fairy Glen runs east-west so can work well at either sunrise or sunset. It is at its best when the low light picks out the conical hills, creating interesting shadows and heightening their dramatic appearance. Rha falls are best appreciated after heavy rainfall and as they are set within deciduous woodland work well in autumn.

*Opposite top: looking to Castle Ewen along Fairy Glen (VP1). Fujifilm X–T2, 10–24mm f/4, ISO 200, 1/180s at f/8. Mar.*
***Bottom left**: marks left from the stone circles below Castle Ewen. Fujifilm X–T2, 10–24mm f/4, ISO 200, 1/340s at f/8. Mar.*
***Right**: Rha Falls (VP2). Fujifilm X–T2, 10–24mm f/4, ISO 200, 3.2s at f/11. Apr.*

The Waternish Peninsula and Dunvegan provide a great variety of photographic opportunities. A unique beach will satisfy the coastal photographer, Trumpan Church the astro-photographer, and Dunvegan Castle is an excellent location for those interested in historical sites. All are located relatively close together and can give a good day and (potentially nights) shooting.

## What to shoot and viewpoints

### Viewpoint 1 – Trumpan Church ♿

At the far end of the Waternish Peninsula is the Trumpan Church. It is an excellent dark sky location, with a fantastic view north for those nights when the northern lights are putting on a show. The church itself has a turbulent history. In revenge for a massacre committed against the McDonalds of Eigg by the McLeods of Skye, the McDonalds of Uist set fire to the church, burning the McLeods who were at Sunday prayers inside. The only survivor was a young girl who managed to squeeze through the window and run to safety. A truly grisly tale for what is now a quite idyllic site. Perhaps the most interesting view is not of the church itself, but from the steep road which leads down to the bay.

The land and sea interlock in the most appealing way, with a sequence of lines drawing the eye to the dramatic cliffs on the horizon.

### Viewpoint 2 – Coral Beach

Skye is blessed with a number of beaches, but they tend to be two tone grey/black sand. Coral Beach however, is pure white and is formed from a hard seaweed known as maerl which has been crushed. It positively glows under the right conditions. Coupled with a fantastic outlook to the Outer Hebrides and some handy hills to provide elevation, it is a great spot to visit. There are also excellent views from the beach back towards the the flat topped hills of Macleod's Tables.

### Viewpoint 3 – Dunvegan Castle

Dunvegan Castle and its gardens are definitely worth a visit. One of the oldest castles in Scotland, it sits on a rocky outcrop with an outlook over Loch Dunvegan. It is best photographed from the lochside at high tide. There is also a seal colony offshore, and boat trips are available should you wish to photograph them.

## How to get here

Coral Beach is located near the village of Claigan. From the car park it is approximately a 2km/1.2 mi walk along a good track to reach the beach. Trumpan Church is located at the northern end of the Waternish peninsula and there is a car park adjacent to the church. Dunvegan Castle is just to the north of Dunvegan. It is £12 to visit the gardens. Alternatively a lay-by on the road to Claigan provides a view back to the castle.

### Viewpoint 1 – Trumpan Church

- **Lat/Long**: 57.555930, -6.6417580
- **what3words**: ///fewer.mixer.liked
- **Grid Ref**: NG224612
- **Postcode**: IV55 8GW

### Viewpoint 2 – Coral Beach

- **Lat/Long**: 57.488989, -6.6208345
- **what3words**: ///ripples.octagon.bulbs
- **Grid Ref**: NG232537
- **Postcode**: IV55 8WF

### Viewpoint 3 – Dunvegan Castle

- **Lat/Long**: 57.447984, -6.5864098
- **what3words**: ///expel.quite.goofy
- **Grid Ref**: NG249490
- **Postcode**: IV55 8WE

### Accessibility

Coral Beach requires a short (2km/1.2 mi) walk to reach the beach from the parking spot. Trumpan Church and Dunvegan Castle are roadside.

### Best time of year/day

Coral beach works well under most conditions, but is at its best at sunset. At low tide it is possible to walk across to the tidal island of Lampay. Trumpan Church is an ideal location for astro-photography as it is in a dark sky area and makes an excellent location for aurora spotting. You are slightly hindered by the opening hours for Dunvegan Castle, but it is best photographed at high tide.

*Top*: the view across to Dunvegan Head from Trumpan Church (VP1). Fujifilm X–T2, 10–24mm f/11, ISO 200, 1/280s at f/8. Apr.
**Middle left**: trumpan church with the Outer Hebrides on the horizon. Fujifilm X–T2, 10–24mm f/11, ISO 200, 1/300s at f/8. Apr.
**Middle right**: a shed with a view at Trumpan. Fujifilm X–T2, 55–200mm f/3.5–f/4.8, ISO 200, 1/900s at f/8. Apr.
**Above left**: looking across Loch Dunvegan to one of Macleods Tables. Fujifilm X–T2, 55–200mm f/3.5–f/4.8, ISO 200, 1/210s at f/8. Apr.
**Above right**: Dunvegan Castle gardens (VP3). Fujifilm X–T2, 10–24mm f/11, ISO 200, 1/25s at f/8. Apr.

*Coral Beach and the view north to Harris (VP2). Fujifilm X–T1, 18–55mm f/2.8–f/4, ISO 200, 1/45s at f/11. Dec.*

*Above*: looking south down Loch Dunvegan from Coral Beach. Fujifilm X–T1, 18–55mm f/2.8–f/4, ISO 200, 1/110s at f/8. Dec.
*Below*: Dunvegan Castle. 10–24mm f/10, ISO 200, 1/180s at f/8. Apr.

# NEIST POINT

Neist Point is a destination. You don't pass it on the way to anywhere else, you don't happen to find it. You might glimpse it from the ferry to Harris or from other far flung islands. But it is a place that you have to make a real effort to get to. The settlements thin out, the road winds its way uphill and round bends before diminishing in size and eventually ending. The end of the road. The end of Skye and the Inner Hebrides with nothing between you and the Outer Hebrides but the lonely lighthouse and the sea. It's a special location and might just be one of the finest sunset spots in the Hebrides when the setting sun lights up the basalt in a fiery burst of colour.

## What to shoot and viewpoints

### Viewpoint 1 – The Upper Cliffs
From the car park, head past the hut and turn right towards the edge of the cliffs. As you proceed along the path you will get your first glimpse of the lighthouse. Perched out on a finger of land which extends south west into the sea stretching out towards the Outer Herbrides, it is one of the most dramatic locations for a lighthouse.

This 100m–200m stretch of clifftop is where you will find the most popular locations for the classic shot of Neist Point. There are plenty of rock outcrops to use as foreground interest, or just as a stable base for your tripod and the views are sublime, particularly at sunset when the basalt glows an intense red. As you head around the coast you gradually lose the view of the land which connects the peninsula, but also gain a better view of the cliffs of An t-Aigeach. It is worth spending a bit of time up here seeking out your desired composition before sunset. >>

*Waterstein Head from Neist Point (VP1). Fujifilm X–T2, 55–200mm f/3.5–f/4.8, ISO 200, 1/200s at f/8. Apr.*

## How to get here
Head west on the B884 from Glendale and take the road on the left signposted to Upper Milovaig. Take the next turn on the left, signposted to Neist Point. The car park is 2 miles further on.

### Parking for all viewpoints
- **Lat/Long**: 57.429908, -6.7781782
- **what3words**: ///notifying.every.atomic
- **Grid Ref**: NG133478
- **Postcode**: IV55 8WU

### Accessibility
The path along the upper cliffs is relatively flat and simple to navigate, although these are steep cliffs so care should be taken in high winds. You can find excellent compositions without going right to the edge. The concrete steps are steep but in good condition with a handrail. The sloping cliffside in VP2 can be dangerous so only attempt if you are confident on steep ground. A slip could be fatal here, so use your judgement; if it looks scary to you, don't attempt it! The rocky shores to the south of the lighthouse are uneven and can be overtopped by waves on days with a big swell, again use your judgment and keep your wits about you.

## Best time of year/day
Neist point is a classic sunset location with the setting sun dramatically illuminating the cliffs, particularly in summer. However, even in winter, the angle of the cliffs mean that they still pick up a hint of colour at sunset. You should arrive a long time before sunset if it is you first visit, so that you have time to explore the lower terrace and the lighthouse. It is a popular location and you are likely to be sharing the clifftop with numerous other photographers on a fine sunny evening so if you have a composition in mind it is best to arrive early.

*Opposite: Neist Point at sunset (VP1). Fujifilm X–T2, 10–24mm f/11, ISO 200, 1/20s at f/11. Apr.*

*The lighthouse from the lower cliffs (VP2). Fujifilm X–T2, 10–24mm f/10, ISO 200, 300s at f/11. Apr.*

*The route to the lighthouse, Fujifilm X–T2, 10–24mm f/11, ISO 200, 1/10s at f/10. Apr.*

## Viewpoint 2 – The Lower Cliffs

At the end of the car park a series of concrete steps descend towards the lighthouse. Towards the bottom of the steps, a wall branches off to the right. If you follow this wall, you will reach an area of steeply sloping grass which provides another great view of the lighthouse. As you have descended, the cliffs of An t-Aigeach now sit above the horizon, further emphasising their height and drama. Be particularly careful in this area as the grass can be slippery and a fall here could easily be fatal.

## Viewpoint 3 – The Lighthouse

Continuing out to the point along the concrete path eventually leads to the lighthouse. The lighthouse itself isn't in the best of conditions, and actually isn't all that photogenic up close. However, the blocky basalt outcrops to the south provide an excellent foreground for the view to it and offers something different from the classic view. There are plenty of opportunities here, and it is worth the walk to explore the rocky terraces. The cliffs of Waterstein Head look particularly dramatic from the lower level.

***Opposite**: looking back to the lighthouse from the cliffs beyond (VP3). Fujifilm X–T2, 10–24mm f/11, ISO 200, 1/200s at f/8. Apr.*

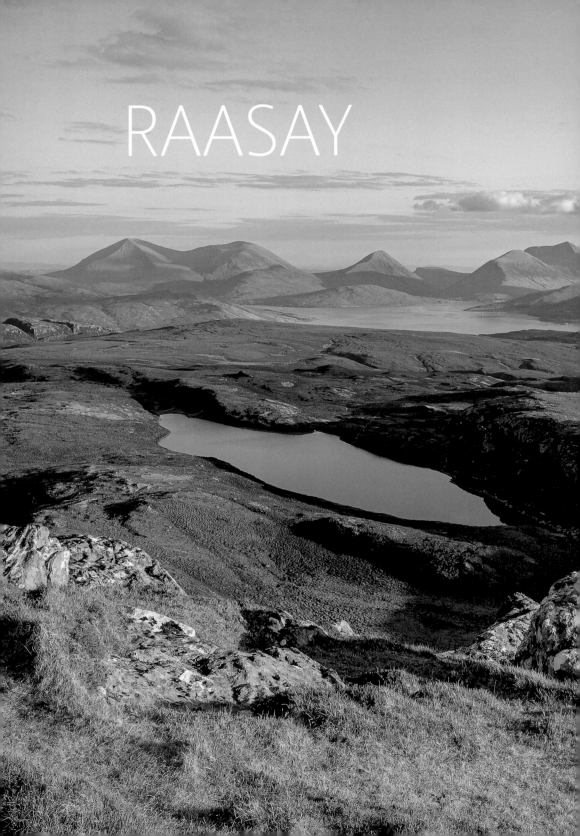

RAASAY

Compared to its larger neighbour, Raasay seems a little bit forgotten about in the mad rush to head to popular locations on Skye. However, if you would like to escape the coach tours and tartan shortbread, then Raasay is the island for you. It has so much photography to offer and whisper it, probably provides the best views of Skye. From the lofty perch of Dun Caan to the pebble beach of Eyre, the island provides some incredible views. However, that is not all that Raasay has to offer, there is a real sense of peace and quiet on the island and it is a place which deserves time to explore.

## How to get to Raasay

### Ferry

It is a 15-minute ferry ride (Caledonian MacBrayne) from Sconser on Skye to Raasay, they leave every hour most days and you can take your vehicle.

| RAASAY | |
|---|---|
| Scottish Gaelic | Ratharsair (Roe Deer island). |
| Area | 24 sq. miles (62 sq. km). |
| Length/breadth | 14 × 3 miles. |
| Highest Elevation | Dùn Caan 444m (1,457ft). |
| Owned by | Mainly public ownership. |
| Population | 161 |
| Largest settlement(s) | Inverarish |
| Vehicles allowed | Yes |
| Car/Bike rental | Bike rental at *raasay-house.co.uk*. |
| Public transport | No |
| Day trips from mainland? | Yes |
| Internet/mobile phone coverage | Yes, but variable 3G/4G coverage, dependent on your carrier. Broadband in hotels/residencies. |
| Power | Raasay Community Renewables: *raasayrenewables.co.uk* and wood fuel. |
| Island website(s) | *raasay.com • raasaydistillery.com • southernhebrides.com visitscotland.com • scotland.org.uk* |
| Festivals/Events | No |
| Accommodation | Two hotels: Ramsay House and isle of Ramsay distillery, two B&Bs and several holiday cottages. There is no campsite and parking up in a camper van is discouraged. Wild camping in a tent is allowed. Book at *raasay.com*. |
| Provisions/Eating Out | Raasay's community-owned shop, Inverarish. |
| Wildlife | Raasay voles, mountain hares, sea eagles, golden eagles, otters, rabbits, seals, dolphins, porpoises and whales. |
| Night Sky Bortle Scale | Class 2. |

*Previous spread*: The view to Skye from Dun Caan. Fujifilm X–T2, 10–24mm f/10, ISO 200, 1/80s at f/11. Apr.

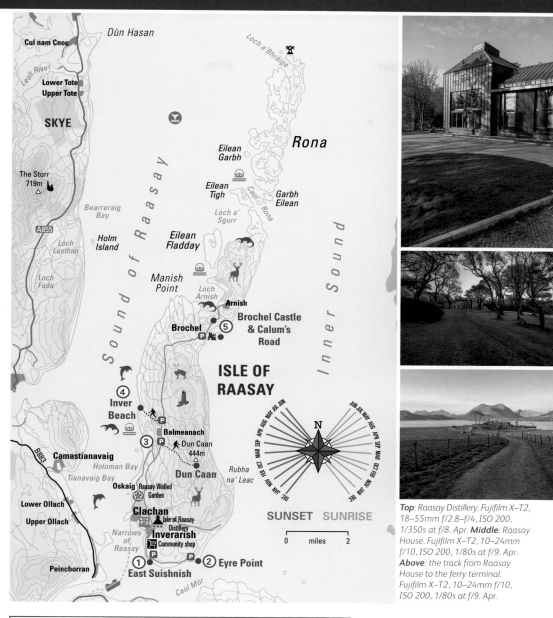

*Top*: Raasay Distillery. Fujifilm X–T2, 18–55mm f/2.8–f/4, ISO 200, 1/350s at f/8. Apr. **Middle**: Raasay House. Fujifilm X–T2, 10–24mm f/10, ISO 200, 1/80s at f/9. Apr. **Above**: the track from Raasay House to the ferry terminal. Fujifilm X–T2, 10–24mm f/10, ISO 200, 1/80s at f/9. Apr.

## LOCATIONS

## Maps

- OS Landranger 24: Raasay and Applecross (1:50 000)

## What to shoot and viewpoints

### Viewpoint 1 – East Suishnish ♿

You may have glimpsed the old pier at East Suishnish from the ferry on its short crossing from Skye. It is in a ruined state these days and access is precluded, however, it does provide a fantastic outlook to Glamaig on Skye which seems to rise straight from the water. The pebble beach provides an interesting foreground and the old pier can work well as a silhouette. **>>**

*Caravan with a view, Fujifilm X-T2, 18–55mm f/2.8-f/4, ISO 200, 1/60s at f/9. Apr.*

*The seagulls follow the trawler in the Narrows of Raasay. Fujifilm X–T2, 55–200mm f/3.5–f/4.8, ISO 200, 1/125s at f/7. Apr.*

## How to get here

Raasay is accessed via regular Caledonian MacBrayne ferries from Sconser on Skye. To reach East Suishnish and Eyre Point, follow the road from the ferry terminal past the distillery and through the village. East Suishness is 2km along the road and there is parking at the old pier. Eyre Point is a further 2km along this road. Dun Caan is accessed from the minor road which runs north from Inverarish. There is a parking area just before Balmeanach. From here, the signposted route runs south east, gradually gaining height before a small lochan is reached. The path then drops down into a narrow valley before rising up the other side and then on to the summit of Dun Caan. Inver Beach is located a little further north, there is a small parking area on the left side of the road but be careful not to block the gate. Proceed through the gate, descending to the right of the ruined building. As you enter the woods, pick up the trail which descends through the woods to the shore. Brochel Castle and Calum's Road are located a further 2km north.

### Viewpoint 1 – East Suishnish

- 📍 **Lat/Long:** 57.332236 , -6.0639336
- 📍 **what3words:** ///paid.apply.offerings
- 📍 **Grid Ref:** NG555341
- 📍 **Postcode:** IV40 8NY

### Viewpoint 2 – Eyre Point

- 📍 **Lat/Long:** 57.333269 , -6.0257556
- 📍 **what3words:** ///latches.hope.genius
- 📍 **Grid Ref:** NG578341
- 📍 **Postcode:** IV40 8NZ

### Viewpoint 3 – Dun Caan

- 📍 **Lat/Long:** 57.389756 , -6.0601556
- 📍 **what3words:** ///inclined.afternoon.bandage
- 📍 **Grid Ref:** NG56140
- 📍 **Postcode:** IV40 8PE

### Viewpoint 4 – Inver Beach

- 📍 **Lat/Long:** 57.399819 , -6.0606889
- 📍 **what3words:** ///tested.juror.cools
- 📍 **Grid Ref:** NG561416
- 📍 **Postcode:** IV40 8PE

### Viewpoint 5 – Brochel Castle and Calum's Road

- 📍 **Lat/Long:** 57.442385 , -6.0292097
- 📍 **what3words:** ///rating.region.chucked
- 📍 **Grid Ref:** NG583462
- 📍 **Postcode:** IV40 8PF

*Opposite top: the dramatic form of Glamaig on Skye from East Suishnish (VP1), Fujifilm X–T2, 18–55mm f/2.8–f/4, ISO 200, 240s at f/6.4. Apr.*

*The pebble beach and old pier at East Suishnish. Fujifilm X–T2, 18–55mm f/2.8–f/4, ISO 200, 1/80s at f/8. Apr.*

*Looking down the road to the old pier at East Suishnish. Fujifilm X–T2, 55–200mm f/3.5–f/4.8, ISO 200, 1/125s at f/4.5. Apr.*

*A grand view of Skye from the beach at Eyre Point. Fujifilm X–T2, 18–55mm f/2.8–f/4, ISO 200, 1/300s at f/9. Apr.*

### Viewpoint 2 – Eyre Point

A short drive along the road leads to Eyre Point, at the end of the road. The beach is accessed via a gated track just past the small parking area. The views from this beach are excellent, with a wide panorama of the Red and Black Cuillin hills arrayed on the western shore. You can fit all the peaks into a wide shot, or alternatively there is scope to home in on the individual peaks and make studies of their fine forms.

### Viewpoint 3 – Dun Caan

Dun Caan is a familiar hill to many, its flat-topped conical summit seen from as far away as the Skye Bridge. Such isolated peaks tend to provide great views and Dun Caan is no exception. It is no exaggeration to say that it might provide the finest view from a wee hill anywhere in the Hebrides. Panning round from the north east your eye will be drawn to the mountains of Torridon, Applecross, the Kishorn hills and the Skye Bridge. To the west, the whole eastern seaboard of Skye is laid out before you with the Cuillins jagged on the horizon. It is even possible

to glimpse Harris on the north western horizon! It's a steep pull up to the grassy summit, with a few ups and downs on the way but it is certainly worth it. During the golden hour, the view across to Skye is hard to beat. *(3.5 miles/5.5km round trip with 319m of ascent, 2-hours walking in total).* »

### Accessibility

East Suishnish and Eyre Point are roadside, however, the pebble beaches are unstable underfoot. The ascent of Dun Caan is relatively simple, on good paths and will take roughly 45 minutes from the parking area. It is steep and there are big drops from the summit of the hill so care should be taken. Inver Bay is 1.5km from the road and is accessed by a steep and occasionally boggy path. Brochel Castle and Calum's Road are easily accessed from the parking area.

### Best time of year/day

East Suishnish and Eyre Point are perfect for sunset, as is Dun Caan. Inver Bay can work at all times however, at high tide much of the interesting formations in the pebbles are lost. Brochel Castle and Calum's Road are great at any time, although work best on days with good visibility.

*Above*: looking over to Skye with Blà Bheinn on the horizon from Eyre Point. Fujifilm X–T2, 55–200mm f/3.5–f/4.8, ISO 200, 1/200s at f/8. Apr.
*Above right*: Beinn na Cro on Skye as seen from Eyre Point (VP2). Fujifilm X–T2, 55–200mm f/3.5–f/4.8, ISO 200, 1/220s at f/8. Apr.

*Above*: the fantastic view of Skye from the summit of Dun Caan, Fujifilm X–T2, 10–24mm f/10, ISO 200, 1/80s at f/11. Apr.

*Left*: Dun Caan from the lochan at Bealach Ruadh. Fujifilm X–T2, 10–24mm f/10, ISO 200, 1/100s at f/8. Apr.

*Right*: Sgùrr nan Gillean on Skye from Dun Caan (VP3). Fujifilm X–T2, 55–200mm f/3.5–f/4.8, ISO 200, 1/480s at f/8. Apr.

*Looking across to Skye from Inver Beach (VP4). Fujifilm X–T2, 18–55mm f/2.8–f/4, ISO 200, 1/480s at f/8. Apr.*

## Viewpoint 4 – Inver Beach

Accessed from the main road north, Inver Beach is hidden away down a steep path through some lovely deciduous woodland. It's a peaceful pebble and sand beach with a great outlook across to the Storr and Portree Harbour. There are some interesting pools formed by the receding tide which have been drawn into sinuous shapes which can provide some foreground interest and the trees clinging on to the steep cliffs at the north end of the beach make a nice study.

*The winding road through Raasay at Brae (VP4). Fujifilm X–T2, 55–200mm f/3.5–f/4.8, ISO 200, 1/320s at f/8. Apr.*

## Viewpoint 5 – Brochel Castle and Calum's Road ♿

As you drive north up the spine of Raasay, the land becomes more unforgiving with rock protruding through the sparse soil. It feels quite remote and the narrow winding road down to Brochel will test the nerves of most drivers. It is worth it though. From the car park at Brochel the castle is located down a grass path alongside a cottage, or it can be photographed from the road itself. There are great views across the sound to Applecross. This is also where the road used to terminate, meaning that residents of the settlements to the north were forced to walk home, contributing majorly to the isolation which was causing the population to decline. One of these residents, 56 year old Calum Macleod changed all that. After unsuccessfully lobbying the local authorities for many years to build a road he took it upon himself to construct it himself. Armed with a pick, a shovel and a wheelbarrow, Calum Macleod spent the next decade building a road in his free time (alongside his other jobs) and eventually created the link between Arnish and Brochel. Walking the route as it traverses bogs and negotiates switchbacks is a great way to pay tribute to his remarkable achievement. The views from up there are not too bad either.

Rathad Chaluim
CALUM'S ROAD

RATHAD CHALUIM

'SE 'OVACH BLIADHNA BE SEO AM FRITH–RATHAD GU ARNA'S –
IVA M'LE CHAIDH A LEUDACHADH AGUS A' DHEASACHADH GU RATHAD
MOR LE 'IOVADAN LE GEIL SEACHAD GU IRE TEARRA HE LE

CALUM MACLEÒID, B.E.M.
(1911–1988)
ARNAIS MU DHEAS.

SHAOTHRAICH E 'NA AONAR AGUS CHUIR E CRIOCH
AIR AN OBAIR AN CEANN DEICH BLIADHNA.

CALUM'S ROAD

THIS FORMER FOOTPATH TO ARNISH – A DISTANCE OF 1¾ MILES –
WAS WIDENED TO A SINGLE TRACK ROAD WITH
PASSING PLACES AND PREPARED FOR SURFACING BY

MALCOLM MACLEOD, B.E.M.
(1911–1988)
SOUTH ARNISH

HE ACCOMPLISHED THIS WORK SINGLE–HANDEDLY
OVER A PERIOD OF TEN YEARS

**Top left**: *Brochel Castle (VP5). Fujifilm X–T2, 18–55mm f/2.8–f/4, ISO 200, 1/350s at f/9. Apr.* **Right**: *Calum's Road. Fujifilm X–T2, 18–55mm f/2.8–f/4, ISO 200, 1/320s at f/8. Apr.*

**Middle left**: *the start of Calum's Road (VP5). Fujifilm X–T2, 18–55mm f/2.8–f/4, ISO 200, 1/50s at f/9. Apr.* **Right**: *plaque commemorating Calum's incredible achievement. Fujifilm X–T2, 18–55mm f/2.8–f/4, ISO 200, 1/250s at f/8. Apr.*

**Left**: *the rugged coast along which Calum's Road leads. Fujifilm X–T2, 18–55mm f/2.8–f/4, ISO 200, 1/180s at f/9. Apr.*

*Looking across to the east coast of Skye from Raasay. Fujifilm X–T2, 10–24mm f/10, ISO 200, 1/180s at f/8. Apr*

## Biography

**Based in Glasgow, Chris has been exploring the Hebrides since he was a young boy on family holidays. For the last five years he has devoted most of his time traveling to all the islands whilst working on this book. Originally a landscape architect, he became a full-time photographer in 2017 producing photography for architects, landscape architects, engineers and interior designers. He also supplies stock images to various clients including the National Trust for Scotland, Conde Nast, the Bank of Scotland and other organisations and publications.**

He has won numerous photography awards over the last ten years, including first place in the *Scottish Landscape Photographer of The Year awards* in 2016 and winner of the *British Wildlife Photography awards* 'Urban Wildlife' category in 2018.

*"My love of the Hebrides started at a young age when we would go on family holidays to the west coast and over to the islands. I've always been drawn to elemental coastal landscapes and the Hebrides have plenty of those!*

*Aesthetically, my approach to photography is always to strive for strong, graphic compositions with a desire to simplify the scene into its base elements. I grew up using film and like to get it right in-camera, minimising the amount of time I spend processing images. I do enjoy using long exposures, mainly to simplify water and skies, and create an ethereal atmosphere but aside from long exposures my images are intended to convey a realistic but artistic impression of the landscape.*

*Understanding the environment is important to me and it plays a big part in my photography. Learning about the geological processes which created it, the natural processes which shaped it or the human history of how the land has been used is all part of my process and helps me to develop a strong connection to place. I'm currently learning Gaelic and even with the little bit I know it has opened my eyes to so much about the landscape of Scotland."*

Find out more about Chris and purchase prints at: *www.christopherswan.co.uk*

*West Loch Tarbert and the Paps of Jura.*
*Fujifilm X–T2, 18–55mm f/2.8–f/4,*
*ISO 200, 1/4s at f/11. Sep.*

# ABOUT FotoVUE

fotoVUE's Explore & Discover photo-location and visitor guidebooks guide you to the most beautiful places to visit and photograph.

Contact: mick@fotovue.com
Website: www.fotovue.com

## Order at: www.fotovue.com and use code: HEB at checkout to get: 20% off all books

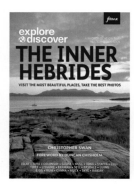 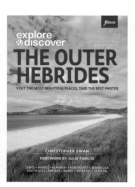  

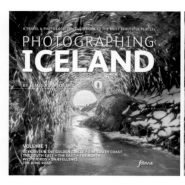  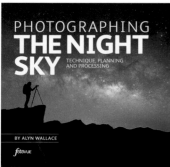

## What people say about fotoVUE photo-location and visitor guidebooks

"The best photographer guidebooks by a mile."
"The quality of product is surpassed only by the attention to highly relevant detail."
"This could be the best location-oriented photoguide I have yet to come across."
"A fantastic book and an amazing travel guide."
"The template for all photography location guides."

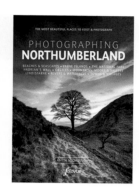

THE MOST BEAUTIFUL PLACES TO VISIT & PHOTOGRAPH

PHOTOGRAPHING
NORTHUMBERLAND

BEACHES & SEASCAPES • FARNE ISLANDS • THE NATIONAL PARK
HADRIAN'S WALL • CASTLES • MOUNTAINS, MOORS & VALLEYS
LINDISFARNE • RIVERS & WATERFALLS • TOWNS & VILLAGES

ANITA NICHOLSON

fotovue

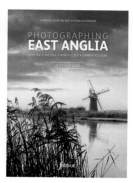

A PHOTO-LOCATION AND VISITOR GUIDEBOOK

PHOTOGRAPHING
EAST ANGLIA

NORFOLK • SUFFOLK • NORTH ESSEX • CAMBRIDGESHIRE

JUSTIN MINNS

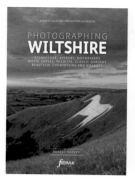

A PHOTO-LOCATION AND VISITOR GUIDEBOOK

PHOTOGRAPHING
WILTSHIRE

STONEHENGE, AVEBURY, MOONRAKERS
WHITE HORSES, WILDLIFE, CLASSIC GARDENS
BEAUTIFUL COUNTRYSIDE AND VILLAGES

ROBERT HARVEY

fotovue

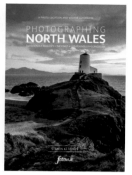

A PHOTO-LOCATION AND VISITOR GUIDEBOOK

PHOTOGRAPHING
NORTH WALES

SNOWDONIA • ANGLESEY • THE LLYN PENINSULA • CLWYDIAN

SIMON KITCHIN

fotovue

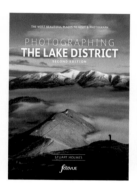

THE MOST BEAUTIFUL PLACES TO VISIT & PHOTOGRAPH

PHOTOGRAPHING
THE LAKE DISTRICT

SECOND EDITION

STUART HOLMES

fotovue

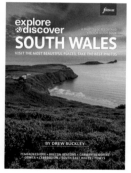

explore
& discover

SOUTH WALES

A PHOTO-LOCATION AND
VISITOR GUIDE MAP

VISIT THE MOST BEAUTIFUL PLACES, TAKE THE BEST PHOTOS

BY DREW BUCKLEY

PEMBROKESHIRE • BRECON BEACONS • CARMARTHENSHIRE
GOWER • CEREDIGION • SOUTH EAST WALES • POWYS

A PHOTO-LOCATION AND VISITOR GUIDEBOOK

PHOTOGRAPHING
SCOTLAND

DOUGIE CUNNINGHAM

fotovue

A PHOTO-LOCATION AND VISITOR GUIDEBOOK

PHOTOGRAPHING
LONDON

VOLUME 1
CENTRAL LONDON

GEORGE JOHNSON

fotovue

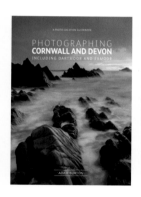

A PHOTO-LOCATION GUIDEBOOK

PHOTOGRAPHING
CORNWALL AND DEVON

INCLUDING DARTMOOR AND EXMOOR

ADAM BURTON

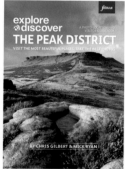

explore
& discover

THE PEAK DISTRICT

A PHOTO-LOCATION AND
VISITOR GUIDEBOOK

VISIT THE MOST BEAUTIFUL PLACES, TAKE THE BEST PHOTOS

BY CHRIS GILBERT & NICK RYAN

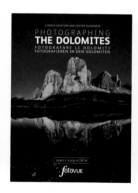

A PHOTO-LOCATION AND VISITOR GUIDEBOOK

PHOTOGRAPHING
THE DOLOMITES

FOTOGRAFARE LE DOLOMITI
FOTOGRAFIEREN IN DEN DOLOMITEN

JAMES RUSHFORTH

fotovue

A PHOTO-LOCATION GUIDEBOOK

PHOTOGRAPHING
WILDLIFE IN THE UK

ANDREW MARSHALL

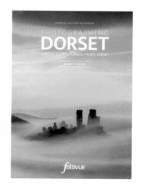

A PHOTO-LOCATION GUIDEBOOK

PHOTOGRAPHING
DORSET

JURASSIC COAST • PURBECK • RURAL DORSET

MARK BAUER

fotovue

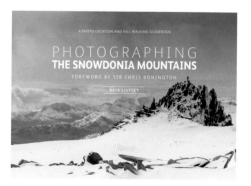

A PHOTO-LOCATION AND HILL WALKING GUIDEBOOK

PHOTOGRAPHING
THE SNOWDONIA MOUNTAINS

FOREWORD BY SIR CHRIS BONINGTON

NICK LIVESEY

fotovue

THE fotovue
ICELAND
adventure
& travel
MAP

A TOPOGRAPHIC MAP OF ICELAND
150 beautiful locations to visit,
enjoy & photograph

# LOCATION INDEX